HOWL

HOWL

A Collection of the
Best Contemporary Dog Wit

From the Editors of The Bark

THREE RIVERS PRESS
NEW YORK

Library of Congress Cataloging-in-Publication Data

Howl: a collection of the best contemporary dog wit /
from the editors of The Bark.—1st ed.
p.   cm.
1. Dogs—Humor.   I. Bark (Berkeley, Calif.)   II. Title.
PN6231.D68H69   2007
818'.6020803629772—dc22   2007013374

ISBN 978-0-307-33839-6

Printed in the United States of America

Design by Lynne Amft

10 9 8 7 6 5 4 3 2 1
First Paperback Edition

We dedicate this book to our mothers,
who are somewhere laughing.

Contents

Contents

Foreword

MY SINGLE GREATEST qualification for introducing this collection may be that I've never had a dog. Stephen Crane was never a soldier and wrote *The Red Badge of Courage*. Likewise, I can be dispassionate and more critical of the cult of sentimentality surrounding "man's best friend." I see things that besotted dog owners cannot see through their slobber-covered glasses.

My friend Catherine, an otherwise self-possessed woman and accomplished filmmaker, used to call me regularly with updates on Jock, her Flat-Coated Retriever: "Jock had his first swim!" "Jock had his first play-date!" "Jock fetched his first ball!" (The retriever part took a while to kick in.) She and her husband, Grant, created a whole history for Jock: He moved from rural North Carolina to Paris, where he wrote beat poetry until he ran out of money. Then he trained to become a hairdresser and ended up running a wildly successful salon in the sixth arrondissement, before moving to Washington, D.C., to become Catherine and Grant's dog. (Huh?)

This kind of anthropomorphization may seem harmless. But as a rational observer of dogs I am concerned that we're bringing dogs down to the level of humans. Dogs are dogs—nothing less. In my book describing the vital role dogs have played in White House decision-making, I recounted how dogs saved us from nuclear catastrophe during the Cuban missile crisis. They'll probably end up saving Social Security. (I also believe we should unloose a Newfie on Kim Jong-il. A good face-licking would soften him up and he'd give up his nuclear weaponry in a Pyongyang minute.)

So enjoy this book. Let dogs make you laugh. Then let them get back to the business of running this country.

—MO ROCCA

Introduction

"A DOG WALKS into a bar . . ."

Cats are enigmatic. Horses have a noble air. Pigs are gregarious. But dogs are by nature funny—they make us laugh. As any comedian will tell you, timing is everything, and have there ever been creatures with better timing than dogs? They always seem to be there at just the right moment, or just the wrong moment, depending upon whom the joke is on. A pot roast left unguarded. An open bedroom door. An ill-timed squat. How quickly tragedy turns into comedy with a dog. A comedy of manners, fish out of water, parody, slapstick—all genres of humor are fair game with a dog.

If indeed timing is everything, then the time seems right to bring out this collection of canine-inspired humor—we could all use a little laughter. And a book of wit and humor seemed like an excellent follow-up to our first book, *Dog Is My Co-Pilot: Great Writers on the World's Oldest Friendship,* an anthology of essays that explored the bonds between human and canine. As founders and editors of *The Bark,* we take our role of reporting on canine culture seriously, but not so seriously that we can't poke fun at the dog world we've chronicled and helped create over the last decade. Admit it, even the most devoted dog lover will occasionally pause and think, *This is crazy!* Or, at least, uncommonly funny.

"A Democrat, a Republican, and a dog are waiting in line to vote . . ."

Do animals smile? Do they laugh? Both science and literature have taken on these age-old questions, and evidence shows that, indeed, animals *do* have a sense of humor. In a paper titled "Do Dogs Laugh? A Cross-Cultural Approach to Body Symbolism," noted anthropologist Mary Douglas sets out to prove that we can divide human from animal along the fault line of laughter. She cites Konrad Lorenz's *Man Meets Dog* and Thomas Mann's *A Man and His Dog* to show how the panting, slightly opened jaws of man's best friend "look like a human smile" and can give "a stronger impression of laughing." (We have daily evidence of this as we sort through the many submissions to our ongoing "Smiling Dog" contest, a *Bark* reader favorite.) Scientists such as Dr. Jaak Panksepp have also shown that rats respond with laughter-like sounds when tickled, and cite studies performed by Patricia Simonet, which note that the breathy exhalations of dogs at play are evidence of a level of joy biologically similar to laughter. It seems that dogs do have a sense of humor, or at the very least, playfulness. This may explain why your dog can make you look like a fool several times a day.

"Two dogs are sitting in a vet's office. One says to the other . . ."

When we began planning this anthology, we thought we'd include a few older pieces, but were surprised to discover how much our sense of humor has changed with regard to dogs. In many of the venerable examples of dog-related humor—over the past century—the dog was the butt of the joke; even worse, humor was found in cruel treatment inflicted upon dogs. Is this any way to treat a trusted friend? It's an indication of how far we have come that we no longer find amusement in their suffering or laugh at inhumane acts perpetrated upon them. As with all cherished friends, we prefer to laugh with our dogs, rather than at them.

Thus, we were inspired to start fresh, to look for what is funny in today's dog world. We also gathered work from a variety of sources—acclaimed humorists (Merle Markoe, Roy Blount Jr., Kinky Friedman), popular performing comedians (Al Franken, Margaret Cho, Marga Gomez), noted literary authors (Haven Kimmel, Pam Houston, Alice Elliott Dark), and accomplished behind-the-scenes comedy writers whose work has provided the backbone for the likes of *The Late Show with David Letterman, Late Night with Conan O'Brien,* and *Saturday Night Live.* We made it a point to include a number of younger authors who have a certain generational edge to their work, as well as writers who have often appeared in *Bark* magazine (Lee Harrington, Alysia Gray Painter, Greg Edmont). We also tapped into noted "fidosopher" Michael J. Rosen's wellspring of humor. In the end, we assembled nearly 70 pieces ranging from personal essays and parodies to satires and aphorisms. Like the dogs we love, no two are alike. We're very pleased with the mix.

Despite the mirth-provoking stories included in this book, we realize that far too many dogs face an uncertain—and definitely not amusing—future. In the fall of 2005, following Hurricane Katrina, we ran a special section in the magazine covering the storm and its aftermath, not only for dogs and their families but also for Gulf Coast humane and animal rescue organizations. The magnitude of the disaster was almost too much to take in, and it inspired us to look for a long-term way to help with the rebuilding efforts, which are ongoing as we write this, nearly two years later. With the support of our publisher and contributors, we have made a commitment to donate all royalties from the sale of this book to these organizations. Your purchase of the book assists with this effort.

We hope the pieces herein bring a smile or chuckle, or even a guffaw. In sharing a laugh, you're also helping some hounds find a way home.

—CAMERON WOO AND CLAUDIA KAWCZYNSKA

HOWL

Here's the Beef

[Bonnie Thomas Abbott]

 "BOYS AND GIRLS, Howls N' Growls proudly presents, direct from a sold-out month at Hollywood's Rin-Tin-Tin-Pan Alley, put your paws together and give a real Chagrin Falls welcome to . . . Gracie!" *[wild woofing]*

Thank you. Thank you. *[wild barks and woofing continues]* Wow! *[yips]* OK, OK. Down, boys and girls. Sit. *Siiiiiit.*

How about those Browns? *[rhythmic woofing]* It sure is cold here in Cleveland. Any of you have electric blankets at home? *[yelps]* Man, I *love* that thing. You just melt into the coverlet. Good-bye stiff hips! And *under* the covers . . . that's even better than sex. Well, almost better. But how would I know? Thanks a lot, Mom! *[yelps from the females in the crowd]* Hey, do you ever leak a little gas in bed and next thing you know, Mom is waving her magazine around, "Jeeze, Gracie." Just when I drop off to sleep again, "For crying out loud, Gracie!" Now Mom's waving the magazine around so hard, the dust bunnies are diving under the bed *[ripple of howls]* and those scratch-and-sniff perfume pages are stinking up the bedroom. I mean, when Mom does it, do I say anything? No, I just politely ignore it, like I didn't notice. And who's got the real nose for noticing, for crying out loud! But let me do it a third time and she's suddenly, "All right, that's it! Get off the bed!" *[light-hearted snarling]*

What do we do when this happens? Everybody?

["SULK!" the audience howls]

That's right! Sulk. Slink over to the quote-unquote dog bed, turn your back, and let out the Big Sigh. Oh, you all know it works every time. Give it ten minutes, tops, and either she's patting the coverlet to invite you back or . . . she's asleep and won't know the difference anyway! *[yelps and howls]* Then it's fart away all you please. She'll never hear you over her own snoring! *[wild woofing and tail wagging]*

You know another thing that bugs me? Mom goes away for the day and leaves the television on "to keep me company." And what channel does she leave it on?

["ANIMAL PLANET!" the audience snarls]

That's it! Now, first of all, how am I supposed to sleep with the television blaring the whole damn day? Second, *Animal Planet*? Do I give a damn about anteaters in Moombazwi or hippos in . . . who knows where the hell hippos live? And those animal cruelty police shows! She can't guess how upsetting that is? *[snarling]* I know *you* know! That's good for a year of visits to the therapist. If you're going to ruin a day's worth of napping at least leave the TV on the Food Channel. How about that Paula Deen? What's better than a breaded and deep-fried pork chop? *[nose whistling]* Nothing? How about a breaded and deep fried pork chop dropped on the kitchen floor! *[wild howling and tail wagging]* Now that's some haute cuisine!

You know what I really hate? Pedicures. *[snarling]* The other day Mom took me to this new place—I thought we were going shopping for biscuits at the mega-pet-mart store—and the next thing I know I'm getting my (bleep) toenails trimmed. "Boy, that was fast," says Mom when the woman returns me to the reception area. "Oh, I just threw her up on the table and clipped all eighteen before she even had time to count to three," the woman says. *[audience flattens ears]* How would *she* like it if the manicurist at *her* salon just threw her into the pedicure chair and slapped on some pearlescent purple polish even before she had time to fish the twenty out of her pocketbook? *[yap, yap, yap]*

Mom used to have a Cocker Spaniel—this is before I arrived in her lap—who hated nail clipping so much that she would nibble them off herself. "So ladylike," Mom always says. If I've heard that story once, I've heard it a hundred times. *That* and how the Spaniel was so afraid of a bath that she hid under the bed and one time her collar got caught in the box springs and how she screamed her head off while, one by one, the whole family tried to squeeze under the bed until the daughter managed to un-buckle her collar. *[gleeful yips]*

The last time Mom went away for the weekend—by the way, a little discussion about whether I might like to go along would be a nice touch—I get taken home by that bottle-blond bipedal sister of mine: Mom's Other Daughter. *[knowing groans]* What a weekend! When Mom's Other Daughter is in the kitchen and the cooking smells are getting to me, she goes, "Get out from underfoot—go watch television." So I follow her into the living room. "Not on the furniture!" *[more knowing groans]* OK, so I find a place on the rug and what does she turn on? *[anticipatory groans]*

["ANIMAL PLANET," the audience barks out] And it's a (bleep) animal cruelty police show! *[groans and howls]*

By now I'm so bummed out, I need a nap. So I go into a bedroom and even before I lift one paw from the carpet, she's screaming, "Not on the bed!" Whatta you gonna do? *[collective sighs of resignation]*

Anyway, she goes back to her cooking and when I show up at the din-ner table, as is customary for family members to do, she announces, like it's some Supreme Court ruling, "Dogs are fed when we're done. And we don't allow begging." *[hackles go up across the room]* Begging! Begging is standing on the street next to an open guitar case. *[woofs of approval]*

The whole weekend goes like that. At least we went for walks every few hours. But I was having such a case of anxiety that I couldn't go. "You'd better do your business or else," she tells me. Um, no pressure there, huh? *Or else what, Miss Talk-to-Your-Cell-Phone-the-Whole-Time?* Don't you hate that! *[snarling]* It's *my* walk too, after all. Would it kill her to show some interest in my sensory experiences? Maybe I'd like to stop to say hello and make some new friends in your neighborhood. *[approving woofs again]*

There was one front yard where I spotted a tennis ball in the grass. *[ears go up across the audience]* Do you ever do that? Go in somebody else's yard when there's no one around, mess with their heads and just kind of "borrow" one of their toys? [tails twitch]

Then the next time they go outside, it's like, "Hey, where the (bleep) is my rubber bone?" [wicked little yaps] Now *that,* boys and girls, is a walk well taken! [triumphant snorts]

Finally Mom shows up to take me home and there's all this, "Were we a good girl? Did we miss Mommy?" [knowing pants] And Not-My-Natural-Sister gushes, "Oh she really enjoyed her little vacation, taking nice walks, smelling new smells, leftover roast lamb."

And did I forget to show my appreciation? Of course not: I left a little hostess gift on the bedroom Persian carpet. [barking]

Not everything ticks me off. How about the Biscuit Buffet at what Mom calls the Doggie Depot? Now it may not be so great for you shorties out there—trust me, on top of that table there's more kinds of cookies than . . . fleas on a porch sofa. They should have a sign: if you're this tall, you can graze. OK, if one of you shorties runs up and doesn't get all yippy with me, maybe [isolated high-pitched yaps], just maybe, a carob pinwheel or two just might "accidentally" fall off the table. [chorus of yips] But you've got to be fast. Otherwise, there's all the decision making, the paper sack to fill, waiting in the check-out line, getting in the car, waiting in the car until Mom dashes into a store for milk, before . . . before you get to eat the goddamned biscuits! [howls] And all the cool toys, right down there where you can pick out ones you'd actually want. (Tell me, who *wants* a friggin' green pepper that squeaks? Now, a TV remote that squeaks and actually changes the channels—that's worth a few bucks.) Maybe Mom or Dad just took you shopping for a new collar and toys weren't part of the plan, but remember, boys and girls, what Colin Powell told President Bush, "If you get spit on it, somebody's going to have to pay for it." [barks of approval]

You ever get a sweater for Christmas? What kind of present is that, clothes? [big sighs] Ask the kids at your house how elated new socks make them at Christmas. And what's up with those sweaters—unless you're a little spare in the hair department, like some of you shorties. You know what I hate? Having to wear one of those (bleep) sweaters and it starts to rain. Hard. Try walking around with ten pounds of stinking, soaking-wet wool clinging to your body. And it's November, but you're still wearing your Halloween sweater so you look like a melted traffic cone with jack-o'-lanterns that escaped from Edvard Munch's *The Scream*. And what's Mom saying? "Hurry up, do your business, hurry!" Well, I'd like to see her try to go, wearing a ski jacket and pants in the middle of a pelting monsoon.

Just wait till we get home and get that thing off of me. Like Jerry Lee Lewis sang, there's a whole lotta shakin' going on.

[yelps and nose-whistles, crowd stands up and circles in place]

Thanks a lot, you've been a beautiful audience. Who says you can't do a sit for more than two seconds? You're beautiful!

We'll be selling personally paw-printed CDs in the lobby. And hey, hold off on the water till you get home. Don't drink and ride on a full bladder. I want to see you next weekend at the Komedy Kennel in Cincinnati!

Good night, boys and girls. *[wild howling and barking, tornadic tail wagging]*

How to Tell the Difference Between Your Mother and Your Dog

[Henry Alford]

THE DANGER IS all too real: you're driving down a quiet country lane, conversing with the greatest source of unconditional love in your life, when something outside your car requires that you pay full attention to the road before you. Taking your eyes off your interlocutor, you're suddenly unable to remember whether this individual is the woman who reared you, or the one whose left hind leg flails wildly when you scratch her skritchy spot.

Alternatively, your confusion might be date-specific. Although it may not be a problem right now, it is very possible that on or around May 14 the seasonal burst of intimacy that you experience with your mother will allow you to see that the similarities between her and your dog are profound. After all, consider them individually. There is your dog: easily distracted, increasingly prone to taking long afternoon naps, eager to impress upon you how little he's been eating. And then there is your mother: easily distracted, increasingly prone to taking long afternoon naps, eager to impress upon you how little she's been eating.

It isn't that your mother isn't beautiful. It isn't that you don't respect your dog for his essential doggishness. It is rather that the world is so over-saturated with phenomena that it is sometimes difficult to keep the most disparate things apart, let alone two things that, on a very foggy day, might actually resemble each other. The more information in your brain, the less at your fingertips; indeed, as a result of information overload, facts that were

6

once at your fingertips can retreat into your person, whereupon they become lodged in your elbows.

Fortunately, help is available on the mother versus dog front. But before
you can articulate the differences between the two entities, you must first
articulate the similarities, so as to establish the playing field. To wit:

Similarities

- have proprietary attitude toward garbage and its disposal
- are responsible for the proliferation of small oval area rugs
- are sometimes asked to stay indoors due to inability to mix well with others
- are uncomfortable with the concept of a Kawasaki Vulcan
- are unable to pivot—must bodily complete large circle in order to turn fully
- would relish the opportunity to have all the living room walls painted bone

Startling, no?
But fear not. The differences should set things right.

Differences

MOM	DOG
Is interested in portion control	Is not interested in portion control
Does not like to spend a lot of time in the basement, lying on the cool cement floor	Likes to spend a lot of time in the basement, lying on the cool cement floor
Is no stranger to emotional blackmail	Is no stranger to public cleaning of own genitals
Has a food-preparation disorder	Has a greeting disorder

Wonders if her new dress makes her look fat	Wonders why Saran Wrap exists
Wonders if, when you meet TV anchormen, their makeup is distracting	Wonders if, when licking TV anchormen, their makeup is like butter or frosting
Would like to buy the new holiday album from that Betty Midler, who looks like *such fun*	Would be willing to lick Bette
Likes to impart guilt	Likes to lick any spots on a kitchen surface in an effort to find a food source

In conclusion, though the similarities between your mother and your dog are considerable, there are enough differences to keep you from embarrassing yourself. For instance, while both these individuals like to be petted, I can report with a certain amount of authority that your mother prefers that any such ministrations steer clear of her lower belly.

However, for some people, confusion between these two entities may still exist. If you notice that the object of this confusion is staring at you ominously on May 15, and seems to be filled with intense expectation about how you might be making her life a little more wonderful, then wait a week. If, after a week's time, you're still getting these looks, then the individual in question is probably your dog: Mother's Day comes but once a year, but a dog's day is every day.

Two Pooch or Not to Pooch?

[Jon Bowen]

ONE YEAR AGO, after three years of cordial cohabitation with our yellow Labrador, my wife and I disappointed our mothers again—our grandmothers-in-waiting—by forgoing the baby option in favor of bringing home a little brother for our pooch. This first year of living with two dogs has been, essentially, an exercise in chaos control.

Having survived, however, I now offer these words of counsel to the single-dog family contemplating an addition, from one who lived to tell.

The road that leads to your second dog purchase is paved with great myths—falsehoods perpetuated by animal behaviorists and obedience school Führers—and they should be faced and debunked before you enter the state of pandemonium that is two-dog life.

Myth 1

Your older dog will serve as a role model for the younger dog and teach him, by adult-like example, to abandon his puppy ways in favor of more mature canine behavior. Nope. Your older dog, witnessing the puppy's boundless capacity for disobedience and his no-holds-barred spirit of carpe diem, will experience a flashback to his own infancy and instantaneously and wholly will nullify all your years of diligent training. Begin rehearsing the "No!" command now. Stock up on stain remover.

Myth 2

Your new dog will provide constant camaraderie for your incumbent dog, relieving you of the guilt associated with your failure to be an adequate playmate for Dog Numero Uno. Not really. The only thing dogs like more than playing with other dogs is playing with humans. So when you set your hounds loose in the yard to play with each other, rather than frolicking together they will turn around and stand still and stare at you, waiting. "Go on. Play!" you'll say, shooing them on from the door, and their sad, supplicating eyes will seem to say, "But we want to play with you." Consequently, your guilt is not cut in half but doubled.

Myth 3

Your dogs will entertain each other while you're away, cutting down on episodes of delinquency. Nope. The capacity for destruction in dogs increases in exponential ratio to the number of dogs assembled at the moment of wrongdoing. Where one dog might be satisfied to simply chew awhile on your sofa pillow, two dogs will shred, unstuff, and scatter the pillow tatters around the house. (The two-dog owner's dilemma, of course, is that when you come home to the wreckage you're never sure which dog, if not both, committed the evil deed.)

Myth 4

Your dogs will fight. No, they won't. Dogs are much more efficient than humans in establishing a tranquil, well-regulated hierarchy. Your older dog will claim his ancestral rank as alpha dog, the puppy will instinctively fall in behind, and they will quickly marshal their forces toward the immediate task of dominating you. The first time you have to command your dogs to quit some bit of mischief they've gotten into together, you will see them look at you, then look at each other, and you'll realize in the bottom of your heart that you are outnumbered, outweighed, and out-willed. Be strong in that moment. If you falter, you will die a thousand deaths.

Myth 5

Owning two dogs really isn't much different from owning one. No. Owning two dogs is like owning two dogs. Be prepared to accommodate a radical contrast in personality and emotional temperament, even within the same breed. Our two Labs, who could pass for identical twins on appearance alone, are as different in their souls as Dr. Jekyll and Mr. Hyde. The three-year-old is dignified and defiant, scholarly and aloof, unmoved by affection, wont to wandering off by himself. On the other hand, our one-year-old is perpetually overjoyed and randy as a frat boy, though prone to crippling fits of unwarranted guilt. He's mischievous and lewd, confident to a fault, iconoclastic in word and deed. (If you want to have fun owning two dogs, start practicing anthropomorphism now.)

Myth 5, Addendum A

Cleaning up after two dogs really isn't much different from cleaning up after one. Wrong. Be properly equipped for the twofold increase in poop—especially if you favor larger breeds—or your yard will quickly become as treacherous as a war zone's minefield. As far as clean-up implements go, I recommend the user-friendly combination poop scoop, available at many pet stores. It's a sturdy mini-rake paired with a chrome-plated scoop, both pieces outfitted with long wooden handles. In a pinch, a garden shovel works fine. You'll also see a twofold increase in shedding, which will transform the inside of your house into a furry cave, unless you act swiftly and regularly to suck up those stray hairs. Get a good dog brush, use it often, and get a powerful vacuum.

Myth 6

You'll regret it. No, you won't. The hardships of a two-dog life are always considerable but never insurmountable. You will learn to adapt to the doggy difficulties that arise. For instance, on walks our older dog likes to loiter while the younger one is forever lunging wildly on, nearly asphyxiating himself on his collar. Solution: By knotting their leashes together—by yoking the puller to the lollygagger—I can leverage the equal and opposite forces of motion and inertia, thereby creating a perfect equilibrium in which one hound counterbalances the other for the duration of our pleasant stroll.

In the end, there's nothing in the list of life's rewards that compares with the deep, abiding, unconditional love that is unique to dogs. Besides, if it's true that people who own dogs live longer, your second dog will push you that much closer to immortality's door.

I Done Them Wrong: How I Wrecked My Daughter's Self-Esteem and My Dog's Sex Life

[Cathy Crimmins]

 MY DAUGHTER, AN only child, has been deprived of sibling rivalry, so she does what comes naturally: She takes it out on The Dog.

"You love him more than me," she'll pout, and of course most times I protest that it isn't possible.

But who could blame her for suspecting differently? When she was nine, Kelly even caught me singing her "special" song to the dog. That was a bad moment. I never confessed that her anthem was once her father's particular song in our halcyon childless days, and I had just adapted it for her. Kelly also went to pieces whenever I called the dog by her affectionate nickname, "Tootsie," and I admit that I sometimes did it intentionally—what fun is being a mom if you can't glory in a bit of passive aggression?

Interspecies relationships are hopelessly muddled in any household, especially since a family usually gets a dog *for* a kid. That's a big mistake, because young kids don't really like to take care of a dog and tend to tire of them the way they lose interest in the newest PlayStation game. I ignorantly passed down the kid/puppy tradition from my own family: I had received a puppy as a gift when I was eight, so I promised my kid one at the same age.

At the time, I forgot that I'd never once taken care of my dog, even though my family lived in a rambling exurban community where dogs didn't even have to be walked. Filling her water dish was my only responsibility, but

I still couldn't hack it—at one point, after paying rapt attention in fourth-grade science class, I tried to convince my mother that my dog's water dish was empty because of evaporation, not neglect. And so it went with my kid, who foisted off the dog care on me on his second day with us.

Sitting every day with me in the home office, the little dog became inordinately attached to me, as creatures are wont to do when you walk and feed them. But I felt swamped with duties, and it was a terrible recipe for family friction, going on for years as I struggled to do my work, stay interested in my marriage, prepare meals, help my kid with her homework, *and* walk and clean up after the dog. The puppy, a pudgy, short-legged Jack Russell Terrier named Silver, became the most pleasurable part of the domestic equation, providing endless hours of writerly procrastination. But when it came to my other duties, I was frequently seething in that way only moms can seethe—in a deep Vesuvian mode where the steam coming from one's head is always present, threatening imminent eruption.

I don't mean to suggest that the dog was perfect, but he was certainly the least demanding member of the household, and, being smart, he caught on to the family dynamic right away. Silver the Dog knew that the kid was important, and he had to pretend to like the young hairless pup, even though she moved quickly and unpredictably and mostly tortured him. As a canine actor, Silver rivaled Brando or De Niro—he was positively Stanislavskian—and any visitor to our house would think he adored the kid. He would let her pick up and fondle him while he fell limp in her arms and traveled to his Canine Happy Place, wherever that was. Maybe it was a mountain made out of rawhide, or, more likely, a wonderland with unlimited access to all of her stuffed animals. But after Kelly fell asleep or let him down from the couch, he would immediately go upstairs to her room and destroy whatever toy she loved the most. It was uncanny—he always knew, and he had puppy teeth that could cut through granite. In a way, he was a doggy Mahatma Gandhi, practicing an extreme form of passive resistance. Hold me, hug me, bug me—but in the end, *I will destroy the material goods you hold dearest!*

Once, when my kid was thirteen and the dog was five, she started descending into her customary self-pity.

"You love Silver more than you love me," she said, waiting for the usual reassurances.

That day I'd had some lousy phone calls and, later, a few glasses of wine. My kid was a teenager, so I figured she might as well know the truth.

"Oh yeah?" I hissed. "You think I love The Dog more than you? Yeah, you're right—why wouldn't I *adore* The Dog? Why not? He's always happy to see me when I come home. He eats anything I put down, and he listens to anything I say. AND I don't have to put him through college!"

Even I felt crummy during the stunned silence. I still feel crummy. That's why, now, four years later, I am offering an olive branch, an apology of sorts. Well, actually, I'm offering my daughter something I think she will enjoy:

> *However badly you feel about The Dog, and my attachment to him, and however much you might resent him, consider this: I once threw away our dog's beloved sexual partner right in front of him. Be glad that I can never do this to you.*

Yes, it's true. When I was moving from the East Coast to California, I stood in my daughter's bedroom, took a large plastic bag and threw a big carnival stuffed bear into it. As I turned around to take the bag downstairs, I saw Silver. He was sitting quietly, looking on, and I know I'm anthropomorphizing, but I could swear I saw a small tear roll down from his left eyelid and hit his furry snout. I was discarding the only animal he'd ever truly loved.

Some background here: of course, my dog was neutered, as all good doggies should be, however traumatic it is for their human relatives. My own mother didn't trust me to neuter my dog, so she offered to take care of Silver when he was five months old, and when she returned him, he was missing some gonads. I thought he was much too young, and was vaguely upset, but figured she was probably right—I might not have done anything until a fellow doggy-park regular showed up on my doorstep with a strange litter of half-and-half Jack Russell Terriers and German Shepherds. Because, from the beginning, Silver had sexual charisma, attracting girlfriends twice and thrice his size. He was a regular Don Juan–Napoleon type with a seemingly high libido for a puppy, and I have the bad back to prove it: one morning at the park, Silver's earliest girlfriend, a Mastiff puppy named Gertrude, ran right through my open legs trying to get away from my dog's advances, and I ended up on the operating table with a shattered disk. Silver always went for the tall girls.

We first noticed Silver's secret sex life with stuffed animals about a year after he was neutered. He would disappear for about forty-five minutes up the stairs and then come back in a triumphant rush, scurrying on his little legs as fast as he could down the stairs, then stopping on a dime and looking up with his eyes glazed over and his tongue hanging out. If he could have produced a human sound, it would have been "Ta-da!" I knew he'd been doing something bad, but when I arrived at the crime scene, I still didn't get that my little boy had discovered himself. I was confused that I didn't find anything chewed up—no pencil shavings, no wooden toy cars half masticated. Instead, there was Kelly's four-foot stuffed whale, marooned in the middle of her carpet. It was always the same: to the dog, size mattered. Kelly had half a dozen oversize toys that suddenly became members of Silver's bordello. No shelf was high enough to prevent him choosing a partner for the evening. I felt like a pervert, or Jane Goodall, following my dog stealthily up the stairs to spy on his sexual sessions with a stuffed whale, two giant teddy bears, a large swan, and, his personal favorite, Cinnamon the Pony. First he would steal the thing off the shelf, using any guile necessary, and many jumping gymnastics. Then he would arrange it carefully face-down, and then . . . well, he would go at it. If I yelled at him, he would leave the room for a bit and then return furtively. I have to admit that I even experimented with positions, seeing if he would "do" an animal if it were lying face up. Despite his small stature, if Silver found one of the animals that way, he would spend as much as fifteen minutes flipping it over and arranging it "doggy-style." Mind you, most of his sex partners were at least twice as large as he. But he was filled with shame if I should interrupt his session, and would walk around painfully, dragging his erection behind him. I felt badly for him—he had been robbed of his sexuality and was only practicing a charade that allowed him to establish his masculinity. For all I knew, maybe he thought that the sex menagerie was there for his use. I should have stopped all the madness much earlier, especially since he eventually slipped a back disk and had to be rushed to the veterinary emergency room after a particularly strenuous tryst.

"Umm, I suppose I should mention this," I said to the veterinary student doing triage. "He was having sex with a large stuffed teddy bear when this happened."

The vet I was talking to looked all of twelve years old and pretended at first not to understand what I was saying. I went on, explaining that Silver had a habit of pleasuring himself with giant stuffed mammals.

"You better put those away right now," he said sternly, although I could imagine him telling the story over beers later that night. "You cannot leave the toys around, or your dog could suffer serious consequences. Do you want him to be unable to walk?"

And so Silver's sex life ended, I thought, that day. It was just as well. I hadn't intended to actually illustrate sex for my child, but I found out a while later that she had often hung out in her bed watching the little dog romance the fake fur. "Eeew," she said when she admitted it. I was horrified. What kind of a mother was I?

A bad one, it seems, for both my human and canine progeny. For although I put away the giant stuffed animals, hiding them on high, locked closet shelves around the house, I forgot one chintzy big bear, a very cheap, stiff old carnival prize that Silver had chosen only once in a pinch—stuffed with cardboard or newspaper, she was not cushy like the others, and her butt was a bit flat for a guy like Silver, who preferred some junk in the trunk. Yet he had certainly dallied with her at least once in a pinch, and now, in the process of moving, I had unearthed her, only to throw her away again as he looked on.

Silver and I were both celibate for a long time in California until I decided he needed a new toy and got a stuffed Labrador Retriever that was certainly not life-size, but a bit larger than his other chew toys. Evidently size no longer mattered to my little dog, who was now middle-aged, and I returned from an errand one day to the familiar huffing and humping I'd heard in his halcyon days. He was doing it again! I watched and let him do what he needed, and then took the new dog and threw him away, too.

Sex partners come and go so quickly in doggy land, don't they? But whenever I feel guilty, I think of how simple Silver's breakups were, and how it might have been better if a few of my lovers had been kicked to the curb in a garbage bag. It would have been especially great to be able to do that with my daughter's first boyfriend, too.

The Dog Mumbler

[Merrill Markoe]

IN THE BEGINNING, like dog-loving Americans everywhere, I was utterly transfixed by "The Dog Whisperer." Between his self described "calm assertive manner" and his earnest, well-meaning solutions to dog behavioral dilemmas, Cesar Millan seemed to represent everything good and smart, sensible and loving about the human/doggy bond.

But by season two, it appeared to me that, like all good media figures, he had begun to accumulate some video mange. His problem-solving techniques, though still impressive, had started to feel repetitious and just a little suspect. I began to wonder how many of those easy solutions of his kept working after he and his calm assertive manner had donned their inline skates, hooked up their Pit Bulls, and headed home.

Still, I kept on watching. Right up until the day I tried using one of his methods of behavioral correction myself. After months of struggling to cope with the impolite leash manners of my overly enthusiastic dog Hedda, I followed Mr. Millan's advice and moved a choke chain high up on her neck, by her ears, as I had seen him do with dozens of Dog Whisperer clients. In the context of the show, that was all that was ever needed to cause a formerly rowdy dog to begin strolling quietly beside (and slightly behind) his or her calm assertive owner.

In my own case, however, about a half hour in to tiptoeing near the uncomfortably restrained, overly upright, lightly choking Hedda, I was convinced that this method of "walking" with her was about half as much fun as it had been when she was out of control and barreling down the street, pulling me behind her like an inadequately tethered caboose.

That was the day when I began to give some thought to becoming a dog guru myself. After all, there are no standardized credentials for this position. Advice taken from a dog guru is an act of blind faith, like buying vitamins or going to a psychic. You pays your money, and you takes your chances. And best of all, by the time anyone can prove that the service isn't very effective, it's so long after the fact, there's no way to get your money back.

Hmm, I started thinking, This could be the career path I seek. Why not weigh in with my own special dog care tips and methods! And not only because dog gurus make a lot more money than I do! But, okay . . . mainly because they do.

FLEXIBLE COHABITATION (PATENT PENDING)

My Dog Training Plan for YOU

FAQ

1. How do I know if Flexible Cohabitation (patent pending) is right for me?

Well, let me ask you this: Do you have the patience and follow-through necessary to work with your dog for an hour a day, every day for months, repeatedly giving stern commands, then reinforcing them with a correction or a reward? If you answered "What if I did it once a week instead?" then I believe that Flexible Cohabitation (patent pending) is the plan for you.

With Flexible Cohabitation (patent pending) all that is required is that you sit back in your favorite chair with an icy cold beverage and enjoy the fireworks. Because unlike Cesar Millan, I was not raised in the macho culture of Mexico and therefore am not inclined to ask my clients to put themselves in harm's way or subject themselves to painful puncture wounds by doing an alpha rollover when their dog appears aggressive. Instead, with Flexible Cohabitation (patent pending) I will show you how to relax and let the dog you love behave exactly as he or she wishes. After all, if I want to be covered in dog hair and mud, I can simply sit down on my own furniture!

2. You can't mean that you are advocating letting dogs run wild through your home?

To this I reply, "Obviously you have never been to my home." Frequent visitors have compared it favorably to the Badlands of South Dakota.

With Flexible Cohabitation (patent pending) I will teach you a form of Zen nonattachment to material goods that your bank account is going to love! Get ready for no more worrying about how to get unusual stains off delicate upholstery or fretting about removing dog nose prints from gleaming reflective surfaces! In fact, no more delicate upholstery, no more gleaming reflective surfaces period!

3. Will I have to employ terrifying guilt-inducing accessories like an electrified fence and collar?

Not only will you have no need for so much as a choke chain, but I will show you how to execute a form of dog walk that I call Asphalt Water Skiing (patent pending), wherein you simply hook the pet to the leash of your choice, and hang on for dear life! In addition to providing exercise for your dog, this highly aerobic technique will shape and tone your calves, thighs, biceps, and abdominals.

And that's not all!

With Flexible Cohabitation (patent pending) you will learn how allowing your dog full access to your plate at meal times can help you cut out thousands of calories a day!

You're going to be amazed at how much more free time you have when you abandon the tedium of traditional dog training and accept living alongside your dog in the harmony and chaos that nature intended! When all is said and done, you will find that they love you exactly the same amount! And all it takes, besides writing a check to me, is doing absolutely nothing!! (Offer good where not prohibited by law.)

How to Change Your Adopted Dog's Name to the Name You Want in under Six Months

[Brian Frazer]

ADOPTED DOG'S NAME *at pound or shelter:* SNOWFLAKE.

Upon your arrival at home, give your new best buddy a loving pat on the head as you show him to his custom-made beanbag chair that matches his fur and begin calling him SNOWBLAKE.

Three weeks later, throw a birthday party for him, being sure to invite all of his closest pals from the dog park. Then, when nobody's looking, sneak into the kitchen and change the inscription on the cake to "Happy Birthday, BLAKE.*" He probably won't notice with all the hoopla.*

An hour after all the guests have left, reward him with a special cookie you've baked and refer to him as BLAKEY.

Ninety seconds later, upon digestion of said cookie, praise him effusively for chewing something that would probably crack one of your teeth by tweaking his name to BARNEY.

A fortnight hence, as you're rubbing his belly, pop in an old Flintstones VHS tape, point his head toward the screen, and dispense his new moniker: RUBBLE.

Twelve hours later, pretend you're drunk and begin slurring all your words as you put your arm around him and start referring to him as RUBY.

Five minutes later, act sober and explain that you had meant to call him RUDY.

A month and a day later, pretend you bumped your head on the fireplace and now have amnesia and can't remember anything . . . except your dog's name—which you swear was ROO.

One week later, cough as you say Roo a few times, then seamlessly sail into KANGAROO.

For the next month, don't call him by any name, just do a lot of whistling or gargling when you want his attention.

Six weeks later, pretend that his name's always been KANGY.

One month later, mumble SUGAR BLOSSOM *in your sleep and hope he's paying attention.*

Congratulations! You've now made the transition a smooth one for your new furry pal! Well done, sir or ma'am!!!

All the Bags and Dante and Me

[Pam Houston]

I T ' S   R A I N I N G   I N   northern California for the sixth day straight and my Irish Wolfhound, Fenton Johnson, is not particularly pleased. Every morning that we are here the routine is the same. I get up, shower, and dress, while Fenton waits in the big yellow chair next to the front door, and then I put my shoes on and hold his red leash in the air and say, *Do you want to go for a walk?* and he hops joyfully up and down with his front legs off the ground, and I put his leash on and we head for the ditch. I know that he is jumping up and down, not only because he is happy to see the red leash, happy about the prospect of going on a walk, but also because he knows that it makes me happy to see him jump up and down. This is one of the simple and beautiful ways that a dog takes care of his human.

It takes exactly one hour to walk the length of the ditch that borders the huge agricultural fields on the north side of town. On a sunny day Fenton will bound happily along the burry edges of the fields, flushing out egrets and rabbits and the low-flying birds he loves to chase. But today he puts his nose to the back of my knees and moves along at my pace, wincing slightly as if each raindrop is doing him some slight but accumulating damage, as if *he* is doing *me* a favor by going on this walk.

"Think of your ancestors back in the old country," I tell him. "They

had to put up with weather like this every day." He gives his shoulders a little shake and tucks in tighter behind me. We walk in the ditch because it is
one of the few places in Davis where he is allowed to be off leash most of
the time, but there is one point along the walk where we come out of the
ditch and cross a busy road to another field, and so I take the red leash out
of my pocket and hold it in the air once again. *Do you want to go for a walk?* I
ask him, and he hops up and down again joyfully, pretending not to realize
that we are already on a walk, giving me another opportunity to get a kick
out of him, to find it funny that he is acting *like a dog* again, when actually
he is acting exactly like the very best kind of human would act, if only they
had thought of it first.

We cross the road and the train tracks with a spring in our step, but
when I take him off leash it is no time at all before he is sulking again. In
spite of all the jumping up and down for my sake, today Fenton hates
northern California. He is missing his sisters, Rose and Mary Ellen, who
are back at our real home in Colorado. In fact, as he walks along with his
head slung down between his powerful shoulder blades, I know that he is
picturing Rose and Mary Ellen romping in the fresh Colorado snow, or
wrapped around each other on the sunporch under a Colorado bluebird
sky, or getting home-baked dog treats, one after another, from the Colorado house sitter Sarah even as the northern California sky spits and spits
onto his nose and into his ears, and he starts to smell more and more like
cinnamon toast. Fenton is the dog who this time has been chosen to spend
the teaching quarter out here with me in our part-time California home,
and today he is pretty sure he has gotten the short end of the stick.

I named my dog Fenton Johnson after my dearest friend, the writer
Fenton Johnson, partly because *that* Fenton is named after an eleventh-
century Irish monk, Fintan, but mostly because *that* Fenton has eight
brothers and sisters, all of whom have children (Fenton himself is gay and
childless), and none of his siblings have named any of their children Fenton.
Not even as a middle name. Fenton was bemoaning that lack of a legacy to
me one day, so I thought I could make it right for him in this small way.
Fenton-the-human was at first not sure how he felt about having a dog

named after him (especially first *and* last name), but he spoke to his therapist about it and together they decided to accept the gesture in the spirit with which it was intended.

In the four years of Fenton-the-canine's life so far (or Fenton junior, as Fenton-the-human calls him), the two have grown very close. In a recent picture I took of them together, in fact, several people have commented upon how much alike they look, and Fenton-the-human is coming to understand that having an Irish Wolfhound rather than a human baby named after you—when you consider their comparative potential for good works versus crimes against humanity, the dog is probably going to win hands down—might be a very good thing indeed. There have been a few rare and slightly tense moments when we are all on a beach walk together, and I have to shout, *Fenton, don't pee on that beach towel!* Or *Fenton, stop humping that little dog!* But for the most part Fenton-the-canine comports himself in a way that makes Fenton-the-human proud.

Last weekend in the little coastal town of Point Reyes Station, I stopped into the Cowgirl Creamery to pick up some cheeses for a beach picnic, and left the two Fentons standing outside, leashed together. As is often the case, an attractive man came over to chat Fenton-the-human up, and in the course of conversation, asked him the name of the dog.

"Fenton Johnson," Fenton said, a bit tentatively, holding his breath for the question he feared would come next.

"I'm Jerry," the man said, just as I came out of the store with the cheese in a bag and saw Fenton looking between the two men, wagging and wagging his tail.

"Hi Jerry," Fenton said, "this is Pam."

"Hi Jerry," I said, "this is Fenton."

"We've already met," Jerry said, looking at the dog, which is when I realized Fenton's predicament: the rock of rudeness or the hard place of narcissism. Either way it seemed best to make a hasty exit, before Jerry, cute as he may have been, came right out and asked Fenton-the-human his name.

That was the last sunny day in northern California, and today, in the ditch, I try to remind Fenton-the-canine of how much fun we had just last weekend. How sunny it was, how we took our cheesy picnic to Limantour Beach, and how those medium-sized birds who bob up and down right along the shoreline kept circling back in front of him so he could chase them and chase them, how the harbor seal kept popping his head out of the breakers as if he was asking Fenton to come out and play, and how Fenton ran and ran until he could hardly keep his eyes open long enough to eat all the organic chicken tenders that Fenton-the-human had brought him from the specialty dog shop in San Francisco.

But it is no use, last week is forgotten and now Fenton misses his sisters. When we get back to the house after our ditch walk, Fenton digs under the sofa for a toy he hasn't been one bit interested in, in the two years since he officially left puppyhood behind. He puts the cartoonishly fat sheep into his mouth and gives me a long look over its woolly back. "This is what you've driven me to," his eyes seem to say as the sheep gives off a strangled dusty squeak.

"Your sisters miss you too," I tell him. I know for a fact that his sisters miss him because *two* weekends ago I left Fenton in California and flew back to Colorado and drove a rent-a-car up to the ranch just to make sure the dogs, the horses, and house sitter Sarah were all eating well and staying warm. Mary Ellen, after an enthusiastic, but very brief, greeting, planted herself on the leading edge of the porch and refused to come inside. Hours later as the thermometer dipped into the sub-zero range, she still couldn't be persuaded and stayed exactly where she had been all day, eyes fixed on the rent-a-car. It was Sarah who finally figured it out late that evening: Mary Ellen was waiting all those hours for Fenton to hop out of the empty rent-a-car. If I was home, she was thinking, he must be home too. This is one way that our dogs teach us about faith.

Of all my dogs, Mary Ellen is the largest, about 160 pounds, and being the largest, is the most insecure. She is afraid of a great many things, including the linoleum that covers the kitchen floor. In an average day Mary Ellen might go out and come back in six or seven times, and lucky for Mary Ellen, we have another door besides the kitchen door, one on the front of the house that opens directly onto the living room, which has nice soft pine floors where dog pads can get a somewhat better grip. Oddly though, Mary

Ellen asks to come in only at the kitchen door, with one sharp scratch of a paw down the wood. At that point Sarah or I will get up, open the kitchen door, and say, "Okay, go around!" and she will bound off the porch and around to the front of the house where we will open the front door and let her in. Why she doesn't just ask to come in at the front door in the first place is one of the things that makes Mary Ellen Mary Ellen, but I suspect it is some complicated scheme she has cooked up to ensure that her humans feel needed. One day Sarah was on her way from the kitchen door to the front door, and she stepped over Rose (who loves the cool kitchen linoleum because she is almost always overheated). "She's going around," I heard Sarah say to Rose, even though Rose was sound asleep, which is how I knew Mary Ellen's plan was working just as she had hoped.

Sometimes I bring both Fenton and Mary Ellen to California. We drive across 50, the Loneliest Road in America, and we have our favorite stops: a quick dip in the Colorado River near Fruita; a stop to chase the ubiquitous rabbits at the giant rest area near the highest point of Utah's San Rafael Swell; the dog-friendly Silver Queen Hotel and Casino in Ely, Nevada; the giant sand dunes just east of Fallon; and the Sno-park on the top of Donner Pass. It is immeasurable how much less lonely the Loneliest Road in America is when you have the good company of one or two or even three Wolfhounds (which, added all together in the back of a 4Runner, provide excellent traction on wet or snow-covered roads, adding up as they do to 450 pounds of dog). Mary Ellen is even a better town dog than her brother Fenton, because another one of the things she is afraid of is having fun. I call her the leashless wonder because leashed or not, she is never less than six feet from my right hand. She is the only dog I have ever owned who simply won't chase cats, dogs, cows, or cars, no matter how much her misbehaved older sister eggs her on.

Which brings me to Rose, who after many years of being my driving companion back and forth across Utah and Nevada with the much-celebrated and now-departed Dante (Fenton and Mary Ellen's uncle), has hung up her traveling booties and retired permanently to the ranch. There she fills her days keeping track of her horses, heading out to the barn once or twice a day to grab a poop-cicle or two, ambling out to the end of the driveway to rough up the rock marmots from time to time. She likes to watch the mountains turn color from indigo to lavender to crimson in the morning, and from tawny to vermilion to cobalt at night. This is the way a dog teaches us about stillness.

Rose is counting the days until summer, when we will all be reunited on the porch in Colorado: Fenton, Mary Ellen, me, Sarah, maybe even Fenton-the-human. Maybe someone will pull out a mouth harp, and Rose will start thinking back to her traveling days, when the rhythm of the tires on the asphalt led her to write the song that made her famous all those years ago:

ALL THE BAGS AND DANTE AND ME

(sung to the tune of "Me and Bobby McGee," by Kris Kristofferson, as Janis sang it at the Warfield)

Stuck in the hot car again,
Windows barely cracked,
Wonder why I'm always in the back.
Dante says it won't be long,
It's just a grocery store.
Man I hope those humans bring a snack.

I took my last dump, at a truck stop near Elko.
Haven't stretched my legs since Wendover . . .
Stuck in back I've done no crime, oh,
Is it ever suppertime?
Is it ever time to take a stroll?

Road trip's just another word for nothing much to do.
Nothing . . . they won't even let me pee.
Oh, the humans love to travel,

But I haven't got no room
Room enough for all the bags and me . . . eee.eeee.
Room for all the bags and Dante and me.

Rooo, roooo, rooo, rooo, rooo, rooo, rooo. Roo, roo, roo, roo, roo, roo, roo.
Roo, roo, roo, roo, roo, roo, Dante and me, rahr rahr. Rahr, rahr, rahr,
rahr, rahr, rahr, rahr, rahr. Rahr, rahr rahr, rhar, rhar. Rahr, rahr, rahr,
rahr, rahr, rahr, Dante and me, rahr. Rahr rahr, rahr, rah-ra-rah, rah-ra-
rah, rah-ra-rah, rah-ra-ra-ra-ra-ra-rah-ra-rah, hey, now, hey now hey
now, Dante and me, yeah. Rah, ra, ra-rah-ra, rah-ra-rah, ra-rah-ra, rah-
ra-rah, ra, rah, ra, hey, hey, hey Dante and me, rahra.

⌠ A dog says "snow" by eating it. —Dan Liebert ⌡

How You Can Help Your Dog Enjoy a Visit to the Vet

[Michael J. Rosen and Mark Allen Svede]

A TRIP TO the vet's office need not be a traumatic experience. A dog who is fearful, trembling, incontinent, blowing her coat, snarling, snapping, or attempting to claw an opening in the freshly repainted examination room door cannot appreciate the fact that you, and those of us here at Green Valley PetroPlex, have only her best interests in mind. Moreover, a veterinarian who is fearful, urine-soaked, and bleeding from both scratches and puncture wounds cannot appreciate your dog's adorable qualities.

And why should you yourself fill with dread as you enter the clinic on the off-chance that we didn't have to hire yet another receptionist who won't know about your pet's previous arraignments?

We have prepared this tip sheet with simple "desensitizing" exercises—that is, things you can do to acclimate your pet to the sounds, smells, physical sensations, and invasive procedures that are a routine part of veterinary care. Remember: after our own lives and limbs, followed by

our anxiety over litigation and the loss of your patronage and potential re-
ferrals, we here at Green Valley PetroPlex value your pet's safety and health
above all else.

Begin slowly. Acknowledge that your dog might not enjoy car rides, or
perhaps a leash. Or unfamiliar places, or strange sounds, or even familiar
sounds. That's okay. Your dog also might not enjoy other dogs, or spending
time on uncarpeted surfaces, or being weighed—especially by patronizing
strangers—or doing most anything that's not just eating what you're eating.
So why is it that your dog loves a ride to the soft-serve ice cream place,
which includes all these same anxiety-producers, except for the weighing
part? Dogs are complicated animals, which is why you begin slowly.

- The weighing thing is no big deal. Tear off a sheet of aluminum foil
  that's as long as your dog's body. Set it on the floor. Place your dog on a
  leash, and have him stand on your "scale." Now praise your dog and give
  him a treat. (At this point, don't worry about a few extra pounds: foil
  scales are notoriously forgiving.)

- Speaking of little rides, if your dog already enjoys driving to the bank
  with you because her favorite teller dispenses dog biscuits through the
  pneumatic tube, have the teller say your dog's name through the speaker,
  along with a phrase such as "This might sting a little."

- For a few minutes every day, wear a brightly colored smock, preferably
  dotted with smiling puppies and happy kitties. Gradually, wear your
  smock for longer and longer periods of time. An extra-large smock
  works overtime as a nightshirt if your scaredy cat sleeps under the covers
  with you.

- Place dog-eared copies of magazines at least two years old on your end
  tables and windowsills. Make certain to include at least one animal-
  husbandry publication and one with graphic images of an untreated
  tapeworm infestation.

- An examination need not create anxiety. Help your dog understand this by poking and prodding your dog when he is calm—upon waking, for instance. Start by simply touching various places on your dog. Name the parts if you like, although it isn't really reassuring if Mommy uses the word "occipital ridge" instead of "the little pointy place on top of your head I like to kiss."

- Eventually imagine that your fingers are a stethoscope: press firmly around your dog's withers, brisket, and raised hackles. Act like you are listening. (If your dog is unaccustomed to your silence, you may hum softly.) You can also pretend that your fingers are an otoscope, an ophthalmoscope, a syringe, and a rectal thermometer.

- Trim your dog's toenails every time you trim your own. Make it a fun routine: let your dog trim one of your toenails, and then you trim one of your dog's. Even if this is unlikely to make the experience more pleasant for either of you, it will help you understand the risks we here at Green Valley PetroPlex face when we see your reluctant little fella.

- To help your dog understand that we do our best to honor appointment times but that delays are an unavoidable aspect of veterinary care, secure your dog on a leash and invite dog-walking passersby to join you in your TV room. Some of the strangers should make small talk; others should remain close-lipped. One should narrate the entire hour in a high-pitched baby voice, while yet another should weep inconsolably into her animal's fur. If convenient, to further dispel possible future tension, invite other members of the food chain to come sit a spell—for instance, boas, bunnies, accipiters, turtles, and Wheaton Terriers.

- In general, dogs do not like slippery surfaces. We don't either, but we're in the business of preventing the spread of disease, not sterile interior design. Help your dog overcome any insecurity about the exam table by clearing the surface of whatever table in your house has the slickest surface.

For the first few days, simply introduce your dog to the empty table. (Find an alternate surface for family meals, stacks of mail with unpaid vet bills, and the rest of your unsorted crap.)

Next, place a dog treat on the table. Provide a "stepping stool" such as your sofa, even if you have a dog who has proven, repeatedly, that he can jump that high—and even higher as on the Thanksgiving he consumed Aunt Nancy's pumpkin cheesecake on the sideboard.

- Being a highly olfactory creature, your dog is sure to remember the smells here at Green Valley PetroPlex: a mixture of disinfecting products, other animals' odors (including a steady stream of colognes and after-shaves), and the aromatherapy candles that our bookkeeper Ginny sells to pay for all the discount veterinary care she requires for the scads of unwanted kittens and puppies she's adopted from the clinic. In order to ensure that these smells are pleasant associations why not take home a few scented candles to make your dog feel "at home" when in "our home"? Ginny offers a six-for-the-price-of-five discount as part of our low-cost spay/neuter package.

- Drive over to the clinic each week. Make us just another little errand on which your dog accompanies you. At first, just drive through the parking lot, point out the other nice doggies, and wave to the drivers circling the lot for the same reason that you are. After a few weeks, roll down the windows, or, if you feel your dog is ready, pull the car into a parking space and talk with your dog in a cheerful manner. Finally, walk your dog around the perimeter of the building. Make up happy stories about the dogs and cats you see in the waiting room; in this situation, your sense of irony is no help.

Thank you for helping us help you help your dog. Remember, it's your attitude that models your dog's attitude. Show your dog that you enjoy visiting Green Valley PetroPlex and your dog will too. Exude confidence and have a confident dog! Keep to yourself why you feel that flea preventives are a rip-off, or why it scares you that a person who spent a small fortune on a veterinary education would believe that a bright purple smock with orange Beagles sniffing rainbows would calm either you or your pet. Your dog will pick up on your skepticism.

Should you need more assistance than these brief suggestions can provide, ask a member of our staff for your complimentary copy of "My Dog Has a Panic Attack If I So Much as Mention the Word 'Vet,'" which comes with a free 30-day sample of CalmDown® (or that would be two 2-week samples if you want to give half to your dog), and our Scaredy Cat Dog Kit ($25) that includes our 64-page Do-It-at-Home Veterinary Care guide, a CalmDown® frequent-buyer discount card, and one of Ginny's Lavender Calming Candles.

CalmDown® *(2-chloro-4[2-(dimethyl-amino)propyl]-10,11-dihydro-4H-dibenz[b,f]azepine monohydrochloride)* **is not for every dog or every dog owner. Talk to your vet about whether** *CalmDown*®, **or even your dog, is right for you.**

Better Than You

[Jon Glaser]

I HAVE A DOG. But this story is not about her. It is about me and how I am better than you. The reason I am better than you is this: not only do I pick up my dog's No. 2's, I also rinse and dilute her No. 1's. Since this is a reputable magazine, from this point forward, "rinsing her No. 1's" will be referred to as "the thing that makes me better than you."

I live in a big city, and I have always been disgusted by how people just let their dogs freely urinate on garbage bags, on newspaper boxes, or even right on the sidewalk. There's no consideration or respect for the sanitation workers who have to handle the bags, the people who get newspapers, or even their neighbors and neighborhood. So several years ago, I started carrying a water bottle with me when I took my dog for a walk, to do the thing that makes me better than you.

Over time, I started to feel myself becoming a little smug whenever I pulled out the water bottle. I was very impressed not only with what I was doing but also with my entire system for doing it. I didn't inconveniently and awkwardly carry the water bottle in one hand. I wore (and still wear) Dickies double-knee work pants. Full length in the fall, shorts in the summer, both of which have a pocket on the side of the right pant leg that also happens to fit a standard bicycle water bottle perfectly. It's almost as if the pants were designed for me. Or designed by me. I have them in dark blue, black, gray, and brown. A friend once asked if the pants were Helmut Lang. Helmut Lang? Good Lord, how much better than you can I be?

On all my walks, I never saw anyone do anything remotely similar to what I was doing, and I gradually allowed myself to believe that I was the only one in the entire city—and quite possibly all of America—who was doing something like this. I wondered if people were noticing me, thinking about me, talking about me to one another after they passed me by.

"Did you see that?"

"That is so great."

"More people should do that."

I fantasized about standing in front of City Hall and describing what I do, showing everyone the water bottle in the side pocket, demonstrating how small and easy a thing it is to do, my voice starting to rise a little with passion. The little things add up to a lot, I'd say. I envisioned doing a print ad for Dickies: a shot of me walking my dog, reaching for the water bottle, with the caption "Dickies: Worn by the guy who does the thing that no one else does."

I didn't go to City Hall. I didn't do an ad for Dickies. And in all the months, and then years, that I walked my dog, waiting to be acknowledged, no one ever said anything. It became obvious at some point that no one else was doing it, and I resigned myself to the fact that no one cared.

My dog and I were in the street when it happened. A woman approached me. She wasn't passing me on the sidewalk or sitting in a nearby car. She was a good thirty feet away, inside a building. She came out of the building and walked over to me. I almost wasn't sure what to do. The moment I always dreamed of was happening, and it caught me off guard. It was like finally accepting the fact that Santa Claus doesn't exist, only to have him come walking through the front door instead of the chimney, on a day that is not Christmas, just to tell me what a great thing he thought I was doing with my dog. (After this, I picture him just standing there for a moment of awkward silence and then turning right around to leave.)

This woman was impressed not only by what I had done but also that I had done it even though my dog wasn't on the sidewalk. Which I guess, in this woman's eyes, made what I was doing all the more noble. We chatted for a bit about this, about how what I had done was so easy, how more people should do it and have respect for their neighborhood. All the things I had imagined people must think when they see me. It was a very short exchange. No extended dialogue about morals or the state of the world or anything. She then walked back into the building, and I walked away feeling very good about myself. I had been validated.

That was all I needed. The confidence in knowing what a great thing I'm doing is back. I'm guessing that this article will inspire copycats. People will claim they wrote this article, and for the most part I'll continue to go on being unrecognized. But some people—the smart ones—will figure out that I was the author. And when they do, they will probably want to tell me what a great thing it is that I'm doing. Let me just say right now that it won't be necessary. Because I already know.

Lucas

[Haven Kimmel]

A FEW YEARS ago I adopted Bosco from a local rescue organization. Bosco was a frightfully attractive dog; he appeared to be some mixture of a Pit Bull and a Great Dane. So while he was lovely to me, to drug dealers he looked like a big pile of narcotics laced with money. How he was stolen and my search for him is another story, but while I was looking for him physically— walking into neighborhoods even the police wouldn't enter—I posted his picture and name and tag numbers on the Internet and with the local shelters and vets' offices, and that's how I came to get an e-mail about Lucas.

Lucas's original name was Dewey, which sounds almost exactly like Bosco. And while Bosco weighed 75 pounds at seven months, Dewey weighed fifteen, and looked precisely like nonconsensual intercourse between a Pit Bull and a Chihuahua. So an honest mistake was made on the part of the shelter. (Both dogs were black, Dewey all over and Bosco in a few places.) The shelter sent me a photograph of Dewey standing on a concrete floor with his very large ears poised like satellite dishes, and even though the digital picture was blurry, I could see that a more abject look of terror had never been affected by a mammal. The accompanying note said, in terms barely concealed by euphemism, that the shelter was full and Dewey was going to be put down. He was an owner-surrender, and had come in with a Poodle companion who was also scheduled to meet the Reaper.

At this point it might be interesting to pursue what happened to me internally, but it would certainly not be profitable, as all signs point to mental illness. I am moved to rescue animals the way others are moved to gamble, or collect aluminum foil, or take many wives. I just can't bear it, the thought of an animal in distress and desperate for intervention when I have the power to intervene; to me all stray animals look like little war orphans. (My mother would point out here, perhaps a tad psychoanalytically, that War Orphan was one of my nicknames as a child, because I was scurvy-skinny and my clothes consistently came out of the dirty-laundry pile. Also the lack of shoes.) The older I get and the more resources I have at my disposal, the worse this becomes. Because what does it cost me after all? Some vet bills, a little extra dog food. I already have to vacuum every seventeen minutes, so what's the big deal? Sure, my family and neighbors and friends fall down prostrate and plead with me to stop before Animal Control gets wind of my behavior and classifies me a "nuisance," but I consider all of my loved ones to be slightly anal.

I called the shelter at which Dewey was smoking his last cigarette and accepting his blindfold. The woman who answered the phone said Dewey had three hours to live, and the shelter was four hours away from Durham, North Carolina, where I live. I tried to explain the discrepancy to the lovely receptionist, but she was unable to grasp the mathematics. I asked her if he could possibly be kept overnight, and I would leave the following morning. The question brought about extreme consternation on her part. Finally she said she thought he'd be okay in his makeshift crate.

"Can you tell me anything about him?" I asked, realizing that I'd committed myself to driving over the Blue Ridge Mountains and into a town doubtless populated by former Grand Dragons of the Klan, in order to adopt a dog I knew absolutely nothing about.

"Well, lahk I said in the e-mail, his owner brought him and said I don't want this dog no more, nor the other one neither. He's a'skeert, I'll tell you that."

"Does he bite? Is he injured, neutered?"

"He done bit Kinny."

"He bit Kinny. Who would that be?"

She coughed for about 45 seconds, apologized. "Kinny works here. He went to take Dewey out of his cage, and Dewey bit him."

"What's his disposition like otherwise? Aside from biting Kenny."

"Well, he's a'skeert, and he pees."

"Is he neutered?"

"No. That's why he bit Kinny, if you ask me."

Our conversation went around and around like this for a long time, and finally I was assured that Dewey could live one more night (under conditions I couldn't have actually imagined), and then I had to explain to everyone I knew that I wouldn't be home the next day because I was driving all the way across the state and over the mountains to rescue a dog I'd never seen and knew nothing about. And why was I doing this? In Bosco's name. Bosco, who was by that time long, long gone.

The drive was lovely, but the location of the shelter seemed to adhere strictly to Zeno's Paradox. No matter how close I got, I was still only halfway there. I followed the map carefully, but still had to stop at a "country store" and ask directions. Country stores are ubiquitous in western North Carolina, and are so called for reasons that escape me, as they generally only carry Sno-balls, cigarettes, and malt liquor. There was a time when "country" meant red-eye gravy and excellent jerky, but now it seems to apply exclusively to NASCAR, by which I mean "country" is a $700 gazillion affair. The woman behind the counter, who was smoking a cigarette and mourning the death of Dale Earnhardt (whom, when my daughter told me he was dead, I assumed to be one of her classmates), explained that the shelter was at the "foot" of the mountain. In Indiana, the land from which I hail, we keep our feet in precisely one place. I tried to explain this, then realized I was *on* the foot of the mountain, and had passed the shelter fourteen times. I passed it because it looked like a cinder-block house next to a double-wide trailer.

———————

I pulled up in front of the cinder-block house and went inside, where I was stunned to discover upwards of six or seven women all wearing Carhartt bibbed overalls, the sort I wear on exactly one occasion, which is when I visit my sister's farm and must deal with her horses. (Dealing with my sister's horses inevitably involves prodigious mud and a temperature of four. This past winter, while visiting home, I listened to the weather report on the radio as I was getting ready to leave for Melinda's house, and when the announcer said the temperature was four, I called my mom and asked could it possibly be true. She said, "I know it sounds less like a temperature than the age of a toddler, but alas.") Wearing Carhartts as a matter of course is a fashion statement not widely understood outside the American South, but I quite respect it. These were women not likely to be afraid of dogs, and who were clearly fine milk-producers for their young. There were hips and upper arms on those women not seen since before the First World War.

I approached the desk and said I was the person who had just driven for many days to rescue the stranger, Dewey. I ended up dealing with the same woman I'd spoken to on the phone, who picked up the phone and called Kenny, the shelter-hand. He was apparently in the double-wide, where the dogs were kept, as opposed to the cinder-block, where the vets were.

"Kinny. That woman is here to pick up the Poodle–Shit Soo mix."

I shook my head dramatically; no no no, I am not that woman. Anyone looking at me would know I'm not even remotely that woman. "I'm here for Dewey," I said, pointing to his little picture, which I'd carried with me like a War Orphan looking for her parents.

"Aw wait. She's here for Dewey." She paused. "Okay, I'll tell her." She hung up the phone and I knew in my bones that he'd been gassed and was on a big corpse pile behind the cinderblock. "Kinny's a'skeert of that dawg and don't want to get him out of his cage. He says ever time he gits near him, that dawg tries to bite him. Kinny's a'skeert."

"So I hear. Do you want me to go get him?"

"I'll go get him," one of the younger Carhartts whispered. Her voice was so quiet I feared she'd been the victim of a rogue tracheotomy. Her hair was long and wavy, her breasts were large, and her cheeks were flushed with high color. She was a child formed by a rapid influx of estrogen, and I didn't dare look at her too closely or too long, for fear I'd make her pregnant. She moved slowly through the clinic, slowly down the steps, and across the drive to the double-wide. A few minutes later she came in carrying Dewey.

I've seen some dogs in my life. I grew up in a town where dogs weren't restrained, and in fact could run for public office. I saw a rabid dog shot in the street, just like in *To Kill a Mockingbird*. (To be honest, the town marshal shot his own hat off and the dog fell down, scared to death.) I've seen dogs limping around barnlots with only a couple of usable limbs, and dogs dying of disease, and dogs hit by cars. But I've never seen anything quite like Dewey. His bat ears were lying flat against his head; his whole body was tensed; and he was screaming as if caught in a trap. He was bleeding from both eyes, and the blood had covered the white patch on his chest. The parts of him not sticky with blood were slick with urine and diarrhea. The girl who'd gotten him out of his cage carried him into an examination room and put him on a table, where he stood trembling so hard I thought he might be seizing. She stood close to the table and let him lean up against her.

And then into the room lumbered Kenny, who was roughly the size of a mature walnut tree, bearded, and built like a military vehicle.

"That dawg bit me good," he said, in a voice that caused the floor to shake. "But he's not bad in his heart."

I turned and looked at him and my eyes filled with tears. I wasn't sure what I was crying about, but the whole situation was so wretched I suddenly couldn't help myself.

"How'd he get this way?" I asked, still not daring to approach the screaming dog.

"His owner got mad at him and that Poodle, kicked them in their heads. This one's been bleeding from his eyes all night."

Anyone who has worked with stray dogs knows that you have to read a myriad of signs before adopting or fostering, and not just the obvious things

like how well they do with other dogs and children. What you look for first
of all, and most importantly, is *sanity*, simple as that. What I was seeing was
the most traumatized dog I'd ever met. Dogs go crazy from lots of things.
Pit Bull Terriers, a breed that loves people more, maybe, than any other, can
be broken from exile in a backyard, just from the lack of human contact.
Abandonment will break the heart of most things, really. This dog had been
brought to a ghastly place, separated from the companion dog with whom
he'd lived his whole life, been forced to listen to the frantic and desperate
barking of all the other dogs who were about to be euthanized. And just as
a bonus, his owner had beaten him within an inch of his life before surren-
dering him.

"The guy who owned him," Kenny continued, "went all the way
through school with me, I've known him my whole life. But I'll never be
able to look him in the eye again."

I approached the table and Dewey wailed even louder, pressing his
body as hard against the Milk Maiden as he dared. There was so much
blood on his head I couldn't tell if he was still bleeding, if his skull was frac-
tured, if those enormous ears were actually attached. I put my hand on his
back just as the vet walked in, and at the sound of the door shutting he
jumped straight up in the air, nearly falling off the table, which caused me
to jump, and Kenny to scream like a nine-year-old girl.

The vet, Dr. Morris I'll call her, was entirely calm and composed and
caused all of us to regain our sensibilities, even Kenny, who was trailing a
string of gauze wrapped around his left hand and who seemed a tad undone.

"His head seems okay," Dr. Morris said, feeling around the dog's eye
sockets and looking in Dewey's ears, even as his screams broke up into yips
and hiccups and he shook until his feet were dancing on the metal table.
"He'll be able to see fine once this blood clears up, and he has a broken rib
or two, but that will heal. His legs aren't broken; I don't think he has internal injuries, but you'll need to keep an eye on him." It was consistently difficult to tell if Dewey was going to bite someone. Half the time he seemed
right on the verge of snapping, and the other half he seemed about to go
into cardiac arrest. "He needs to be neutered, and I'll give him his vaccina-
tions before you leave today."

So that was that. I didn't need to fill out an application or explain whether I had a fenced-in yard or if I intended to test my bathtub LSD on Dewey's little brain. No one there could afford to act as if it mattered. Dewey was going to die if I left him; if I took him and abused him, he'd at least bought a few more days on the planet, for what that was worth.

I went out to my truck and brought in the baby wipes and towels I'd brought, along with some biscuits and rawhides. I'd imagined having a normal meeting with Dewey, the sort one has with dogs wherein you offer them a treat and they see you as the Big Treat Giver and know you are Good. Now the whole bag looked paltry and naive.

After Dr. Morris was done with her exam and had given Dewey his shots, I asked that he be put on the floor, where he at least might feel comfortable in the knowledge he wasn't going to fall off the shiny steel table. Large Hormonal Girl insisted on moving him, still afraid he might bite me. Kenny stepped back into a corner. I sat down next to the dog, and slowly began wiping some of the blood off his face and chest with the baby wipes (added benefit: no diaper rash). He trembled and cried, his tail tucked between his legs, his back arched like a cat's. Kenny shook his head and clucked. The Large Girl looked down at us dreamily. "He's going to be so happy with you, I can just tell," she said, slowly. I nodded. Everyone in that clinic was completely mad, I now understood. Because Dewey was never going to be happy again, not anywhere, not with anyone.

"By the way," Kenny said, scratching his chin under his thick beard. "I don't think old Dewey there has ever seen grass. He was kept in a kennel outdoors with a concrete floor. When he first got here I tried to take him out to go to the bathroom, and when his paws touched the grass he jumped back like he was on FAHR."

I wanted to ask, What more? What more could you possibly tell me? He's a bearer of monkeypox? He's packed with explosives? I cleaned him up as best I could, then just accepted what I'd done, like the good little existentialist I used to be. I put the collar on Dewey I'd brought from home, and the leash, and tried to get him to follow me out the door. As we passed the front desk, all the women in their Carhartts waved, wished me well. They were distracted. Dogs and cats were coming in, going out, dying and being saved all around them, all day. They were doing the best they could. The dog made it out the door, then began howling and trembling again as soon as his feet touched the grass. I picked him up and carried him to my truck.

During the four-hour drive back home, Dewey regressed into catatonia. In many ways this was preferable. He didn't raise his head, move a muscle; I didn't even see him blink. He stared at the glove box, silently. I considered what I'd just done. Not only was I bringing this dog home to live with my children, I was (and perhaps more important) inflicting him on Harry and Fay, the mayor and deputy mayor of Dogland. Harry (my dog) and Fay (my daughter's) were so perfect, so dear and well-behaved, so trusting of my judgment, I feared they would see Dewey as an astonishing betrayal. I glanced over at him. He didn't move. To my shock and horror, I realized he looked less like a Chihuahua/Pit mix than a *hyena*. A hyena crossed with a fruit bat. Hyenas are another of God's little reminders that the world is a horrific place best not considered with too much precision. If anyone reading this is a charter member of the Hyena Lovers Foundation, don't even bother sending me hate mail. I know the truth about hyenas, which is that they have hinged jaws, they can swallow and breathe at the same time (allowing them to eat on the hoof, as it were); they chomp right through bone and swallow it, and their poop looks like chalk as a result. CHALK-POOPERS. In addition, the females have an enlarged clitoris known as a hemipenis. All of this is nasty and grotesque and nightmare-inducing and not to be borne. And Dewey was one of them, I could clearly see. We drove.

When we got home he continued his nefarious plan of motionlessness. I had about twenty-five minutes before my son and daughter got home from school, and I decided the best way to use the time, and to exploit Dewey's catatonia, was to give him a bath. I couldn't do anything about the whites of his eyes, which were still bloody, but I could at least make him a little more presentable before Kat and Obadiah saw him.

I put Harry and Fay outside before I brought Dewey in, so as not to traumatize any of them, then carried Dewey over for his bath. He sat in the sink without any fuss, as would the dead. I was careful of his broken and bruised places, and watched the blood and foulness from his two days at the shelter swirl away down the drain. Then I wrapped him in towels and sat down with him on the couch. He leaned against me, shivering periodically. I thought to myself, I just drove eight hours; I crossed over a mountain range; I stopped at a country store; I met Kinny; and I brought home the Jack Nicholson character from the end of *One Flew Over the Cuckoo's Nest*. Postoperative Jack. Here he is on my lap. He is my dog.

Kat pulled in the driveway after picking up Obadiah from kindergarten. Dewey was a fine test of character for them: Obadiah was a kindergartener; Kat was a seventeen-year-old senior in high school. As they walked in the door, I said, "Don't make any sudden moves; I've got this weird crazy dog on my lap." Kat noticed that his towel configuration resembled Palestine. (The comparison to Yasser Arafat's headwear was prescient, and I took note of it.) For just a moment, this story is about my dear children, who, even though they're separated by gender and twelve years, reacted exactly the same way. Neither said, "You brought home THAT?" Nor did they move too quickly or frighten Dewey. Both simply said, "Poor sweet little fella," and got down on their knees to look at him.

What a different story this would be if he had bitten one of them! Ha! Because I could end the essay right here with "And then I killed Dewey." Instead, his tail began to wag just slightly. It would have wagged more, but he was completely swaddled by the Gaza Strip. I unwrapped him, and he stepped over to Obadiah, smelling his hands, timid, but clearly happy to see a child. After we'd all petted him and talked to him and told him what a good boy he was, we decided to let the other dogs in. Fay and Harry, who were both then twice Dewey's size, approached the couch gingerly. And here is a classic example of how One Just Never Knows: Dewey sprang off the couch, his tail curled tautly over his back, staring the other dogs in the eye and smelling their nether-regions, as is customary in Dogland. All the dogs became very stiff, if I may. I wasn't sure whether a scuffle was brewing or not, and then Dewey did something I've never seen a dog do before. He leapt straight up off the floor, all four feet at once, and turned 180 degrees. It was positively freakish. He looked first at Harry, then leap! turn! at Fay. Everyone found this breathlessly amusing, including the dogs, who lowered their chests to the floor in the bow that signals play, and after that they were off. They wagged crazily, bit one another's lips, exposed bellies, rolled around like doughnuts, ran in circles. Happy happy happy. Happy to be alive, to meet another of their tribe. There wasn't a moment of tension between them. Eventually I opened the back door and off they went into the yard, where they played until bedtime. I told Kat that whatever had happened to Dewey in his brief, sad life, it hadn't been done to him by other dogs.

I couldn't continue to call him Dewey, and not just because of how much it sounded like Bosco. I didn't want him going through life hearing that name, given the contexts in which he might have heard it before. So I renamed him Lucas, and he came running the first time I called him. Smart boy.

More must be said about the fact that Lucas wasn't neutered when I brought him home. Specifically, I must be honest about his testicles. I decided not to have him neutered immediately, because I wasn't sure of his age (his grown-up teeth were brand-new), and because he was so traumatized. I decided to wait a month and let him settle in. Fay had been spayed, and there was no chance Lucas could get out of our fenced-in yard and make more little hyenas, so I didn't worry much about it. But I'd never had a, shall we say, intact male dog before. I prefer females (a real dog person would write "bitches" there; oh, and I shall). I prefer bitches. Walk around saying that. The only male dogs I'd had were already taken care of in the reproduction department.

The first thing I noticed about Lucas's parts was that they were really noticeable. He'd been with us only a couple of weeks when my daughter gave him the nickname Fat Tony, because he swaggered like a wiseguy in the Mob. In fact, he acted in all ways like a mafioso; it had something to do with his demeanor around dogs much larger than he (he came to us weighing about sixteen pounds to Fay's fifty, for instance), as if he had nothing to talk to them about because he was packing greater heat. Not to put too fine a point on it, but he was packing the genuine article, and his testicles were visible with every step he took. I couldn't get over it. I'd see him run through the house toward the back door: testicles. He'd jump up on the couch with me: there they were. I wasn't sure where to look.

And also I didn't know how adorable those little guys can be. Lucas slept sitting up like an old man in a recliner, with his head thrown back. He also snored. He preferred to do this leaning up against me. So one night Kat and I were sitting up late talking; I was in one corner of the couch with Lucas on my lap. He was sound asleep, bent like a question mark. Kat was at the other end of the couch. I pointed out to her (in an educational way) that Lucas's testicles resembled little furry eggs. I said, "Look! Look how cute they are." Perhaps I had said this a few times already.

She said, "Yes, Mom, I see them."

"Do you think he'd notice if I just poked them?"

"Oh for the love of God," Kat said, exasperated. "No, I don't think he'd notice."

So I did that. When Kat tells this story now, she makes a little gesture with her first and middle fingers together and says "poke poke," which was exactly what I did. They *felt* like little furry eggs, too, which I took to be a bonus. Lucas not only didn't mind, he didn't even stir. He just kept snoring through his black lips. He slept so hard he eventually slid down my left arm and ended up on his side on the couch.

Maybe fifteen minutes had passed, and Kat and I had moved on to more important topics of conversation, like Kant, or the death penalty, something like that, when Kat suddenly leapt off the couch screaming, "OH MY GOD!" and pointing at Lucas.

He was enjoying what I learned in seventh-grade health class to call a *nocturnal emission*. I'm sorry to say that it wasn't merely the nocturnal part occurring, but also the emitting. I too jumped up with great haste, but was unsure what to do after that. Does one awaken an ejaculating dog, or does one absolutely not? For his part, Lucas appeared to still be sound asleep (although quite happy). I decided to just let him have his moment, as it were, and headed toward the laundry room for towels and upholstery cleaner. Kat covered her face and said, "I am scarred for life. I am SCARRED for LIFE."

By the time I got back to the living room, Lucas was awake and seemed confused. I picked him up and put him on the floor, and began cleaning the couch cushion. "Okay," I said to my daughter, who was by this time pacing, "when you get into therapy in a few years, you're welcome to say that I poked at the little furry eggs. I encourage you to be honest. But please don't jumble this all up in your mind and make it look like satanic ritual abuse." I was afraid of losing the right to ever open a day care.

I eventually had Lucas neutered while I was out of town. That was the only way I could go about it. I never expected to feel the way I did: me! Ms. Neuter All of Them! Including most human men! But when it came right down to it, I didn't want anyone to hurt Lucas, and I didn't want some of his little parts to just vanish. I kept thinking of his days at the shelter at the foot of the mountain; how diminished he was when I found him. He'd emerged with almost nothing but his big personality and his, well, other things. And I couldn't help feeling like he deserved to hold on to what he had, what he'd entered the world with. But in the end, so to speak, I did the right thing. When I came home and saw him prancing around, just a little blank space between his legs, I felt a moment of real sadness, then considered what a better world we might have lived in if someone had done the same thing to Lucas's former owner. Kinny would have done it at a discount, I'll bet.

Ball and Chain

[William Wegman]

Dog of the Day

[Laurie Notaro]

MY DOG MAEBY has always gotten good grades.

Every evening when I pull into the driveway at the doggy day care center that she attends, Maeby, a fluffy Aussie/Lab mix, is waiting for me, along with her daily report card.

Although it is fanciful thinking that one day the center might provide classes in "The Mailman Is Only in It for the Pension and Not Your Territory, Therefore the Barking Looks a Little Silly," "A Fart Is a Fart and Not an Invisible Stench Rocket, So Stop Looking for It," or "Picking Up Your Own Poop," my dog consistently got good marks in areas of interest such as playing nicely with others and making new friends, and was apparently well heeled in the saucy arts, since it was reported that the flirty miss had a new boyfriend every week. While I wasn't exactly proud that my little Lady was shaking it up for the Tramps on the playground, I was delighted when she was promoted to the position of "greeter" at the center, which is a dog who is assigned to play with new dogs in the doggy day care pack to get them adjusted and make their transition easier. She was even asked to participate in a marketing video for the day care center in which, according to her report card, "Maeby stole the show with her playtime skills."

I mean, really. That one is *still* up on our refrigerator.

So, honestly, I was a little surprised when day after day, week after week, I would pick Maeby up from day care, get her report card, and glance at the chalkboard of honor that stands at the entrance to the center, only to see that the Dog of the Day—the highest honor of distinction that any dog could receive—was proclaimed to be Blackjack.

Last week it had been Mossimo.

The week before it had been Sammie.

The week before that, Ziggy.

The previous week, it went to Hercules Wu, whose parents had once taken our leash because theirs looked similar and then returned it a week later with HERCULES WU written across the back side of it in black permanent marker, along with Hercules Wu's phone number.

You know, I thought to myself as I drove home with Maeby fast asleep in the back of the car, I don't know what's going on here, but something's got to give. Look at her, so busy greeting and teasing all the boys on the playground that she falls asleep the minute she gets in the car! My dog is a hardworking hussy, pouring her heart out, *giving her all,* and what does she get in return? A nice report card. A scratch on the ears. That's not enough, I said to myself; that is not enough for my dog.

"I hate to break it to you," my husband said that night at dinner after I had voiced my Dog of the Day concerns. "But I highly doubt Maeby is upset about not being The Chosen One. She is far more concerned at the moment with licking the floor where you dropped a hot dog yesterday."

"That's not the point," I argued. "Do you not remember that Maeby was the one who *stole the show with her playtime skills?* Because if you've forgotten, I can show it to you."

My husband sighed. "She doesn't know how to spell 'Maeby,'" he offered. "Just point to the sign the next time you're there and tell her she is the Dog of the Day."

I was stunned. "If that's how you prefer to handle a crisis—with deceit and trickery—then I don't even want you in this house when I finally have to tell her she's adopted," I stuttered.

"Did you ever think," he finally said, "that maybe those dogs got the distinction because they earned it? That maybe they just gave a little bit extra?"

I gasped, not knowing what to say, but my mind began to race. Was it possible that the other dogs got better grades than Maeby? Could it be true that other dogs contributed more, were harder working? How could that be? Maeby was a greeter, showing new dogs the way, making them feel at ease, helping them with the introduction to the group. That was real dogitarian work. What could the other dogs possibly be doing that could outshine that? Was Sammie brokering peace accords between Indian and Pakistani dogs? Was Mossimo peacefully fighting for the rights of dogs not to be forced into wearing hats and sweaters if they chose not to? Was Black-jack removing land mines, making the playground safe for everyone else? Had Ziggy finally talked Mr. Winkle into retiring? And what was Hercules Wu doing, besides stealing leashes? Was Hercules Wu a greeter? I really doubted it. Was Hercules Wu asked to be in the video? Probably not. Did Hercules Wu steal the show with his playtime skills and his appropriated leash? Not very likely.

So I decided to do the only thing I really could do, and that was ask. I wanted to know what the Dog of the Day criteria were, what the mitigating factors might be, and then tackle the problem from that angle. But when I went to pick Maeby up after her next day at the center, I was not at all prepared for what I saw.

It was an empty chalkboard.

No one had been proclaimed Dog of the Day yet.

This was my—and Maeby's—chance.

I stood still for a moment, listening. I heard nothing, not the rustling of collars, or leashes, or barking. Everyone, it seemed, was outside on the playground.

Maeby stole the show with her playtime skills.

Maeby stole the show with her playtime skills.

I took a step forward toward the front desk.

Maeby stole the show with her playtime skills.

Where they keep the chalk.

I took another step. And another. And another, my steps becoming quicker as I neared the desk. And the chalk. And my dog's redemption.

And I saw it, a pink, slim tube of chalk, right there next to the computer keyboard. I was a step or two away from reaching over and grabbing it, because it was lying right there in the open, when I stopped.

Maeby stole the show with her playtime skills.

It was true. But how would Maeby feel if she knew that I stole the title of Dog of the Day and gave it to her, with her name written all over the back of it in pink chalk? I didn't take another step. Instead, I waited there for Mandie, the center's owner, to bring Maeby out with Hercules Wu's leash, and then told her that Maeby would be coming in an extra day that week because I had finally made an appointment to have my terminally ill nineteen-year-old cat, Barnaby, cross over into the Kitty Light. It would be better if she spent that day shaking her milkshake on the playground at the likes of Ziggy and Blackjack, I told Mandie, than to be at our house when something sad was going to happen.

And I was right; the day we sent Barnaby to a hereafter stocked with an all-you-can-eat buffet of Fancy Feast and Pounce was awfully sad, beginning with the moment we brought Maeby over to his cat bed to say good-bye to him. She nudged him gently, licked his head, sat and waited for Hercules Wu's leash, and was off to day care.

When I went to pick her up later that day, I couldn't wait to see her. Although Barnaby's passing couldn't have gone any smoother due to our sympathetic and patient vet, it was as emotional as any experience of letting a friend of nineteen years go could be. My eyes were red and puffy when I arrived, and as I walked into the lobby, Maeby bounded in through the side door.

"What a good girl!" I said as I scratched behind her ears and she jumped and hopped around with excitement. "I'm so happy to see you!"

"That's not all you should see," Mandie said, and I looked up to see her pointing away from us.

I looked in that direction, and that's when I saw it. The chalkboard, on which Maeby's name was written in pink, swirly letters.

"You're Dog of the Day?" I asked as she jumped and I jumped a little too, as I petted her head and she panted with excitement. "That's wonderful! Look at that! Maeby is Dog of the Day!"

Mandie handed over the leash and we were just about to walk out the door when I realized I still had a question and was dying for the answer.

"So," I said before I pushed the door all the way open. "How do you know who's Dog of the Day? In what way do you judge who deserves it?"

Mandie laughed. "It's not who 'deserves' it," she explained as she smiled. "It's who needs it the most."

"Oh," I said as I smiled back. "I think that's a great way. That's really nice. Thank you."

"Don't forget her report card," Mandie said as she pulled it from her pocket. "Maeby has two new boyfriends on the playground, you know."

Back from scattering birds, all dogs swagger a bit. —Dan Liebert

Home on the Mange

[Neal Pollack]

ONE NIGHT IN January, my family sat on the couch, watching television. We'd just moved to Los Angeles and we knew almost no one. A terrible freezing rainstorm had driven us inside; we cuddled for warmth and friendship.

There was a knock at the door.

My wife, Regina, and I looked at each other, a little annoyed and a little fearful. In our previous neighborhood, in Austin, Texas, we'd been constantly bothered at home by people asking us for money. One night I'd chased a couple of guys off my lawn because they were fighting over a prostitute. Then, the week we'd moved into this rental, Regina had answered the door to reveal a one-armed woman who was asking for money to benefit the family of a teenage girl who'd been slain in some random act of gang violence. Regina gave her a dollar. A panicked call to the neighborhood beat officer later revealed that this had been a scam. All the gang violence had moved either six blocks to the east or to the south, he assured us.

We'd learned to be skeptical of knocks at the door. But on nights like this, even scam artists stayed home. So I got up.

Through the slats of our door-length plastic blinds, I saw the French-woman who lived in the house behind us. A Ph.D. candidate in bioengineering at USC, she made a good neighbor: quiet, rarely home, and prone to taking weeklong surfing trips to Hawaii. We were friendly enough with her, though she never thanked us for the Christmas cookies we left on her doorstep.

"I have a leetle problem," she said.

"What?" I said.

"Eet's a dog."

She opened the door further. Behind her was a medium-sized terrier. Its white fur had been torn away in chunks from its torso, leaving a hideous vista of red-raw skin and sores and eminently visible bones. The dog was soaked and desperate to come inside; it stank like an entire animal shelter full of filth, with that certain kind of desperate putridity that presages death.

"Eet followed me home," she said. "I don't know much about dogs."

"We have a dog!" I said proudly.

"I know," she said. "That's why I'm asking you for help."

Our dog was a neckless Boston Terrier named Hercules. His hobbies included eating cat barf, licking my ankles under the bedcovers, and moping on the couch. When we did take him for walks, we had to lift him over puddles because he was afraid of water. Particularly compared with the other dogs in this neighborhood, hungry-looking Pit Bulls and Boxers who spent their entire lives shitting in concrete lots enclosed by wrought iron, Hercules was really more Muppet than dog. Owning him hardly qualified me as an expert in canine care.

But I'd only been in town for two weeks, and was feeling neutered and useless. This was the perfect mission to break my slump. A great surge of heroism and duty welled in my chest. I began barking orders.

"Regina! Get me some dog food! And a bowl! No! Two bowls! And a towel! And some treats and some doggie shampoo! We're going to clean this mutt up!"

A few minutes later, we walked through the rain to the back house. The French girl's place already smelled like the dog throughout.

"Eet's a he," she said. "I looked."

The stray hovered in her kitchen. But when I offered him doggie treats, he just looked confused, like he'd been hungry so long that he'd forgotten food's purpose. So I skipped that step, picked him up in a towel, and carried him to the bathroom. Then I placed him in the tub, soaked him with water from a cup, and scrubbed him down with Johnson's Baby Shampoo. He behaved himself. At least the water was warm.

When we were done, he still smelled like death, but at least now it was a clean death.

"Now what do I do?" said my neighbor.

This woman had obviously spent so much of her youth in microbiology labs that she had no idea how to function in the world of the mundane.

"Um," I said. "Call a vet?"

For some reason, instead of making the call herself, she handed me the phone book and phone. I dialed the Eagle Rock Emergency Animal Hospital.

"Yes, hello," I said. "I have a dog here. I found . . . well, actually, my neighbor found him on the street and took him home and then I gave him a bath. Where should I send him?"

"You need to get in touch with the Humane Society," said the man on the other line.

"OK."

"And, because you handled the dog, you might have mange."

"What?"

"Mange. Scabies. You should check with your doctor in two weeks. It usually doesn't set in for a month to six weeks. And if you have it, then everyone you come into contact with will get it too."

"Are you saying I shouldn't touch anybody for a month?"

"Just to be safe."

"Mange?" I said. "Are you *sure* I'm going to get mange?"

"Go to your doctor," he said. "You have mange."

This seemed impossible. I'd bathed the dog with disinfectant shampoo and washed my hands afterward. I've come into contact with stray dogs many times. And yet mange is not on the list of diseases I've contracted. Nevertheless, I ran home in a panic.

"We have mange," I said to Regina.

"What?" she said.

"You need to take off all your clothes and put them in the washer."

"You're kidding."

"Do it! NOW! And take off Elijah's clothes, too! And Hercules's collar!"

"Oh, come on."

"Dammit, Regina," I said. "We have mange! Mange!"

"Nooooo!" said my son. "I'm cold. I don't want to take off my clothes!"

If anyone is trying to decide whether or not to become a parent, let me provide you with this image: Regina and I forcibly undressing a three-year-old because his clothes might be infected with mange. If that doesn't dissuade you, let me try another image: All three of us in our underwear, shivering, afraid of having contracted mange, and watching *Monsters, Inc.*

What the hell were we doing here?

We quickly determined that Hercules's heartworm medicine protects him from mange. Also, we learned that while people can contract mange, it's an entirely different disease from the one that afflicts dogs. So we were safe. By the time we went to bed, our frenzy of disinfecting had ended.

That night, the French girl took her sad mutt to a shelter. A couple of days later, Regina came into my office bearing a concerned look.

"I'm worried about that dog," she said. "Will you call the shelter?"

Some dogs are born into families that dress them in argyle sweaters and feed them steak, while others are destined to walk the earth in misery, desperate for the sweet relief that death provides. It's never pretty when you run into one of the latter dogs. I called the shelter. Of course they'd put the dog down immediately.

Rather than putting us off from dogs, this incident actually made us like them even more. Regina started sidling up to me, just as she had right before we adopted Hercules. She put her head on my chest. She stroked my hair.

"Puppy, puppy, puppy," she said. "Puh-peeeeeee! Puh-leeeeese! Puppy!"

"Oh, God," I said. "Not again."

"They're so cute."

"We don't need another dog," I said.

"Of course we do," she said.

As of this writing, we're still a one-dog family. That probably won't be the case by the next writing. Recently, we put in an application online for a Boston Terrier named Shaq, but he had a dozen other suitors and we lost him. We found an adorable little Pug named Ella whom we liked, but to acquire her we had to go meet her at a fair, which we found out about too late. Regina liked another Boston named Chloe, who sounded cool from her online description. I rejected Chloe because she had a nasty-looking overbite. My wife was getting frustrated.

"It's just so hard to find a dog in L.A.," Regina said.

Not true, I told her. Dogs are ubiquitous here if you want them. You just have to be prepared to deal with a little mange.

Dog Whores

[Margaret Cho]

I LIKE WET dog noses resting on my skin, and feeling the fine, downy soft hairs of a sweet muzzle underneath. I love dogs, mostly all dogs. Possibly one or two I have met in my lifetime rubbed me the wrong way, but of the many thousands I have petted and cuddled, that isn't too bad.

When I am away from home, I put pillows on my body so that when I fall asleep, it still feels like my dogs are there. Pillows don't radiate heat or curl around my neck like a Chihuahua can, but when you are a dogless nomad, these and other people's dogs are all you have.

I think that there should be dog prostitutes. High-priced Great Dane gigolos. Miniature Doberman hustlers, in tiny white tank tops and studded leather collars. A fancifully beribboned Bichon Frise, a little aloof, but with kind eyes, to coo over and stroke all night. I want a mixed-breed Midnight Cowboy, to warm my bed and ease my lonely heart. Of course, in the end, when you have to go to your early-morning flight, with no time to check in any odd-sized baggage or go to the vet to get a travel certificate, you would have to pay them to leave, just like you paid them for the extras, like maintaining a down stay for an extended period or any particular canine agility.

I would spend a fortune on dog prostitutes, most likely fall in love more than once, filling up my home with dog whores from all over the world.

Lhasa Apsos and Labrador Retrievers. French Poodles and English Bulldogs. Chows and Irish Setters. All mine for the night, then all mine forever.
I have the potential to be one of those crazy people who take in hundreds
of strays and then irresponsibly die, only to have all my dear pets eat me. I
will have someone look in on me now and again to ensure that does not
happen.

A Catwoman in Dogland

[Kathe Koja]

THANKS FOR HOLDING the gate . . . yes, I'll watch my step. Honestly, it's a lovely country you have here, with such strange and wonderful objects—the Burberry leash, the Mutt Mitt, the fluorescent-green Kong— the like of which we've never seen in Fresh Scent Litter Land—which I abhor, by the way: I would rather smell my oldest cat's ammonia-drenched scat forever than that perky "pine" reek. Although we clean the box twice a day, I swear. We have to: We have three cats.

We also have friends, and some of those friends have dogs, and one of those friends, Jay, is as close to me as a sister. So when she adopted T.S., big and gangly and beautiful, a brown-eyed, blue-eyed (yes, one of each) half-Dane/half-who-knows-what, all at once this confirmed catwoman found herself, like Alice tumbling down the rabbit hole, squarely in Dogland.

Of course I like dogs, and always have: they're furry, they're animals, what's not to like? But cats are my ur-animal. Their quirks and flings and ailments, their small determined moods, their butting heads and twining tails—well, you get the idea. The three we live with now are members of a long and loving line, dating all the way back to when my husband and I were children. We are, in all senses of the word (well, maybe not the Paul Schrader–movie sense), cat people.

So I had to wonder, how would it be, now, with Jay and T.S.? It was like she'd gotten hooked up with a new boyfriend, one whose language I didn't speak, and whose expressions (the bark!) were a little strange to me. But I was game.

The shelter adoption process held no surprises: It is what it is, forms in triplicate, neuter, shots, and tags. Although T.S. didn't go home in an adorable purple-paw-print cardboard carrier; he couldn't fit, natch, and anyway he would have eaten it. My first real lesson in Dogland came at Jay's, with the concept of the crate. In our little suburb of Cat World, the "crate"—den, safe house, time-out chair—is my office. Unless it's the sofa in the living room, or the downstairs bathroom sink. Or the exact middle of the bed, in the exact middle of the night. Or my face. Wherever, it's the cats who make the call. So "What if he doesn't like the crate?" I asked Jay.

"Well, he'll be trained," she said.

Second lesson. There is no such thing as training, period, in Cat World. Some people claim to have trained their cats to stay off the furniture with deadeye squirt bottles or double-sided tape, but actually these people are delusional, and their cats laugh quietly at them behind their backs. The people at the obedience classes I attended with Jay and T.S., however, didn't seem delusional, although a few of them needed training far, far more urgently than their chubby Pugs or funky little Terriers. For six weeks, I stood on the taped-off sidelines, observing as the dogs learned—with a combination of firmness, praise, and the occasional (OK, in the beginning, the constant) jerky-treat reward—to sit and stay, to walk at heel, to trace a serpentine route between one another without leaping up for play or combat. It was kind of like watching contra dancing, except half the dancers had four legs. Originally I didn't care much for the instructor, because she liked to wear a floppy sweatshirt that said IT'S A GOLDEN THING, YOU WOULDN'T UNDERSTAND, and I didn't. But it turned out she had many nuggets of exotic wisdom to share regarding proper leash length and those cute collapsible water dishes you see at Pets & More (a godsend, according to her). And I admit, I was secretly enchanted by the concept of rules as applied to human-animal relations. To ask an animal to do something that s/he would then, you know, *do:* Wow. And apparently with no hard feelings afterward, either.

The dog park was some more terra incognita. T.S. had come from a sadly solitary situation; i.e., he was a yard dog, but he learned quickly how to play with the others, to catch the ball and the Frisbee, to solicit pats and fondling from the dog parents. As I hung around listening to them talk, and occasionally tossing in a comment ("Oh yeah, T.S., he's so not dominant"), I marveled at the way the dogs, sized from Humvee to compact, chased and rolled, nipped and yipped, in a big perpetual-motion canine mob where no one ever really got hurt, unless a human happened to get in the way of the rolling scrum and got bowled over; still, no harm, no foul.

But trust me, there's a reason why there's no such thing as a "cat park." Not that my cats don't adore playing with one another—they definitely do (until they definitely don't). Run, chase, pounce, tussle, even the eldest of the three can turn kitten on a dime. But play with a *strange* cat? A cat of unknown provenance, possibly with testicles still attached? Oh boy. A few years ago I briefly sheltered a midnight stray, but had to hustle him to a neighbor's when my cats went seriously emotionally AWOL, and tried to claw through the door to get at him and his ballsy little behind. Even if he'd been neutered, no amount of ass-sniffing could produce a workable détente in less than a calendar week, if ever, and never is a long time to stand around outside making conversation with a guy in a Polarfleece vest.

Other things about Dogland were instantly, comfortingly familiar. The worship of crinkly snack bags remained just the same, as did the daily task of shedding (black hair on white sweater, brown hair on black dress, etc. etc.). Everybody, dog and cat, wants to know what it is you're doing behind that bathroom door, and how they can become actively involved in it. Chef Barkley's Organic Beef Canine smells exactly like Organic Beef Feline, except maybe when it comes out the other end, but who's counting? The ritual greeting at the door—dog people don't think cats do this, but they do, the little faces pointing up as soon as you walk in, the little tails swishing, impatient with delight. And climbing on laps—same deal, whether you weigh seventy-five pounds or fifteen. All you really want is to get some love, and give it.

So we go down different aisles in the pet store, we plan our trips differently—she calls the doggy day care, I hunt down the home-care gal—does it matter? Dogland, Cat World, they're just neighbors on the same big continent, although one has more scratched-up couches and the other is damper from drool. It's the passport that really matters, that truly separates Jay and me (not to mention T.S. and my cats) and all of us—dog people and cat people, bird and rabbit people, that guy with the bandanna you see walking his iguana—from the place where animals, all animals, from the shelter to the zoo to the veldt to the forest, are a toy, a nuisance, a commodity, a nonentity, the place where it's only humans, all humans all the time.

And the passport out of that empty land is the empathy that realizes, that cherishes, that the dog, the cat, seeks what you seek, and offers it too: the love, the bond between beings. Expressed by a run around the block rather than a twisty string across the floor, still, a thumping tail equals a purr equals the clean and wordless joy of being close to a friend in whom you trust, who trusts you, who knows you. When Jay walks T.S., when I snuggle my cats, when you hug your critter of choice, the love is the same. The love is exactly the same.

So now, when I hear the inevitable question, at the dog park or the vet's or the pet supplies store—*Are you a dog person or a cat person?*—thanks to T.S. and Jay, I can truthfully answer *Yes.*

Kirby

[Al Franken]

 I HAVE TO be careful when I get home to kiss my wife before I kiss my eight-year-old black Lab. Franni takes offense if I kiss Kirby first. It's just that sometimes he comes to greet me and she doesn't.

Also, Kirby has never been mad at me. As anyone who has a black Lab knows, they are sweet dogs who love their masters. It's not that Franni doesn't take care of him, especially when I travel, it's just that I lavish him with so much affection that he knows I'm the alpha male. Actually, I'm not sure that lavishing affection is an alpha trait—but now that Franni and I are empty-nesters, I'm the only male in the house—alpha or not.

Franni won't kiss Kirby or let him lick her. This isn't because she doesn't love Kirby. It's because he eats dog poop.

Not all the time. Only when he can. Other Labs do this, and it can be a nasty trait. When I walk Kirby, I have to be super vigilant, always on the lookout for stray dog poop. If I go to a dog run, I have to walk the entire place looking for poop and picking it up before I can let Kirby off his leash. As a result, I've developed an almost irrational hatred of people who don't pick up their dog's poop. Every once in a while I find another Lab owner who has the same problem and we bond like crazy.

Kirby's very sly. If I steer him clear of some poop on a sidewalk, he will remember where it is. For days. Day One, he'll lunge for it, and I'll pull him back before he gets it. On the way back home, he'll lunge again and I'll catch him again. Day Two, I'll be ready and pull him away just as he begins his lunge. By Day Three, Kirby will walk past it all nonchalant and lull me into a false state of calm. On Day Four, he'll spring, grabbing the dried dung before I'm even aware of what the hell is going on.

After I know Kirby has eaten dog poop, I won't kiss him for at least a day. By then he's had three bowls of kibble and a lot of water and I figure all the poop molecules are gone. If not, I figure I'm building up immunities. The trouble is that we use dog walkers to walk Kirby and I can't be completely sure when he's eaten poop. I can't really expect a dog walker to be as vigilant as I am, because basically I'm a nut about it.

There have been two occasions where dog walkers have failed egregiously on this score and the result isn't pretty. Twice now, once in New York and once in Minneapolis, Kirby has eaten so much poop on a visit to a dog run (dog park in Minneapolis) that, several hours after returning home, Kirby has gotten sick and vomited lots and lots of partly digested dog poop (if you can digest poop).

In New York, he threw up on the couch. It was absolutely horrendous. I cleaned it up as fast as I could, but we ended up having to throw the couch away. As you might imagine, Franni was not happy, and this might have been the low point in their relationship.

In Minneapolis, Kirby threw up in the middle of the night. The retching woke me up and I ran downstairs to see him throwing up on the hardwood floor, thank God. He continued throwing up, on and off, for a couple hours, and I successfully steered him away from the rugs and furniture and managed to save my marriage.

That day I talked about the episode on my radio show. I thought it was relevant because I hadn't got much sleep and was tired, but some members of the audience were disgusted. Some, mainly dog owners, were amused and even delighted.

I've received lots of advice about Kirby's "problem." A lot of people get it in their heads that he eats his own poop and suggest putting something or other in his food. But that's not what he does. He eats *other* dogs' poop.

Some have suggested using a collar that can give him a shock whenever he eats poop. I'll admit that I tried that once, but I just couldn't bear to shock my dog. Recently, someone said that they knew a holistic veterinarian who believes that this is caused by some kind of nutritional deficiency. I can't imagine that's what's going on here, and I am not taking my dog to a holistic veterinarian.

My solution, of course, is harsher penalties for people who don't pick up after their dog. I'm talking first time a fine; second time, prison. It's really a quality-of-life issue if you think about it. The enforcement could more than pay for itself. People without dogs would certainly get behind it, and responsible people with dogs (and that's most of us) would too.

In the interim, while this new legislation works its way through Congress, I would ask my fellow dog owners, pick up after your friggin' dog!

Show a dog the time and he sniffs the leather watchband. —Dan Liebert

A Second Act

[Alice Elliott Dark]

A NOW INFAMOUS controversy arose last year in the usually warm and furry world of dog books when Raw Bones, the mutt who penned the best-selling memoir *A Million Little Reeses*, was exposed by the Internet media watch site The Steaming Pile as having fabricated many of his claims. *A Million Little Reeses* was already a best-seller before it was chosen by Orpah Doxie as a book club selection for her wildly successful show on the Animal Planet channel. As always, her imprimatur sent sales through the doghouse roof! It seemed every dog everywhere was reading the book. At dog runs only the puppies gamboled in the dust; any dog who'd learned to read could be seen stretched out against a fence, snout buried in the tome.

The attention paid to this dramatic story of one dog's descent into chocolate addiction and his self-styled recovery barked to thousands. There was new hope, especially for all those dogs who'd tried the methods offered by 12 Step programs, only to find themselves stymied when they simply couldn't conceive of a higher power to whom they might turn over their runaway appetites. Raw Bones's tale of old-fashioned determination appealed to those who were unable to find a place for themselves in the pack at meetings, or who were precluded from attending altogether, often by means of a rope tied to a tree. In a population not always aware of its options, Raw Bones had provided a fresh trail, and many rolled onto their backs with gratitude.

Then the accusations of hyperbole, if not outright falsehood, hit the airwaves. Was it true that the book was a lie? At first many of Bones's fans scratched the counterclaims as being jealousy. When a dog gets famous, particularly a mutt from nowhere, other dogs can get a little weird. Some come out from under the bed to hound him; some seek a butt-sniffing familiarity with him; and some criticize him for thinking he's best in show. Soon, however, it was clear that Bones had indeed claimed to get chocolate poisoning many more times than he actually did. Nor had he ever reached the end of the line at the pound and had an X placed on his cage. In fact, he'd only spent one night at a kennel, and a rather plush one at that. The story unraveled, and Bones, accompanied by his editor, made a famous appearance on *The Orpah Doxie Show* to offer an apology to her and to his packs of readers. Book sales plummeted, and Bones disappeared from the public eye with his tail between his legs.

We at *Mea Culpa* magazine followed his story closely, and recently sent a reporter to visit Bones. Our readers are always curious to see how such cataclysmic experiences and public apologies shake out after some time has passed. Bones was willing to talk to us and invited us to conduct the interview at his place. He lives in a gorgeous doghouse—he did make a lot of money—overlooking the ocean, in a location he asked us not to disclose. Suffice it to say he isn't an American dog anymore—not that he'd be eligible to join any of our kennel clubs anyway. One look at him and you immediately see generations of unpedigreed sires and dams stretching back into his past.

Not that that matters. The real question on our minds was: had Bones really changed? Read what he told us and decide for yourself.

MEA CULPA: Thank you, Mr. Bones, for having us. Our readers are very eager to know how things are going for you today.

BONES: Call me Raw.

M.C.: Okay, then, Raw. I guess we may as well begin with the big question. Why did you write so many lies in your book and then claim it was a memoir?

BONES: You know, you get tired of being at the bottom of the heap, kicked around by people who don't even bother to try to understand you or your needs, signals, and vocalizations. You see all these dogs who aren't nearly as intelligent as you leading these cushy lives, being carried around in expensive purses, going to restaurants and premieres and offices. Basically never being left alone. Over time seeing the unfairness that goes on all around you can create a low growl in your throat that just doesn't go away. Even if you're not a sight hound you can see that no one is going to give you a chance. You realize that if you're going to have any luck in this world, you'll have to make it yourself. That's what I realized. So I wrote the book.

M.C.: That explains your motivation, but not the lying.

BONES: I didn't lie! I embellished the truth to make my point stronger. Only the details are lies. I really was a chocolate addict.

M.C.: Stop pacing back and forth. We're not going to be able to communicate with you while you're so agitated.

BONES: I'm sorry. Without the chocolate, you see, I have nothing to calm me down.

M.C.: Wow. That's rough. But it's so great you quit. Chocolate addiction is really dangerous for dogs. Did you know you could die from chocolate?

BONES: Oh, sure, I knew. Addicts know these things. You have to. Heroin users know how much they can handle. Dogs know about chocolate. I had the stats firmly in my head. It's all calibrated to weight. I weighed about 50 pounds when I was eating a lot of chocolate. At that weight, toxicity sets in at 200 pounds for white chocolate, which isn't really chocolate, of course. For milk chocolate and semisweet, it takes about 2 pounds; for cocoa about two-thirds of a pound; and baking chocolate or dark chocolate, about 5 ounces. Dark chocolate was the most lethal and also, naturally, my favorite.

M.C.: Five ounces is a lot, though. A candy bar is about 2 ounces, right?

BONES: Right. But two candy bars in the course of a day is nothing. I could have eaten ten if I didn't want to stay alive to eat more. I wasn't completely self-destructive, you know. I mean, I never ran across a highway or anything like that. No death wish. I would push the envelope and eat the two candy bars. Yeah, that made me pretty sick, but I'd just go into the fireplace and eat a bunch of charcoal to set myself straight.

M.C.: That seems like a plan that so easily could go wrong.

BONES: Sometimes it did. I had two incidents in the book that showed how on the edge I was living. There was the time the fireplace got cleaned while I was outside in the yard; I didn't know about it, so the next time I needed a hunk of charcoal it wasn't there. I was a pretty sick puppy that night, let me tell you. And then there was the time I was at the house of a person who had a whole bag of Dove miniatures under her bed. I knew I shouldn't eat them, that I probably wouldn't be able to save myself if I did, but an addict is an addict and that kind of reasoning means about as much as most language does when your nose is two inches away from some other mutt's fresh puddle of pee. I had to go to the emergency vet that time.

M.C.: So that was true.

BONES: The book was mostly true!

M.C.: Stay calm. We're not here to accuse you of anything.

BONES: I know, I know. I'm still a bit skittish. You can't imagine what it was like. I mean, I've been beaten before, but having the Bones name spoken in harsh, scolding tones over and over and over . . . it really hurt.

M.C.: We can imagine. It's too bad you couldn't have published the book as a novel.

BONES: I wanted to! My editor said it would sell better as a memoir.

M.C.: Maybe. But it was such an exciting book. Your writing is really strong. We think it would have sold anyway.

BONES: I can't think about that. Alternative life trajectories are really hard for me to wrap my mind around. A few memories, an appreciation of the present moment, maybe a thought or two about dinner—that's about it. I'm really a very simple guy.

M.C.: Are you working on anything now?

BONES: I'm thinking about it. I haven't come up with the right idea yet. *A Million Little Reeses* was so me.

M.C.: We can see where it's a hard act to follow.

BONES: It's hard to learn a new trick.

M.C.: You look very well. That's good.

BONES: I am well. I've lost ten pounds. One of the terrible side effects of a chocolate addiction is you get fat. I've dropped my chocolate weight and I'm working out a lot. I put in an electric fence and I'm running inside it, twenty, thirty times around the perimeter of the property in a day. I'm also doing stairs, and I'm eating grass once a week to cleanse my digestive tract.

M.C.: That sounds like a rather abstemious regimen.

BONES: I'm doing what needs to be done. Chocolate has a grip that's hard to describe if it hasn't had its choke collar around your ruff.

M.C.: Just as long as you don't push it too hard. People can become addicted to the cure too.

BONES: Huh.

M.C.: What?

BONES: Oh, just something you said. Hey, did I say I ran around the property thirty times a day? I meant thirty times an hour. I do it five or six hours a day. And I've eaten most of the newly seeded grass in the neighborhood. . . .

Every hair on a Pointer shouts *"Here!" "Here!"* —Dan Liebert

Littermate

[Marga Gomez]

M Y N O S T R I L S B U R N when she licks them, but it's either that or on my pursed lips. If I'm slow, my dog will slip me the tongue. It's because she left her litter too young and wasn't properly socialized. I'm not her only conquest. The singer Tennille (of Captain and Tennille) was so taken by the smooth coat, the brown spot on the butt, the floppy ears, and the naturally black-lined eyelids that she bent down on one knee to make friends. It was alarming. I wanted to shout, "Get up, Tennille! Move away from the dog," but it was too late. Tabasco had already reared back on her Jack Russell haunches, aimed, and stolen another French kiss. I apologized profusely as we were led away from Tennille's dressing room in the Tampa State Theater. She was starring in *Victor/Victoria*. I was working next door at the smaller Tampa State Theater Annex, which doubles as a storage unit most of the year. It wasn't the greatest week of my career, but Tabasco liked the blistering sun and the fresh scent of armadillo outside our Holiday Inn.

I'd like to say that Tabasco was named after the town in Mexico, but really she was named after the hot sauce my girlfriend sprinkled on her eggs at a roadside diner on the way to pick up our puppy. Getting a dog was her idea, and we were so in love that I would have agreed to any name she liked, from Cornflakes to Decaf. If we merely had a baby instead of a puppy we'd probably still be together. But I quickly fell under Tabasco's spell.

Instead of bringing my girlfriend flowers, I bought Tabasco a new squeaky toy every week.

I got custody after the breakup even though the dog clearly favored my girlfriend. When dogs sense fear, they may attack, but when they sense codependency, they pick you last. It's not the worship I expected from a dog. She's stingy with the tail-wagging, and getting a kiss from her is like pulling fangs. So when she affectionately swabs my sinus cavities, I tell myself it's genuine, not because she wants something. Then I fix her food—half a cup twice a day, presoaked in spring water and not one kibble or biscuit more.

I wish I had somebody to control *my* meal portions. While my weight fluctuates, Tabasco's compact form has never exceeded 13 pounds. She has the dimensions of a six-pack of beer, just small enough to slide under an airplane seat in her FAA-approved Sherpa travel bag. Some airlines offer two spaces per flight for pets small enough to remain confined under the seat for the duration of the trip—flight attendants go postal if they see a paw poking out from the blanket on your lap, trust me. No doubt they're envious of the divorced, bankrupt former flight attendant who invented the Sherpa bag, became a millionaire overnight, and sent little dogs packing coast to coast. Tabasco and I have become versed in where to find trees and shrubs at JFK and LAX, and dog-friendly hotels in America. These seem to fall into two categories: the high-end establishment that caters to the Chihuahuas of the rich and famous or the going-out-of-business dump that will take anybody and their dog, cat, or ferret for an extra fifty bucks—in other words, the downtown Tampa hotel of our first road trip.

It was a rough road to single parenthood. Tabasco sniffed our dreary room from wall to wall and opted to spend the first night brooding under one of the twin beds. I lay awake wondering what she was thinking or if she was thinking. Was she homesick? Did she miss my apartment or my ex-girlfriend's apartment? Or was she pining for something primal that no human could provide?

We got her from an old-fashioned country vet on a horse farm. He showed us her mom, long-legged and slim, hopping around the barn in a cast after being stomped by a horse. The dad dog was tied to a tree, all muscle and medium height like Tabasco. The vet claimed this dog enjoyed watching cartoons, which sounded cool but may have been another fabrication, like telling us Tabasco was eight weeks when she was only seven weeks. Finally, we were taken to the puppies. It's impossible to feel like an adult at a time like that. I was clapping my hands and squealing like the six wild balls of fur at my feet. If I could design my afterlife, it would be populated with puppies, specifically Jack Russell puppies, no disrespect to the other breeds. The puppies would be born in heaven, not taken from earth, because that would be sad. Tabasco was the runt, getting tackled and sideswiped by the pack but persevering. We lifted her out of the melee and she wiggled joyfully in our arms. She was a happy puppy until we drove down the gravel road and past the wooden gate, at which point she let out a long mournful howl, followed by another. Aliens in a Volkswagen spacecraft were abducting her. Where were her brothers and sisters?

I'm no pet psychic but I *am* an only child, and I recognized alienation when I saw it under that bed in Tampa. There was only one thing that could draw her out. Food. Food changed everything for us. Tabasco got a bonus meal in the middle of the night. She looked up at me with love while she chewed. Not love for her master, because I fawned too much to ever gain that distinction. It was love for a long-lost littermate, a partner in play, a source of body heat for cold nights, and a really big dog that had her back and would never go away. It was what we both were missing.

My roll-aboard suitcase became her exclusive dog bed for the week. I pimped it out with a pillow and threw in my dirty socks for that lived-in aroma dogs crave. I moved the easy chair and ottoman to the window, giving her a two-hop viewing stand of the occasional bird flying by. We enjoyed many walks along the nearby creek and an up-close armadillo encounter that stirred her killer instinct and made her tail quiver with excitement. But for Tabasco, nothing compared to kissing Tennille in that special way reserved for the Captain. It was a bold move from a creature of habit turned adventure seeker. Tampa was our territory. Now we roam new lands as a small but fierce pack of two, masters of our destiny. She anticipates each voyage before I start packing. She sits by the suitcases before the airport shuttle arrives. Howling is in the past. All we hear is the call of Tennille.

I will, I will, I will, I will
Be there to share forever
Love will keep us together

In antique photos, only the dogs still seem alive. —Dan Liebert

Dog Mad

[Lee Harrington]

 WELL, IT HAS finally happened, as I feared it would. I have officially become a Crazy Dog Lady.

How can I say for sure? Well, just last weekend, at the local dog run, I was chatting with my fellow dog parents about the usual subjects—anal sacs, diarrhea, undescended testicles, and the like. And I thought it perfectly fine—even appropriate—to announce that my dog's breath had begun to smell like urine. "I follow that Berkeley-water-conservation rule, to, you know, not flush every time, unless it's necessary, and I forgot to put down the lid. With Ted gone, there's no one to crab at me about putting it down. So when my dog came up to give me a kiss, there was this awful smell, and I knew what he had done. I knew he had drunk—"

Slowly, my fellow dog parents backed away.

Even the man who was just, not minutes before, describing, in excruciating detail, the contents of his Terrier's most recent Riverside Park vomit ("Cigarette butts! Part of a Cuban sandwich! Even some partially digested human feces"); even he put his dog's leash on and hurried off, stiffly, like Charlie Chaplin, as if I were a disease he might catch.

I was left standing alone, in a cloud of dust, wondering how it had happened. And so quickly! I was only in my third decade, and had had my dog only four years. I didn't even get a chance to tell them that the urine drinking was a onetime incident. That I had learned my lesson and now flushed. But it was too late. I had been pegged.

Meanwhile, far, far away, from across the run, I heard someone bring up the subject of bull pizzles. And I thought: What separates me from them? Where does one draw the line between Normal, Paranormal, and Crazy Dog Person?

I mean, before I got a dog, I had a definitive, admirable style. I knew how to pair vintage sweaters with the latest Tuleh sundress. I wore platforms from the seventies a year before they came back into style. And the extra-long-hem-over-stiletto-shoes-and-jeans trend? That was me who started it. The tank tops under mesh? Me again. A real downtown chick.

But now look at me. Open my closet and you'll find all the feather boas and leather skirts pushed neglectfully to the far reaches. And front and center are mom jeans. With pleats. To accommodate all the liver treats and poopie bags in my pockets. And then there are T-shirts (which say things like LOVE ME, LOVE MY DOG or, of course, DOG IS MY CO-PILOT) covered with paw prints and drool. I never bother to wash these T-shirts, because why bother? There's a Sisyphean quality to having a dog that says, for every hair you brush off your black velveteen jacket, twenty more will appear. And speaking of hair, mine, which I never have time to style anymore, is always pulled back in a hurried "the dog has to go to the bathroom" ponytail, and I barely bother to color it any more (or "enhance" it, as we say here in New York), because who sees me but the dog? And a bunch of other Crazy Dog People?

My one comfort is that I suspect I am not alone. Oh, you know who you are. You have two, three dogs, and you volunteer at the animal shelter. You like dogs more than people. And you are no longer loath to admit it. Come on, 'fess up. And don't be ashamed.

There are loads of us out there. And it seems that no matter how educated you are, no matter where you stand on the corporate ladder, no matter how intelligent or savvy or well-read—if you have a dog, you are at risk of contracting this degenerative disease.

And how do *you* know when you have contracted Crazy Dog Lady Syndrome? Perhaps this little quiz I devised will help. So put down your bull pizzle, pour yourself a gin and tonic, and grab a pen. The pen that says "I ♥ Cockapoos" on it. Or the one with your vet's address.

The following seven questions will help you determine where you stand.

When asked a simple question, such as "How are you?" do you:
1) Say, "Fine, thank you, and you?"
2) Say, "Fine, thank you," and then tell the person who inquired how your dog is?
3) Immediately launch into an extended monologue in which you prattle on about the consistency of your dog's stool?

Does the term "heavy petting" conjure up images of:
1) Being groped in the backseat of an Impala by your first high school boyfriend?
2) Worrisome images of the kind of thing your prepubescent son is viewing online? Right now, as you read this!
3) Your dog?

Where do you store your liver treats?
1) In your pockets.
2) In your mouth.
3) I don't carry treats! My dog loves me for me, not my freeze-dried animal products.

You've set some money aside for your children's college education. You:
1) Actually send your children to college.
2) Donate most of it to your local animal shelter.
3) Blow it all on cosmetic dentistry for Willy the Weimaraner when he chips his incisor on a bone.

Your children complain that you love your dog more than them. Do you:
1) Say, "That's not true"?
2) Say, "That's not true." And then, "Come here my little Muffy

Wuffy and give Mummy a kiss" (and your child is not named "Muffy")?

3) Say, "And your point is?"

Your husband leans toward the nape of your neck to kiss you. Does he smell:

1) J'adore by Christian Dior?

2) Notes of dog breath and liver (from being licked on the ear)?

3) Urine breath (from you-know-what)?

And finally,

At the movie theaters, when they get to that part where the heroine finally finds her One True Love, do you:

1) Grab your date's hand and thank your lucky stars?

2) Scoff at the idea of a One True Love?

3) Think weepily of your dog?

Okay, now, put down that I ♥ Cockapoos pen and tally up your scores.

If your score is 8, you're fine. You're at Stage I. You can hold your head high as you walk down the neighborhood sidewalks. You will be happily admitted to the Belmont Country Club and to any dog run in the fifty states. And feel free to help yourself to another glass of gin.

If your score ranges from 8 to 16, you are at Stage II and are what they call a High Functioning Dog Person. This is similar to the High Functioning Alcoholic, a problem drinker who still manages to keep himself together in public by performing admirably at his job and maintaining healthy relationships, et cetera.

Before the urine-breath incident, I myself was a High Functioning Dog Lady. I prided myself on the fact that I could attend a Junior Members reception at MoMA (looking fetching in my Pucci-print blouse and custom-painted Pumas), and, at my creative writing workshops, could wax poetic on the merits of the intimate third-person point-of-view. Meanwhile, back at home, I'd be singing little ballads I had composed about my dog to my dog. No one knew of my sordid underworld, and therefore, no one was harmed.

But then came the urine incident. And then it was time to acknowledge that I was weird. Smart, but not normal. I wondered if I had begun to look like my dog. Or if I smelled like one. *Did the people at work notice?* I began to wonder. The way they'd notice gin on a High Functioning Alcoholic's breath?

And how could I be sure the smell was real, or acute, or if it was just my own paranoia? One can become desensitized to a chronic smell, after all (just ask a Cat Lady). But just to be sure, I called upon Chip, Ted's bluntly honest friend. We invited him over for Appletinis, and I prepared by putting out the cheese plate and lighting a scented candle from the excellent French company Diptyque. And after we had exchanged our human pleasantries and taken our first sips of drink, I asked Chip, very directly, if our apartment smelled like dog. He didn't hesitate. He didn't even sniff the air. This meant the answer had been on his tongue for a long, long time. "Yes," he said. "It always has."

Which brings us to Stage III. If you scored 18 to 21 on the above quiz, you have contracted full-blown Crazy Dog Person Syndrome. But don't worry. It's not fatal, after all. And we're here to help. Let us remember that life is full of milestones: birth, marriage, the day you find your first gray hair (on your pubis, no less). Dog people simply have additional milestones to contend with: puppy's first play date, puppy's first solid poop, the first time your adopted dog responds to his name. And perhaps the most significant milestone is the day you realize you have gone over the edge.

Mine, of course, was the urine-breath announcement. My friend Karen knew she was a Crazy Dog Lady when she canceled her long-dreamed of trip to Hawaii to take her Lab to a doggy summer camp instead. Another friend, Lisa, a devoted wife and mother of two, wears an antique locket on a chain around her neck that contains a photo of her new Malamute, not her kids. The list is endless. You see a man at Zoomie's dog boutique buying an amethyst and garnet collar for his Bichon while his wife complains that they can never afford to go out to eat. You see a man at an outdoor café on Second Avenue who *can* afford to go out to eat and brings, as his date, his giant English Bulldog, whom the waiters allow to sit across from him at the table, in a chair. There is the woman at the office who communicates with her dog through a walkie-talkie; one that she keeps on her desk, the other that is fastened, back at home, around the dog's neck. At four o'clock every day she buzzes the dog and asks him what he wants for dinner. The dog doesn't say much, just as that Bulldog at the café doesn't say much, but their guardians *know* just what they'd like to order that night.

So who's to say whether these people are Stage II or Stage III? It's all subjective, I suppose.

But isn't the first step in changing a problem acknowledging it? There's a technique in Cognitive Behavioral Therapy in which you wear a special string around your wrist to remind yourself that you are repeating bad habits. I have started to wear the string, to remind myself to wash my clothes once in a while, and not to use my screechy Crazy Dog Lady Voice while out on the streets. At the dog park, I try to limit my conversations to human topics, such as the unbearable heat waves, or the summer-in-the-city smell of festering garbage and molten tar. These subjects always lead to the dogs, of course—they hate the heat, they love the smells. And when it gets to that, I close my mouth and nod my head, wearing the tight, closed expression of a recovering alcoholic at a bar.

If people ask about the string, I'll simply say I am a member of a cult. What cult that is they need not know. All I can say is there are no Madonnas or Britneys or Ashtons as members. At least not yet. Perhaps they simply have not yet come out of the Dog Closet. It takes a strong person to admit her weaknesses.

My name is Lee. I am a Recovering Crazy Dog Lady. And I am not ashamed.

Confessions of an Amateur Pickup Artist

[David Malley]

I'M WHAT DOG people call a "flincher." I try not to be, and I used to believe that, much in the same way I taught myself to appreciate the salty goodness of an anchovy, I could also learn to cherish a warm canine tongue lapping at my face like it was the inside of an empty bucket of KFC Extra Crispy. But instead, just as soon as a fuzzy little nipper called Tulip or an adorable Akita called Sunshine starts with the licking, my head involuntarily jerks back, my palms begin to sweat, and I commence with nervous laughs designed to give off the appearance of confidence.

For years, I had a list of about a dozen excuses I would routinely use to explain to friends the reason for my doglessness. They started with "I would, but I'm . . . *allergic!*" and ended with bad jokes like "The only time I strap a leash to *anything* is when it's dressed in latex and has a gag-ball in its mouth!" In reality, the whole flinching process probably started when I was five years old, when a sneering Doberman Pinscher kept its breed-standard body nicely toned by chasing me up and down the streets of the genteel Oklahoma City neighborhood where I grew up. But, while the catalyst for my flinching is a set of snarling teeth, it all climaxes with the hind end. I'm very sensitive to foul odors, and aside from the whole Eau-de-Poo-Poo breath problem, it would be incredibly upsetting for me if I happened to, for example, acquire a dog that was routinely gassy. Really, it can all be very emasculating.

I'm not squeamish about everything. In fact, when I sit and contemplate things scatological, I find that it's mostly things that come out the rear exit that make my stomach turn. I'm mostly okay with vomit. I don't even wince while exchanging spit during a French kiss, which I do often. I'd say I have a very reasonable, probably even healthy, aversion to snot, boogers, and loogies. No, I don't often mull over such grotesqueries, but now as I watch my youthful early thirties recede like Count Chocula's hairline and my wife starts to drop those not-so-subtle hints about maybe bringing some little ones of our own into the world, I feel it's time to start confronting my paralyzing fear of poo.

I think babies are bundles of bliss as long as they're cooing and cackling at my jokes. And not dirtying their diapers. Yes, I know, baby poop smells of sweet yams and figgy pudding . . . until they start eating real food . . . which they will do. That's when the yams get rotten and the pile starts looking and smelling no different from something John Goodman might eject after a night of nachos and daiquiris. And just when you've finished your full-time job of opening little white packages of stink, you find yourself hunching over toilets, making blind swipes at an ungrateful toddler's stinking anus.

Try taking care of a dog before you go making babies. It's not an original idea, just an old good one. The ol' training wheel puppy. I take comfort in this plan. If we crash and burn with the dog, I know a couple of good dog-loving people who'd save me in the end (I call them Mom and Dad), but there's no nice way to do that with a baby. Besides, every parent I've ever known, including my own mother and father, says that crying, drooling, crapping kids aren't that bad when they're your own. I imagine the same goes with a dog.

The Scoop

Of course my first real experience looking after a dog involved excrement and misery. Six years ago, I spent ten days dog-sitting a handsome mixed-breed named Skye in New York City, and discovered that I was firmly on my way to becoming poop phobic. From our first "shake," Skye had my number, and that number was 2. Every half hour or so, the whining would start (first him, then me), and I would find myself being led around a frigid downtown block near where I was living. The Humane Society says that the average canine needs a constitutional walk about fourteen times a week, but Skye seemed to need about fourteen a day.

On our first trip onto Manhattan's streets, I hadn't prepared for the not-so-little package Skye proudly left for me at the corner of Broadway and Broome. I panicked.

Thankfully, there was an empty cereal box (Cheerios, I think) in the nearby garbage can, and as I tried to ignore the bewildered looks of passing pedestrians, I held my breath, flinched, and scooped. Then I scooped again. And again. And then some poo touched my finger.

So, sure, this story isn't so crazy. It's nothing a real dog owner hasn't gone through at least a few times. It goes with the territory. And I suppose that's really my point. Dog owning is a territory, a faraway, war-torn territory that's riddled with land mines. And now here I am, the pacifist, lined up alongside the trigger-happy loonbird dog people, plastic produce bag over my fist, awaiting my four-legged, stink-dropping mission.

How Do You Doo?

First, if I'm going to be responsible for any kind of animal, I need to do some risk assessment. And I've still got some time.

After a few clicks on the Internet, I fear it's just as bad as I always thought it was: "Ebola Virus: From Wildlife to Dogs." The article comes from a French science journal—*L'institut de recherche pour le développement*—and explains that humans get Ebola from "infected carcasses of chimpanzees, gorillas and certain forest antelopes" and further, it goes on to point out, in heavy, barely understandable scientific terms, that it is entirely possible that I could have gotten Ebola from my old pal Skye's excretions. Of course, he would have to have dined on infected gorilla carrion, which is probably pretty hard to find in Manhattan, but still . . .

As I absorb this helpful information, National Public Radio's Eleanor Beardsley is bellowing out of my computer. I pause to listen because she's talking about the benefits of being a trash collector in Paris, and I know, after spending some very romantic evenings dodging sidewalk bombs, Paris is a perfect example of why this world doesn't need more dog owners. According to the book *Sixty Million Frenchmen Can't Be Wrong: Why We Love France but Not the French* there are around 200,000 dogs in Paris. Those dogs leave ten tons of dog waste behind every day (that's 4.38 million pounds each year or about the same weight as a fully fueled space shuttle!), and each year, over 500 people break bones slipping on unseen doggy slicks.

But Eleanor Beardsley assures me that's all changing. "Garbage collectors show up with a Dr. Seuss–like arsenal of cleaning machines," she says, and that includes "pooper-scoopers" and "side-walk scrubbers." It turns out that today's most effective mechanism for keeping Parisian streets clean is "the $200 fine for dog owners caught leaving canine ejection on the side-walk," and after I work out just exactly what Ms. Beardsley means by canine-ejection, I begin to realize that if even the French government has mandated that *Parisians* need to pick up after their pets, there must be a good, disgusting reason for that mandate, and I have a feeling it has nothing to do with dead gorillas.

It turns out that aside from spreading Ebola with their excrement, dogs have bacteria in their stomachs that can be transmitted through their feces to potentially turn your human gut into oatmeal—gruesome things like *E. coli* and salmonella and giardia. So what? Disregarded doggy dirt biodegrades into local watersheds, and because of the icky bacteria I mention above, that's a bad thing. I finally understand why Parisians have been so keen on bottled mineral water for so many years before we tap-water-swilling Americans. What's worse is, according to *USA Today*, 40 percent of American dog owners don't bother to scoop poop. And if you're one of the people not picking up, keep this in mind: Back in the 1990s, a well-intentioned biochemist at the University of Leicester introduced a way to collect DNA from derelict dung to help coppers trace negligent nuggets back to offending owners, and it's an idea that big cities around the world are taking seriously. A 2005 *New York Times* article even suggested that each of the more than one million dogs in New York City should submit a DNA-rich saliva sample upon being licensed so that delinquent owners could be tracked down and fined. The result would be twofold: cleaner streets and increased revenue from the fines. Frankly, there's only one thing that makes me more nervous than effluence, and that's the fuzz. If I get a dog, I'll pick up. I promise. Same goes if I have a kid.

A Call for Help

In the vulgar mulling over this subject, I decide to pick the brain of my good friend Ian Tyndall. Ian is a landscape architect and has been what he calls a PCG (Principal Care Giver for his "doggies") for forty years. He has two Welsh Corgis named Rose and Rocky whom he's constantly taking on walks through Washington, D.C.'s parks, and since he is, in part, responsible for planning and designing D.C.'s parks, I know for a fact he's an avid picker-upper.

"I am a big fan of the *New York Times* delivery bag," he says, when I ask him about his methods. "It's free, it comes regularly, and it is sturdy. By carefully taking advantage of the long narrow shape it is easy to pick up a second, and even a third, poop, if things come out that way. Of course, its disadvantage is that it only comes once a day."

Ian says that when he doesn't have a spare newspaper sack, he's like lots of dog owners and grabs a bag from his local supermarket. He prefers the ones from his local Safeway because they don't use double bags unless it's absolutely necessary. Of course, the drawback to this Earth-friendly plan is that single bags often get punctured—what I imagine to be a near-tragedy for dog owners who don't notice the perforations until it's too late.

After Ian tells me this, I've decided that the riskiness in using grocery bags just doesn't seem worth it to me. So, as I find myself researching strength and permeability of plastics, I discover a Web site run by an Englishman named Paul Mundy, who, in his free time, collects and exhibits exotic examples from "the magical world of airsickness bags." Somehow his fascination in the bags found on airplanes tucked between the in-flight magazine and the aircraft safety card naturally led him to the world of "doggy bags"—bags especially made for collecting doggy-dung. On his Web site, Mundy displays more than sixty different doggy bags from around the world; many of them come complete with explicit "how to pick up" instructions. In Mundy's collection, the bag that particularly interests me is the Mutt Mitt. It isn't the most colorful bag. That would be the "Fido Bag" from China. Nor is it the most innovative. That would be the "Gassi" from Austria, which is a combination of a box *and* a bag. But there's a subtle sophistication about the Mutt Mitt, and I can actually imagine wrapping one of them around my hand.

I reach out to Rod Lukey at Intelligent Products in Rabbit Hash, Kentucky, where the Mutt Mitt is manufactured. I explain my whole not-being-a-dog-guy problem, and then I ask him why on earth anyone should spend hard-earned money on something that grocery stores hand out for free.

"The Mutt Mitt's protection and functionality are what separate it from a bag," Rod says. "It's constructed with a degradable film approximately twice as thick as that of an ordinary grocery bag."

And that's where he's got me. A normal plastic grocery bag is only between .5 and .75 millimeters in thickness, which is great for carrying boxes of Hot Pockets and Hamburger Helper, but for picking up caca, I'm gonna need the full 1.25 millimeters of protection that bags like the Mitt provide. Also, grocery store bags end up festering in landfills for hundreds of years, while the Mutt Mitt "degrades" or decomposes in any environment.

"And, unlike a regular bag," says Rod, "the mitt has a pouch, which provides an area to store the collected material."

Rod, who has a yellow Lab named Boone, then goes on to describe the types of people who use products like the Mutt Mitt. I am most interested in his fourth category:

Squirmers.

"Squirmers," he explains, "fear the idea of picking up after their pet, but recognize it as a social expectation. They consider the process discomforting, and will often walk away from the problem rather than confronting it. We estimate that squirmers are 95 percent male and 5 percent female."

That's it! Not only am I a flincher, but I'm also a *squirmer*. As a kid, I was always amazed at my mother's ability to handle grossness without cringing (let's just say that when a kid is five and he has to go, he really has to go), and I assumed it was just because she grew up on a farm. But it was because she's a woman! All of this unrelenting emasculation I've been feeling during all these years of doglessness was just in my head. As a guy, I'm simply not hardwired to handle gross stuff.

I think that, with a little help, this is a hurdle I can actually overcome. Twenty-six-year-old Kate Morris, who founded Vancouver's Doody Duty, seems to think I can. Doody Duty is one of those services that comes to your house once or twice a week and takes care of the doody, so you don't have to. Obviously, if I had a yard, this would be the perfect choice for a guy like me (my wife tells me they have such services for baby diapers too!), but I'm contacting Kate, not to order her service, but for some sound advice.

"I recommend a visualization technique," she says.

Good. Go on . . .

"Picture the doody being something other than what it is."

Such as?

"Something like clumpy dirt or soggy bark," she says. "However, for our company we see it as gold."

She's not joking. Some estimates say that the poop-pickup industry in America pulls in a cool $20 million a year, in part, no doubt, because these types of services charge around $20 a week for a thorough cleanup. I'm beginning to consider a career change.

A Call for Help II

I call my friend Ian again. I confess to him that at the heart of my original call is a need to cure myself of this aversion to things that look like soggy bark.

After some tongue clicking and sighing, he says, "Look, changing my kids' diapers was never a problem for me, and it was good training for picking up after our dogs."

"Hmm," I say, "maybe some day I'll get one."

"One what?" he asks.

"A dog," I say. "Whaddaya think?"

"You don't deserve a dog," he says.

Head Case

I finally do what I probably should have done from the start. I get in touch with a psychiatrist. I tell her that I like dogs and babies and all, but that maybe my wife's right, maybe I'm not responsible enough to have either. I tell her about my history of excuses, how I fear commitment, and worse, that my new excuse—that I'm disgusted by dung—while true, might not be a very good one. This is a woman with decades in her field, credentials out the wazoo, and I know for a fact that she's treated just about every kind of psychosis imaginable. Still, I'm almost shocked when she tells me that she once treated a poop-phobic patient.

"We worked for weeks walking around poop," says the psychiatrist, who'd prefer not to be identified for fear that she'll somehow be forever associated with this particular subject. "Then one day I moved into putting poop on a stick and showing it to her. That day she literally used one-quarter can of Lysol on her body. Back then we didn't know that a single phobia is sometimes a healthy alternative to total anxiety. I think she became germ phobic."

"Crap," I say, "I can't become germ phobic, too!"

Pretty soon she stops sounding like a shrink and more like a dog owner. She tells me that she has a seven-month-old Lab who is almost completely potty trained, and that she really loves it. Then it becomes clear that she has absolutely zero compassion for my plight, and she might even consider me a . . . wait for it . . . nincompoop.

"Hey," she says, "when I smell crap, it makes me want to throw up. In fact, now that I'm a grandmother, I only change pee diapers. Still, the only way to do it is *immediately.* Buy good-smelling poop bags and attack the foul stuff pronto. No human being enjoys any other living thing's poop. It only happens a few times a day, and the snuggles the rest of the time make up for it."

She's right, too, and besides, how long does it take to actually pick up? And millions of parents change their babies' diapers every day. Perhaps it's possible that the good far outweighs the bad, and to be honest, forever being snuggled doesn't sound too terrible. But still, I wonder, all things considered, is all of that unconditional love really worth it?

When your dog barks with other dogs, you feel a bit left out. —Dan Liebert

Pillow Talk

[Gregory Edmont]

ALTHOUGH MY DALMATIAN'S prognosis was good and his body had been spared the potentially unpleasant side effects of eighteen weeks of chemotherapy, he seemed to be taking leave of his senses. At first I thought it might be a result of sunstroke—so that we could more easily commute to UC Davis for bimonthly injections, we had taken up residence in Palm Springs, and JP would not be dissuaded from basking his liver spots all afternoon in the desert sun. But an oncologist friend and fellow anthropomorphist diagnosed his uncharacteristically gregarious and happy-go-lucky condition as "chemo-brain."

His irreproachable table manners were the first to go. He had not missed a single meal during treatment, and for that I was grateful, but his healthy appetite became a ravenous obsession with all things edible (mostly mine) and some things not. He had never so much as eyed a table scrap, and yet, at a gathering in his honor, he celebrated his good fortune by helping himself to a prime slab of marinating rib-eye. Before I realized that I was one short on the grill, he had methodically tenderized it with his incisors and devoured it, much to the amusement of our friends, who thought it unnecessary to alert me, and all the more reason for them to marvel over his recovery. Used napkins, worn socks, and pretty much anything else fragrant began to disappear . . . only to reappear a day or two later, partially digested, atop JP's personal compost pile in the backyard. But the most noticeable personality shift occurred a few weeks later when he developed a newfound appreciation for less savory things: loud, shrill toys . . . and children of any pitch.

"Get off me!" JP and I were awakened by a mechanical, meowing voice that screeched from somewhere too close as we lay by the pool on a warm, windy day. "G-g-g-g-get-get off me!" it stuttered, before emitting a clown-like guffaw, followed by human squeals of delight. JP's hind legs stopped chasing the beasts of his slumber, and he eased open one eye as if to determine which state of consciousness held the current menace.

"He bite?" asked a steely-eyed, charcoal-haired boy of about seven loudly enough to drown out the pleas of a talking cat-shaped toy pillow, on which he jumped up and down while brandishing a plastic gun. JP opened his other eye and exhaled dramatically when he realized that he was awake, and that the new gardener had arrived with a motorized hedge trimmer and an equally earsplitting child. "He better not . . . or else BAM!" He took aim with his weapon and jiggled an index finger on the trigger.

"He hasn't so far. . . ." I said. The boy frowned, as if disappointed by JP's noncombative nature.

"Jacob!" shouted the gardener, a rugged man in his late thirties with the same long black hair and cold expression as his son. "I told you not to speak to the clients! And wash that dirt off you!" The boy's face and shirt were smeared with it.

"It's not dirt, it's candy," he corrected, shaking his head in smug exasperation. Chemo-brain or not, JP's extensive vocabulary hadn't suffered, and at the word "candy" his nose perked up. He slid off his lounge chair, stretched his aching muscles, and strolled over to Jacob.

"Where'd you steal it?" his father demanded. Jacob was silent, preoccupied with JP, who had begun to lick all traces of the brown, sugary substance from him. Once Jacob was cleaned and glistening, JP stared at him for a long moment, thoughtfully, with one of his unwavering, soul-piercing looks, until the boy cracked a wicked smile. With impressive speed and disconcerting strength, he shimmied up a small palm tree, tore off a fan and then tossed it into the pool. "Fetch!"

"He doesn't fe—" I began. JP turned around and propelled himself into the air, legs splayed, and landed in a belly-flop in the pool. If JP had previously found anything to be on a par of undesirability with rambunctious little humans, it was coming into contact with cold, chlorinated water. With the palm fan clenched diagonally in his teeth and spanning nearly the length of his body, he dogpaddled to the steps, climbed out, shook himself off and began to gnaw at his prize, all the while eyeing the cat pillow.

"Want it?" Jacob teasingly snatched it up.

"No, he doesn't," I said. Of one thing I was still certain: no matter how tired he was, JP only ever liked to sleep on fabric that bore my unique odor—it was a comfort thing. Nonetheless, Jacob defiantly tossed the pillow at JP . . . who proceeded to lie down on the grass and bury his nose in the center of it.

"'Night, 'night," the pillow cooed. JP sighed, closed his eyes and drifted off, oblivious to my astonishment, and to the tedious popping sounds and rubber balls of ammunition that flew past his head.

The next three Saturday mornings, JP lay in the front yard until the gardener's truck pulled in the drive and Jacob leapt out to greet him, flourishing Mr. Cat, his moniker for the talking pillow with its never-ending repertoire of quips. A bewildering and profound attachment soon took root between the two dissimilar beings: after brief but fatiguing bouts of roughhousing between young boy and old dog, in which the latter would tongue-bathe the former from finger to chin, JP and Jacob would lay their weary heads down on Mr. Cat and doze until the lawn was mowed.

At noon on the fourth week, his sidekick hadn't arrived. JP grew restless, started to pace and then bark. I managed to buy his silence, briefly, with a pig's ear, but his anxiety subsided only when a soft tapping at the door later in the afternoon revealed Jacob, disheveled, red-eyed . . . and alone. In one hand he carried a raggedy overnight bag, in the other, Mr. Cat. JP gently took the pillow from him and carried it away. For the first time, Jacob made tentative, pleading eye contact with me . . . and then followed JP to his room.

Jacob had managed to conceal himself beneath a tarpaulin in the flatbed of the gardening truck when he saw his father being arrested. The police department advised me that the man faced a lengthy prison sentence and that his son had no capable relatives to care for him. I was referred to a local child welfare agency, which sent two particularly dog-friendly officials to the house—even though I was required to undergo the background check and psychological evaluation, it was the canine-human bond JP shared with Jacob that convinced them he belonged in our home.

By the time of the adoption interview later in the year, I had long ceased to question why JP had so hungrily accepted the child. I assured the social worker that I had no regrets—in a matter of months, Jacob had become as docile and loving as JP, and we had all three become an inseparable family—although Jacob admitted one discontentment to her: in his haste to reach JP, the first creature ever to slobber him with affection, he had forgotten to pack the key to the talking pillow's secret compartment, which concealed a package of York Peppermint Patties. It didn't matter whether we owed our familial bliss to a temporary case of chemo-brain; a soul's desire to live more fully after a brush with death; or a sweet tooth, pure and simple—it was a true story of dog rescuing human. I smiled at JP, who lay beside Jacob, his nose nestled in the fragrant belly of Mr. Cat.

The Seven-Month Itch

[Nancy Cohen]

 KENYON SLEEPS in our bed. And not just *in* the bed, but nestled between my husband and me, mostly against me. I fall asleep holding his tiny Terrier ribcage in my palm with his warm back pressed against my chest. As I synchronize my breaths with his, I often think we could open a doggie/human pranayama yoga studio teaching this stuff. (I live in L.A.) And sometimes, if the mood's just right, he uses my head as his pillow— which, of course, I take as quite the compliment. He's my twenty-two-pound dose of Xanax.

I awake one morning to Kenyon licking my face like I've just dipped it in squirrel-flavored ice cream. Although this feels damn good, I can't help but wonder if my canine alarm clock is telling me something's wrong, like the time he wagged his tail extra hard not to show how much he loved me but because he had a kidney infection. So I get up to see what the big deal is re: my face. EWWW! I have swollen red welts under my eyes and around my mouth, neck, and jawline. Hours later, the welts morph into bigger, redder welts. And later on, they puff up. Then flake off. Now I have clumps of dry, scaly wrinkles. This is not pretty, especially in L.A. No wonder Kenyon woke me.

I pack K-Mutt in the car. (I recently counted; Kenyon has twenty-four nicknames.) We head to a fancy dermatologist in Beverly Hills, which Einstein Eyebrows is up for, because as long as there's an open window and air shot up his nose at 65 mph he's happy. The doctor gives me a prescription cream to use sparingly. "It can tear the facial skin," he says. What's not pretty in *any* city? Seeing a woman's veins through her face.

My neighbor with perfect skin notices my complexion through Wiggly Worm's nose-printed car window. "You have to see my ayurvedist," she insists, even after I insist I have no idea what one is. Finally Captain Triangle-Teeth and I agree to some ayurveda-ing and wind up at the only not-nice house in the Pacific Palisades. But he refuses to budge from the car, even for a privet hedge sniff-a-thon.

After a cursory examination, this sixty-year-old with a ponytail four times the length of Kenyon's tail informs me that I'm allergic to sulfites. "Avoid food and drink containing them," he tells me through a yawn, during which I see his uvula. (FYI, sulfites are what they put in food to make it last beyond a day. Another FYI: Kenyon's uvula has black spots on it, as does the entire inside of his mouth.) I get back in the car and tell Señor Waggles the news. Licking his sulfite-riddled pig's ear, he gloats, as if simultaneously coughing the word *bullshit*.

Nevertheless, Scruffopolis and I are off to the health food store to pick up a couple hundred dollars' of sulfite-free wine, organic vegetables, and biodynamic cold cuts. And that's about all you can get for two hundred dollars in a health food store.

For the next two weeks, my velvet-eared friend and I live additive-free. For the next two weeks my face is still itchy and splotchy and Pancake Ass can't get enough of it.

"Want to go for a ride?" I ask C.P.C.E. (Curbside Pizza Crust Eater), who's already on board, sniffing my Uggs at the door.

We arrive at the office of an allergist, recommended by my fancy Beverly Hills dermatologist. While Swan-Neckia Jr. pants rhythmically into the car window guarding my sunglass case and Thomas Guide, I lie on a cot on my stomach as a porcupine's worth of needles are thrust into my back. Half-naked and itching, I'm mostly fretting about how long I've left my pal in the car. When the doctor returns, he informs me that I am a very allergic girl.

"No, not sulfites," he says, "dust mites, grass, pollen, cats, and dogs."

"DOGS?! NO WAY!!" I reply. But then he pokes the itchiest part of my back, the spot where he'd injected me with canine. "You'll have to get rid of your dog," he instructs me, as if he were telling me to keep all of my receipts for income tax purposes.

When he notices my eyes welling with tears, Needles (the allergist, not another nickname for Kenyon) relents a bit. "At least don't let the dog in your bed."

"But Kenyatta Malone has *always* shared our bed! We can't take that away or he'll think he did something wrong! Plus, hugging him helps me relax and sleep!"

Needles responds: "Don't you have a husband?"

I drive home, crying hysterically. Our Leader looks at me quizzically and offers his paw. I take it, look deep into his cocoa-brown eyes, and give it to him straight. "There is no way I'd ever ever EVER get rid of you." He wags his tail heartily, licks my elbow, and takes another hit of air out the window. My hands shake on the steering wheel as I worry whom my husband would pick if he had to choose between us.

The next day I leave the Prince-of-K sunbathing on the shag carpet and visit a different dermatologist, also fancy, also in Beverly Hills. She gives me the same face-dissolving cream the first one doled out. When I get home the Barrel-Chested Creature barely looks up; he knew this would be a waste of time. I lie down on the floor and hug him as I wonder if we

should just leave L.A. and go someplace where people don't judge women with blisters and flaky lumps on their faces. He breathes into my ear as if to say everything's going to be okay. Easy for him. He hasn't lost his looks.

Weeks later and still welty, a Sherman Oaks acupuncturist suggests I make the Bearded Wonder an outdoor dog. When I run this by Kenyon, he flashes his pointy little grin. But what does he know? He thinks coyotes are just extra-fun dogs with no parents, not vicious beasts who want to lure him into a game of tag and eat him like it's sunset after Yom Kippur.

At the dog park, I share my woes with a sympathetic stranger who writes down the number of her West Hollywood homeopathist. The homeopath, an exuberant German in a halter top, mixes me a potion of liquid dog hair to put under my tongue three times a day. I do so in the bathroom mirror—as if I can't find my tongue otherwise—while the Little Man watches, giving his body a good shake that causes a bouquet of dog hair to fly into the air. A simple reminder that I could've gotten this particular remedy for free.

My sadness continues, my welts remain; nothing works.

I resolve not to cuddle Beetlepooch. I only pet him with my feet and he's confined to the bottom-right-hand corner of the bed.

And since Sir Barks-a-Little is accustomed to sitting on my lap in the passenger seat while my husband drives, nuzzling his neck against mine as he sucks in his fresh air (okay, it's smog, but I haven't told him yet), I let His Highness have that seat while I ride in the back. He occasionally stares at me, as do other drivers and pedestrians, wondering why we're separated by two feet of seat, carpet, and my Rollerblades, which haven't seen asphalt for the past six years. "It's temporary, Pup-Headia. Mommy will be with you as soon as she gets better," I say, and pray—but not on my knees or anything.

This lasts for two days. Just like when I was single and had too much to drink at bars and hugged men I shouldn't, now I'm having too much to drink at home and hugging my dog when I shouldn't.

The clerk at our neighborhood pet shop, who also fixes computers for $35 an hour less than our computer guy, gives me the card of a Chinese herbalist in San Gabriel. Since we adopted Teddy Bear Nose in nearby El Monte, I have a good feeling about this referral.

In broken English, Dr. Tsao, who has cinnamon-y breath, tells me to smear baby oil onto my face three times a day. The oil is to be followed by Dr. Tsao's special white lotion that, unfortunately, doesn't exactly absorb into the skin. (Good thing I work at home, because I look like a porn star about to finish her shift.) I'm also instructed to take fifteen of his herb pills a day, refrain from hot showers and workouts, avoid mango, red meat, dairy, sushi, coffee, and wine for two solid weeks. I go back to the car and inform Growls McGee that it all seems doable, except for the coffee and cabernet part. He licks my wrist and sticks his head out the window. Maybe he can smell his parents in El Monte.

For two days I smear baby oil and white ointment on my lesions while Kenyon watches. For two days my husband gloats because he's getting 100 percent of Ferret Face's attention. Miraculously, on the third day, I'm cured! No itches, no splotches, no redness. I have normal skin again! I hug Kenyon to celebrate! I eat dairy to celebrate! I buy mangos and ruin my favorite T-shirt while cutting them to celebrate! I even call Dr. Tsao to thank him.

"Good! No let dog sleep in bed anymore."

"But I have to!"

"You no have husband?"

I hang up and look at my Monkey. They just don't get it, do they?

Seven months to the day, it's hats off to Eastern medicine, because Kenyon and I are cuddling at night and at least twice during the day. And I'm proud to report that not only has my head become his permanent pillow, but my shoulder is his ottoman. Although I still ride in the backseat of my husband's car because I kinda like it—and Sock-Pawed Giraffy Legs prefers having the front seat to himself.

Play Dead, My Darling

[Jeff Ward]

 THE DOGHOUSE IN question was a slope-roofed affair out back, about as pretty and pretentious as a mud fence. I liked it. An honest little shack, probably the only one in California—the kind where you can stretch out and roll around and lick yourself without fear of *Architectural Digest* coming to poke around with a photographer. I lay there, still smarting in the flanks, with no plans for the rest of my life. I was seven years old and feeling forty-nine.

After a couple hundred years, the tassel loafers came out and kicked at the portico of the house.

"Come on—walk," he said. "Go for walk."

Chain off, leash on, and once again we were dragging each other around the bleached-out block between Sierra and Gardner. For the first time in my life the exercise felt hollow, even ridiculous, like a wild, romantic hump on your first day after being fixed. The other dogs on the walk were lurid and grotesque, and I saw only their sins. Prince, the Great Dane who had dragged three children into a burning building. Mr. Alexander, the Saint Bernard whose improvement on the traditional rescue had been to show up staggering with an empty cask, just in time to slobber on the dead. And Muggles, the mincing Dalmatian who yammered endlessly about his affairs with Asta and two of the Lassies. With a terrific effort I managed to make small talk with these parading champions and sniff their crotches.

And even this sorry spectacle was too good to last. At the corner of Gardner and Hollywood I spotted a familiar squat figure—a hatless woman holding a leash that trailed down and disappeared into a hedge. When she saw us, a jack-o'-lantern smile turned her big, angular face even more so. She had a skull that I could have picked out from a table full of skulls if I had to—which, given the week I was having, seemed a pretty likely scenario.

Then Sheba emerged from the hedge and there was no more past, only the blinding radiance of her innocence. She was like a pristine snowbank on a leash. It was just how the Virgin Mary would have looked if she had been a good deal holier and a Beagle. The blood hadn't been washed from her coat—it had never been there.

Anyway, it was a good act. It fooled me. It would always fool me. Our owners chattered about the weather and their darlings. Our girl, I learned, had heartworms and was due in the shop for repairs at the end of the week. Sheba's brown eyes leapt hopefully from one speaker to the next, politely avoiding me. I guess we'd never been properly introduced.

"Come on, now, Sheba—good girl!"

And the woman moved on, her little fur saint floating behind, and they were gone.

How could I have resisted her? How many others had looked into those eyes, at those wet black lips, and fallen over backward with their paws in the air? How many more would kill for her, just because she said the word? My advice to the heartworms: Don't waste time looking, fellas. Find yourselves another bitch.

"Okay, s'go home now, let's go," said Tassel, tugging me toward Sunset. "But if I have to throw out another rug, I'm throwing you out as well."

It was naptime, but I wouldn't be sleeping. I would be thinking of something that could have been—which is to say, of nothing at all. I had no plans and no plans to think of any. At three o'clock the mailman would come and I would burst through the doggie door and bite him hard enough to split his calf, but my heart wouldn't be in it.

Where the Dogs Are

[Dan Zevin]

 THE DOG PEOPLE are the people who gather at dawn to throw saliva-soaked tennis balls around parks nationwide. A while ago, I wouldn't have said they were my kind of crowd, as five A.M. was frankly not an hour with which I had much familiarity. But a while ago, I didn't have Chloe, the orphaned Lab mutt who appeared frisky—as opposed to frenzied—when she first conned me into taking her home from the pound. To say that Chloe's internal alarm clock goes off at five A.M. would be misleading, because it would suggest that she requires sleep. In fact, she requires Ritalin. Either that or forty minutes each morning with the dog people.

I feel very close to the dog people, though I do not know any of their names. We remember only the dogs' names, you see. As for our identities, we're just "Chloe's father," "Augie's mother," or "Sadie's parents," to name but a few. Our mission is the same: to chuck the tennis ball until Chloe, Augie, Sadie, and the rest collapse from acute canine exhaustion so they'll spend the remainder of the day sleeping (or, in Chloe's case, "resting") rather than dining on our speaker wires.

The only time it is permissible to stop chucking the ball is when one of the dogs needs a time-out to "poop." Canine excrement, I have learned, is referred to only as "poop" by the dog people. I once made the mistake of using a more colorful term, and was met by stunned silences all around.

But now that I've got the lingo straight, the other dog people and I talk every morning. We don't small-talk, either. We engage in the kind of deep, meaningful conversation you can only have with someone who is outdoors at five o'clock (A.M.) using a plastic Star Market bag to pick up a pile of dog shit. Poop, I mean.

"Hmm, looks like Chloe has diarrhea again," I proclaim.

"Yes, I see what you mean," Augie's mother concurs. "Must be eating too much grass."

"Sadie ate a washcloth last night," interjects her father. "Vomited it up like a Super Ball."

I cannot emphasize enough the significance of these morning chats. With each discussion of Sadie's swollen anal sacs or Augie's weakness for squirrels, I feel a little more connected; a little less like the only father in the city whose daughter does not come every time (okay, *any*time) she is called. Who else but the dog people would have clued me into the Drs. Foster and Smith catalog, featuring hickory-smoked Choo-Hooves at rock-bottom prices? Where else but at the dog field would I have learned that, when it comes to problem "hotspots," the guck from an aloe plant is nature's alternative to cortisone cream? We are all about support and sharing and honesty. Show us a playground full of real parents and we will make them look like amateurs.

One evening I saw one of the dog people at the Sir Speedy copy shop I go to. We were both without our dogs. We looked at each other in that fleeting way people do when they think they know each other but aren't really sure. Then it occurred to me: Sadie's mother! What was she getting copied? Where does she live? Has she seen any good movies lately? Both of us stood there stupidly by the lamination machine until I finally decided to break the ice.

"Uh, how is your dog?" I said.

———

It took a long time to find the canine clique that felt right to Chloe and me. In my neighborhood alone, there were three major scenes going on. We started at Fresh Pond Park, where most of the dogs seemed like they just came out of the Westminster Kennel Club, and most of their mothers and fathers seemed like they just came out of the Harvard Faculty Club. The dog people there didn't really throw the tennis ball as much as they stood around observing the animals' behavioral responses with regard to retrieval-avoidance pack interaction. Plus, a woman with a giant black poodle named Margaret asked me—swear on a stack of Drs. Foster and Smith catalogs—if Chloe "has a problem with ethnic diversity."

Chloe, at the time, was barking at this guy who happened to be black. I immediately experienced that familiar self-consciousness that only we dog people understand: the sense that strangers are passing judgment on us based upon our dog's behavior. *What has Chloe's father been telling her about people of color to make his dog so prejudiced?* Margaret's mother was obviously thinking about me. I felt ashamed, though I knew the truth: Chloe was barking because the guy had a tennis ball.

The dog people at Danehy Park were an entirely different breed. This was the salt-of-the-earth dog scene, and rarely did we see anyone with a purebred anything here, much less a poodle named Margaret. Danehy doggie mothers and fathers just chucked a few balls until they finished their cigarettes, then went home and got ready for work. The couple of times I actually spoke to any of them, we covered the customary subject of effluvia, of course, but they all seemed preoccupied with the man I've come to call "the bad guy."

From what I gathered, the bad guy is some sort of official canine cop who protects parks from the threat of dogs who are not properly licensed. According to Bo's mother, who was holding a load in a CVS bag at the time, the bad guy also issues fines to dog people whose pets are "off-leash." I split this scene pronto, worried that I'd be booked on two counts: unleashed and unlicensed.

And so it was that I stumbled upon my doggie scene of choice: a lesser-known softball field abutting a parking lot and a graffiti-covered grammar school. We're a misfit bunch, Sadie's parents, Augie's mom, and me, but we are going to be the next big thing, I tell you. Why, just this morning we were joined by a potential new member—Rocket's mother—who found herself displaced when the Tufts football field was closed off to canines (surely by decree of the bad guy). I'm amazed at how well I got to know her in the forty minutes we spent chucking the ball and picking up poop. For example, Rocket has ear mites, is scared of luggage, and likes to sleep in the bathtub.

I hope she (and her son) will be back tomorrow, and will one day become permanent members of our little scene. For we are the dog people, and everyone is welcome. Everyone except the bad guy.

A Plea for Canine Acceptance

[Phil Austin]

AS CANINE-AWARD shows steadily flood the cable channels, you may have noticed that many popular breeds of dog are never officially recognized. These excited television programs feature the same panoply of carefully groomed animals dragging around oddly dressed humans of varying sizes on lengths of string as, over and over, the same old favorites— Labrador, Cocker, Pekinese, Shepherd (German and otherwise)—are awarded the prestigious trophies, as if they alone were the only worthy recipients of the public's televised affection. (A side note: If this is a sport, then why can't the human handlers wear at least warm-up suits and running shoes for a properly athletic look? Why dress like Rotary members and school-board supervisors? But, to my point . . .)

I'd like to suggest that it would be wise to take a look at some dogs whom innovative breeders and handlers are promoting these days and, indeed, some whom the public finds increasingly attractive. Please consider several newish breeds that I think deserve not only recognition and attention, but above all, love from people for whom dogs are something more than mere award-winners. These are valued family members with skills more directly tied to modern times than those outmoded skills celebrated by herding, sporting, toying, working, and terriering. The AKC may not find them worthy, but I think you will.

Nova Scotia Cell-Phone-Minute-Counting Retriever

A thoroughly modern breed of companion dog, this slim animal can keep track of minutes, make calculations up to nine places, remember calendar events, and store an extensive list of phone contacts. The Nova Scotia is friendly, flat, and colorful. The breed's ability to take pictures without being seen has been found useful by the insurance industry. The Nova particularly enjoys running with children, especially on weekends and after five o'clock. It may charge an extra amount for an early termination of its plan.

Breed origins: Bred from the larger Flip Hounds and crossed with Hungarian Text-Messaging Herders, the Nova can be taken anywhere, though there is growing resistance to its presence at Broadway shows and intimate restaurants.

Day-Old Danish Pointer

Also known as the Rack Dog in its native Denmark, this marked-down favorite of the urban young is a rare favorite. Two colors, cheese and prune, give the breed a distinctive look. It can be trained to track wounded game and can be found, tightly packaged, even in places like Utah roadside mini-marts, but it most readily adapts to urban environments and has indeed been specially bred for them in Europe. A strong taste for sugar makes it unacceptable as an all-season outdoor dog, but indoors it becomes an excellent coffee companion. This is a thick-boned, hearty breed of modest habits. The dog enjoys the Sunday *New York Times* and can even make hopeful phone calls to attractive young women.

Breed origins: Descended from the Black Pastry Hound of central Europe, these dogs historically pointed at things in Vienna, particularly Puff Poodles.

Liberal Kansas Gundog

For the several hundred years in which black wild-eyed howling gundogs were active members of the Wild Hunt—ducking and retrieving, bullets flying overhead—it was presumed they were willing and able participants in that ancient Germanic ritual. But early gunpowder firearms were remarkably inaccurate, spewing fire and shot in all directions, and the traditional use of alcohol in the ritual continued unabated with the passing of years. Rumors swirled through the canine community in the 1700s that the number of loyal animals actually shot by drunken hunters was increasing at a rapid rate. In America, by the late 1900s, several strains of gundog began to exhibit traits that would eventually lead to the crossing of the Duck-Grabbing Retriever with the Cimarron Pointer by a breeder in western Kansas to create the Liberal Kansas. This is an extremely unusual gundog, naturally adept at taking guns away from hunters. The NRA has declared it to be an even greater threat than weeping inner-city mothers. The Liberal has been known to physically force inebriated hunters into twelve-step programs. It particularly enjoys digging shotgun-size holes for the burial of weapons.

Breed origins: Of an ancient lineage, the friendly Liberal may be ultimately descended from primitive Gimme Dogs in Wales and northeast Germany.

Bernaise Mountain Sauce Dog

The handsome Bernaise will guard $\frac{1}{2}$ cup white wine vinegar and was historically used to draw carts filled with 5 shallots, minced, and at least 2 T. minced fresh tarragon. It is an excellent herding dog, particularly with $\frac{1}{2}$ tsp. white pepper, but is equally willing to gather 4 egg yolks, $\frac{1}{2}$ cup of boiling water, and even 1 cup of warm clarified butter. It uses its size and strength to beat constantly with a wire whisk. Keeping the butter at the same temperature as the egg mixture can modify a tendency toward unprovoked aggression.

Breed origins: An altogether ancient breed, it is said to be descended from the complex Hollandaise Dog.

Britney Mouseketeer Spaniel

This most popular breed enjoys worldwide renown, not the least of which comes from its distinctive seminudity combined with the charm of a relatively empty head. The dog excels in mindless whispering while performing cheerleading lap dances. It inhabits huge stadiums and Internet dreams, where it can be readily Googled. It should not drive an automobile. The standard is for the dog to be heavyset, notwithstanding its tendency toward bulimic behavior. Easily bred, waterproof, and steadfast, it will endure pointless marriages of very short duration.

Breed origins: The Britney almost died out in the early years of this century, but was reconstituted in larger form by determined American breeders. These dogs were originally used to haul in the floating nets of Armenian fishermen on the Elephantine Coast.

Iditarod Refugee Dog

This active Spitz-type dog, described by Jack London in *The Abysmal Race* (1919), is strong and athletic and will happily battle anyone in its pack at the flimsiest excuse. Still, this furtive charmer is frightened of sleds and will try to go south given any small opportunity. Shy and timid, it especially distrusts TV crews and has bad dreams about lonely athletic women who love dogs to the exclusion of everything else. One interesting trait is that of refusing to be numbered. The breed has been known to demand lucrative television contracts. At its worst, it simply runs away.

Breed origins: This large dog originated in motels along highways leaving Alaska. It was originally bred for hauling loads of bulk gold bullion in impossible weather at high speed with only minimal amounts of dog food available.

Insatiable American Food Hound

Now said to be the most common of all American dogs, the Insatiable is quickly gaining acceptance worldwide, thanks to the rapid proliferation of delicious dog food to all corners of the globe. This breed, more than any other, recognizes the urgent need for dog food and demands it upon every occasion. These animals can purchase airline tickets, rent cars, and open cans, especially the pull-tab variety, in their quest for more and more dog food. Certainly stalking is the ancient origin for this behavior, but the viewing of television food commercials—something this dog will do for hours—has largely taken the place of lynx, bear, and vermin hunting.

Breed origins: At one time, nearly every small town had at least one of these dogs. When each had two, and their sexes were not the same, expansion of the breed was inevitable.

A dog's reasons are always reasonable to a dog. —Dan Liebert

The Good Place: A Play in One Act

[Roy Blount Jr.]

The stage is all green. Here and there, above, is a puffy white cloud. Soft, pleasant music plays. A man in a dark suit, MICHAEL, is lying flat on his back at center stage. He begins to stir, then sits up suddenly.

MICHAEL

Where am I? All I remember is—oh!
(wincing, noticing a lily in his hand)
But where . . . ? Hey!
A mixed-breed, self-possessed dog, SASHA, enters, and starts licking his face. Michael, delighted, pets Sasha.

MICHAEL

Hey, there, fella. Nice dog! Can this be . . . ? It must be! I'm in heaven! And there's dogs!

SASHA
(stops licking)
Welcome.

MICHAEL
(jumping to his feet)
Talking dogs!

SASHA

Yes, you and I can converse. But only during Orientation.

MICHAEL

"Converse." I love it—and it makes sense, you know? Because maybe I wasn't so good to people all the time—but that was mostly Wilson, my partner, who did the rough stuff. . . . But I was always nice to dogs.

SASHA

That's why you're here, Mike.

MICHAEL

I knew it! I always thought, there's something in a dog's eyes . . . if a person truly honors the eyes of a dog . . . You know my name, huh? Wow. But Michael. It's Michael.
    He looks around, blissfully.
I always wanted to talk to dogs. Tell me, what's it like? Being, you know, a dog.

SASHA

Here, it's cool. On earth, some complaints.

MICHAEL

Tell me about it. The things I had to do, to make a living! I guess I must've never seriously hurt anybody, though, all that much. Wilson, okay, Wilson was a thug. I would tell him, Wilson, you've got to clean up your act, that stuff you pull reflects on both of us—and sure enough, he got whacked. Me, though—well, I did too, get whacked, true, but . . . Hey, I just realized . . .

SASHA

For instance, when people go out, and leave us all day in little apartments—just take us out briefly "for a walk," so we won't soil their floors. On a leash, so we can be pulled away from checking out the smells. The SMELLS. That's the sweetest part of outdoors, the smells. Duh. A walk to a person is a straight line, toward—who knows what? Not toward smells, that's for sure.

MICHAEL

. . . I don't have to worry about what I did anymore. I made it to the good place!

SASHA

Smells, people jerk us away from. Food, people linger over. If you could watch people eat through the eyes of a dog—it's disgusting, all that slowwww chewing. People know we're watching! People know we're salivating! But they just draagggg it out, and talk, and nibble, and fiddle with . . . what are those things, spoons and things. But when people leave something lying around that *cries out* to be chewed on, and so, of course, we chew on it, we get yelled at. Shoes. How can people walk around in shoes, and not want to eat them?

MICHAEL
        (looking around, not really listening)
Wow.

SASHA

And throwing a stick, like, *twice*? A dog can fetch a stick forever. And people want to throw it *twice*? Mike! Are you listening?

MICHAEL

Hmm? Oh, yeah. I guess people have more time up here, huh?

SASHA

They have forever.

MICHAEL

So I was essentially a good person. This is all just so . . .

SASHA

It takes some getting used to. People have to get over their earthly selves.

MICHAEL
   (chuckling)
Oh, is that so? So tell me about yourself—what breed are you?

SASHA

I'll answer that with a question. What breed are you?

MICHAEL

Oh . . . Scots-Irish on my father's side, mostly, except his grandmother was of Dutch extraction. On my mother's—

SASHA

You could say I'm a Cockapoogle-Labmation.

MICHAEL
That's some mix.

SASHA

Inbreeding is no dog's idea, Mike. My last puppies were with a Boston-spitzihuahua.

MICHAEL

Puppies? It's Michael, by the way. Puppies. There's, uh, sex in heaven?

SASHA

You'd prefer to play the harp?

MICHAEL

Sex in heaven! Hot dog! Sorry. You know, you remind me of a dog I had when I was a kid. I think I'll call you—

SASHA

Sasha. My name is Sasha.

MICHAEL

Sorry, I wasn't thinking. I'm not used to talking dogs.

SASHA

That's why we have Orientation.

MICHAEL

(petting her on the back)

Which is really cute, by the way, for a dog—for you, I mean, to be my
Orientater. But I was thinking, like speaking of sex. For instance. Or just
generally meeting . . . people. Where do I go—

SASHA

Not there. The good place.

MICHAEL

(stops petting)

Excuse me?

SASHA

Base of each ear, and in between. More of a kneading action.

MICHAEL

Well lah-di-dah, Miss Sasha. Base of the ears, it is.

He addresses himself to that area. And chuckles as he follows her instructions.

SASHA

Mmm. Little farther back. Now both hands, both ears. A little harder. Not
that hard. There, that's pretty good. We can work on that. Now, Mike, the
belly, light rubbing.

She rolls over on her back.

MICHAEL
You got it. But, it's Michael.
    He rubs her belly.
MICHAEL
You haven't been missing any meals, I see. What do you eat up here?

SASHA
Squirrel.

MICHAEL
Oh! Somehow, I didn't think . . .

SASHA
You expected ambrosia?

MICHAEL
I don't know, I just—it's not exactly heaven for the squirrels, huh?

SASHA
What a ridiculous notion.

MICHAEL
I guess. Enough rubbing?

SASHA
No.

MICHAEL
    (rubbing some more)
Oh, yeah, you like that, don't you? So. Where do I go from here?

SASHA
    (standing)
You're free to roam. Don't worry, I smell you wherever.

MICHAEL

(chuckling, looking around)

That's okay for you, but—I don't see any buildings. I don't even see any trees.

SASHA

Trees? Trees *would* be heaven for squirrels. I smell one now! Squirrel! Squirrel!

Sasha takes off running, barking.

MICHAEL

Hey, come back! Sasha! You come back here! Doggone that dog. Hey, there's somebody . . .

(waving his arms)

Helloooo! Brother!

He blinks, taken aback by what he sees approaching, which we *see suddenly: a vicious man, dressed in rags, bursting onstage, thrusting his face into Michael's and growling.*

MICHAEL

Get back! What is this? Wait a minute! *Wilson?*

WILSON

(slowly circling)

Grrrrrrr . . .

MICHAEL

You're here? What kind of heaven—

Wilson jumps on Michael and starts pummeling him and trying to steal his suit.

MICHAEL

Help! Get off!

Sasha runs up.

SASHA

Quit that fighting! Willy! Mike! I had to stop chasing that wonderfully pungent squirrel to come over here and deal with you two. What do you think we're going to eat, if you interfere with my work? Shame on you.

> *Wilson stops pummeling. He and Michael pick themselves up—Wilson looking guilty, Michael dusting himself off, looking dumbfounded.*

SASHA

Git!

> *Wilson gits.*

SASHA

Be thankful *you're* not a stray.

MICHAEL

Look here, Sasha, you can't talk to me like that. Enough of this "conversing" with, I'm sorry, but after all: a dog. Take me to somebody who can explain . . . Wh-whuh . . . what . . . kind . . . uhf. . . . Whuhf.

SASHA

Orientation's over, Mike—don't let me catch you fighting with that Willy again. And get your throwing arm warmed up, there's a good fella.

MICHAEL

> *(struggling to speak)*

Whuh-uh—Wuff. Woof. *Woof?*

SASHA

> *(softening, rubbing herself against his leg)*

Come on, boy, stop oozing fear, it throws off the scent of—

She sniffs. Turns.
Another squirrel! I've got to run!
　　She runs off.

MICHAEL
Woof! Woof! Ah-oooooooooo.

Curtain

Untitled

[Gary Baseman]

This Dog's Life

[J. P. Lacrampe]

WE EXPRESSLY TOLD Emily, "No." "Absolutely not." "We're not mature enough." "We're too poor." "Never home." "Completely irresponsible." "Barely able to care for ourselves." "No way."

The next day there he was—tiny and freckled and whimpering in a cardboard box in our clapboard kitchen, six weeks old: a beautiful Dalmatian puppy. A Nerf ball with eyes and a tail.

Seven of us—five boys and two girls—lived in largely self-imposed squalor in a five-bedroom house in Tempe, Arizona—the host-town of Arizona State University. The house itself was not bad: three large-size bedrooms and two smaller ones. In back, it had a screen-window solarium, the screens long since shredded from misuse. And a kidney-shaped swimming pool, which, during our short tenure, had turned an unfortunate and hesitating shade of lime-green. The place was trashed.

Individually, the seven of us may not have been slobs, but, as a collective, our house was an atrocity—an unkempt monument to filth. Weeks of grunge-caked dishes towered in Pisa-ian leans on our kitchen counter. Bags and boxes of fast food scuttled the floors. Half-empty beer bottles patrolled the furniture, unclaimed.

So, it wasn't so much the *place,* as it was *us*—our gross negligence and irresponsibility. Our major concern with this being, that if we have trouble

126

taking care of a large, stationary, and inanimate object, what sort of chance do we stand with a delicate and eclectically mobile puppy?

Collectively, of course, we caved. We caved the way anyone does when confronted by a soft ball of fluff and snivels—immediately and absolutely. We peered into that cardboard box, and our snarls of protest miraculously ceased. "Just *look* at him!" we said. "Isn't he adorable?" A twenty-year-old's version of "Oh, can't we *pleeease* keep him?"

And suddenly—collectively—we were dog owners.

So, the seven residents of 2012 South Kachina congregated in referendum to name our newest and least bipedal member. From the corner store, elder Duncan purchased a 30-pack of Milwaukee's Best—the beer to act as the group's chief facilitator—and, with all of us huddled around the cardboard box, our meeting was called to order.

The suggestions immediately poured forth: "Benito?" No. "Hatchet?" No. "Charlie Rose [the TV was on]?" No. "Leftwich?" No. "Lothar?" No. "Lewis-Meriwether?" Ehn.

More beer; more suggestions: "Whatadog?" "Vache?" "Doctor T?" "Whistle?" "Her Majesty's Secret Service?" "My Liege?" "Dexedrine [Terrence was ADHD]?" "Lord Nelson?" "Doglodyte?" "Yip-Yap?" "Worry?" "The Hydrant?" "Robot?" "*Robot?*"

And there he was—Robot.

Our little Robot.

Sure, objections were voiced; words like "potty-trained" evoked in a cautionary, questioning manner. For it was unanimously decided that we'd enough shit in our house without any need for the more literal form. Cleanliness was already a hot-button issue for some (albeit, purely in its vocal form), and the addition of a puppy seemed a lot like trying to clean a dirty window with a dirtier rag—cute, but counterproductive.

Yet, one look at our puppy's blazingly white-and-black-spotted coat and it was hard to imagine Robot as being anything *but* clean. He seemed immaculate. Radioactive, even. Plus, there were our impromptu housekeeping solutions: "We could train him to be some sort of canine-maid." "Or teach him to chew a stick and push him around like a Swiffer."

Our little cleaning Robot.

The fears of messiness were misplaced. And, in subsequent months, while the seven of us remained completely smitten with Robot—shamelessly parading him around ASU's campus or at parties—it was becoming clear that *he* wanted out of the entire situation. As Robot outgrew his puppy-box, I think he became disillusioned over the fact that the cardboard-kennel he was to leave behind comprised the house's cleanest spot. Our dog, it seemed, appreciated a different sort of lifestyle than the one he had been unluckily borne into. Robot, funny enough, liked clean carpet. And fresh smells. And the calm of quiet solitude. He was sort of like Jack Lemmon in a fancy fur coat—completely exasperated to be cohabitating with seven Walter Matthaus.

And so, our beloved Robot would barricade himself in Emily's relatively clean and quiet room—exiting only for matters of food and business. It was largely a self-imposed exile that we all hoped would soon end. We all hoped that our little Robo would grow to accept us; grow to enjoy the pros *and* cons of commune-style living—the joys of not doing the dishes until Flag Day.

Robot had his own plans.

His first attempts at escape were primitive, simple. A door left ajar, a window slid open too far and Robot was *vamoose* in a black-speckled and furry flash—his tongue waving "Ciao" as he sprinted from the malt-sour smell and garbage-strewn linoleum of our house into the sweet, crisp air of Arizona's winter.

And, suddenly, there we were: pouring onto the streets—on bike, in car, on skateboard—scanning the flower beds of neighbors' lawns, screaming ourselves hoarse: "ROBOT?"

"Here, boy!" "*ROBOT,* come back!"

A fleet of half-drunk collegians in an ear-crunching search for robots.

"No, ma'am—*our* Robot."

When Robot finally had the seven of us trained to shut tight our doors and windows, he began taking more ambitious measures—namely, revenge. And it should be noted that Robot's appreciation for life's finer things shined through even his vengeance. He ruthlessly—and exclusively—pursued our wallets, expensive leather shoes, orthodontic retainers, and once the green card of a Canadian friend. Our morale's low point came when Terrence discovered a batch of "puppy truffles" meticulously arranged as his pillow's centerpiece.

But Robot's sabotage was largely a thing covert—sort of an underground resistance. In front of us, he remained his cute, lovable self—playfully launching himself about the room, howling in tune to Louis Armstrong records, and occasionally deigning to allow some casual petting. Beneath this friendly surface, however, our Robotty was systematically trying to tear apart the fabric of our lives as though it were an expensive leather couch—which, to his dismay, we did *not* have.

When we refused to buckle to his revenge tactics, Robot turned the broad breadth of his attention once again to escape. Tunneling in our backyard was an arduous process—the dusty desert soil flaking away piece by tiny piece. But Robot was a dog undeterred. A hard worker. And while we laughed in carefree whimsy from the shallow end of the pool, Robot was busy at the house's flank, moving earth. Building his channels of escape, into the simmering Arizona spring.

Again, the serenity of the neighborhood would shatter under our shouts: "ROBOT?" "Where are you, ROBOT?" "ROBO, here, boy!" Our voices cracking with the promise that *this* time we'd do better.

"What in the hell are you kids looking for?" "Our dog." "Well, what's its name?" "Robot." "*Robot?*" "Robot."

Optimism forces me to search for the positive in this situation. We eventually located Robot's tunnels—collapsed and filled them. But I'd like to think that we all found some measure of compromise in the last months of our senior year. Collectively, we were beginning to outgrow the romance of squalor—in no small way thanks to Robot's integrity and spirit. Sometimes, in the moment, it's tough to see who's helping you and how. And it's especially tough when, at that moment, you're drinking beer poolside in Arizona's endless summer.

Robot's final—and successful—escape occurred just after graduation day. Emily's mother generously assumed custody as the seven of us disbanded across the country. Robot happily traveled to Mrs. Lyons's clean abode, stashed away in the silvery tranquillity of Longmont, Colorado; to a loving, quiet household with a serene and sweet-smelling garden. To a place you'd be crazy to run away from.

My only hope is that Robot (who now goes by Charlie Rose) misses me about half as much as I miss him. And that he forgives us all for being far more the puppy.

Ciao, friend.

[Our dogs tugboat us home. —Dan Liebert]

Why I Write About Dogs

[Susan Conant]

I CAN'T THROW. As a child, I was spared the humiliation of never being picked for either team in baseball by my friend Debbie, a prodigy with ball and bat who always chose me. She was a sort of one-person Red Sox Dream Team. Because of Debbie and in spite of me, our team always won, which is to say that hers did. Because I love dogs, I have never inflicted myself on a Golden Retriever or a Lab.

For the last twenty years, I have lived with Alaskan Malamutes. One of the mysteries of dogdom unexplained by science is why the fetch gene is extremely rare in a breed that evolved in the snowball-perfect environment of the Arctic. But rare it is. The typical Malamute has a powerful desire to fly after and seize moving objects but requires that the poor things be edible—squirrels, chipmunks, rabbits, moles, and mice. What's more, Malamutes don't share. If we bipeds want rodent delicacies for dinner, we're expected to hunt them down ourselves. As to playing fetch, the Malamute attitude is that if you wanted those balls, you shouldn't have thrown them away.

Or so I always believed. Then along came my Django, who is named for a legendary jazz guitarist but who should properly have been called Lou, Babe, or Mickey. The dog is a fetch fanatic. When the rare gene manifests itself in Django's breed, its effect is typically suppressed by competing genes

131

that prevent Malamutes from engaging in such servile activities as picking up after members of a useful but lesser species. My late Kobuk would return a ball to me five or six times before he'd reach the disappointing realization that it was not going to spring to life and turn itself into a snack. My Rowdy never once retrieved anything but her obedience dumbbell, which she correctly viewed as currency exchangeable for beef and liver. She regarded Django's insatiable appetite for fetch as stupid and treasonous; in her disdainful eyes, he was a brainless traitor to a proud and predatory breed. Rowdy's scorn bothered Django not at all. Malamutes don't give a damn about the opinions of others, including the heretofore universal opinion that I can't throw.

So we play ball, Django and I. As I toss the ball, I follow the advice of athletically gifted friends: just as Debbie used to advise, I keep my eyes on the spot where I'd like to have the ball land. Meanwhile, all on its own, the ball leaps out of my grasp and comes to rest elsewhere. On some occasions, it mysteriously drops to the grass at my feet before I've had the chance to launch it into the air. When the mood strikes it, it travels great distances and lodges itself in the depths of hedges. Once in a while, it perversely decides to roll under the gate and out of our yard.

True pitching, as I understand it, occurs when a human being sends a tiny little round object soaring through space in such a fashion that it miraculously arrives at a predetermined place. In my experience, true pitching is thus an aberration, perhaps, or a freakish coincidence, the kind of bizarre phenomenon that happens once in a trillion times and then only by accident. It has never happened to me.

Does Django care? He does not. Never once, even while digging through forsythia roots after his ball or while watching it fall like a dead thing at my feet, has he ever accused me of being unable to throw. On the contrary, he enjoys the delusion that I am Debbie. In his view, the Red Sox lost gold when they lost me. If you ask Django what he thinks of my pitching, he'll tell you that by comparison with me, Curt Schilling throws like a girl.

And that's why I write about dogs.

What My Dog Has Eaten Lately

[Bonnie Jo Campbell]

 GIVING ANTIBIOTICS TO the cat is a big deal. First, we have to catch the cat—he always suspects something is up and hides. Then we wrap him in a towel to restrain him, pry open his mouth, shove a pill down, then hold his mouth closed until he swallows. On the other hand, when I need to give the dog some medicine, I need only place the pill near some food. Eating is what my dog does best.

When Re-bar, a spotted Lab mix, was a puppy, he ate a lot of shoes. He also ate our couch, or enough of it anyway, that we put the rest of it out by the road for yard pickup. Unfortunately, because of cuts in township services, the yard pickup truck did not come for three months. To our surprise, we found that we enjoyed drinking coffee while sitting with Re-bar on what was left of the couch in the driveway in the mornings. Our neighbors often shouted to us from their cars, "When in the hell you getting rid of that thing?" My darling Christopher and I held up our coffee cups in neighborly greeting.

Now that Re-bar is getting to be middle-aged he hardly destroys anything anymore. And because of an accident with a car on Sprinkle Road, he has only three legs, so he doesn't travel far from home. We only wonder about what he's been eating when he's flatulent or throwing up. Or perhaps when we catch him eating grass, which is what he does when he feels ill and which results, of course, in his throwing up. Once Re-bar ate a dish towel and attempted to throw it up for days. By the time he managed to digest the thing, he had practically mowed our lawn.

Sometimes the dog throws up because of what I feed him. I am pretty brazen about the possibility of poisoning myself or Christopher—I never remember to refrigerate the meatloaf or roasted chicken overnight, and sell-by dates mean nothing to me. I have even less fear of poisoning the dog, since I figure he can just throw up whatever I gave him if it turns out to be bad. So if I'm cleaning the refrigerator and find something questionable, I toss it to the dog.

I wouldn't go out of my way to give my dog really bad food. Nor would I give him especially good food. I would no more feed great food to a dog than I would feed it to a kid. Like a kid, Re-bar is just as impressed with a hot dog as he is with a filet mignon. And it would take him exactly the same amount of time to eat either the hot dog or the filet mignon—one and a half seconds.

There is a category of food that Re-bar rates above hot dogs, filet mignon, and even rawhide chews. That category is dead stinking things, the deader and stinkier the better.

And now that government cutbacks have mandated that Kalamazoo County Animal Control no longer pick up dead wildlife along the road, there is plenty of rotten stuff to gnaw on. (As if to prove that they're really not going to pick up dead creatures anymore, the Animal Control has left a dead male mallard on the road in front of their building on Lake Street for two months.) My dog is grateful for the budget cuts, since chewing on a flattened possum or duck is, to him, an excellent way to spend the evening.

My Lakewood neighbors are the kind of people who, if they hit a deer on the road, will bring it home and dress it out. A little after midnight one night last year, our neighbor Bob was making a lot of noise outside our bedroom window. Chris and I dressed and followed Re-bar outside to discover Bob driving his lawn tractor beneath his basketball hoop. He was pulling a chain through the basketball hoop, and attached to the other end of the chain was a deer carcass. Re-bar barked in delight. A day and a half later, after the deer was in Bob's freezer, Re-bar brought home a deer leg, hoof intact, which he chewed in the yard for a week, a leg that Bob claimed he knew nothing about.

Most impressive to me is the way Re-bar bites and kills and eats wasps. He seems to do it without getting his tongue stung, with a series of rapid jaw snaps. Watching him reminds me not to ever get my fingers between Re-bar and his food. Re-bar also has an irrational desire to bite fireworks, and sometimes even disposable lighters if they've been used to light fireworks.

People are nice to my dog. Last week, when Re-bar and I visited Grandpa, he gave Re-bar a lamb bone that was bigger than Re-bar's head. When Re-bar and I visited my brother Tom, he and some friends were cooking up a dishpan full of smelt, and Re-bar caught and chomped at least eighty smelt tails. Because Tom is too busted up from his recent moped accident (he hit a bus) to cook, his friend Monty made him a venison stew; not only could Tom not stomach the stew, but even his cats wouldn't eat it. We put the pan on the floor for Re-bar and he submerged his whole head in it. Luckily I realized in time the folly of letting a dog eat five quarts of aged stew and then having him ride home in the backseat of my car, so I put the stew into quart containers that I borrowed from Tom, brought them home, and gave Re-bar one quart of venison stew per day until it was gone.

To really cheer my dog up, I let him spend the day at my mom's while I'm working. My dog was born at my mom's house and his litter sister lives there, so together they swim in the creek, bark at the donkeys, and harass woodchucks who live under the woodpiles. By the time I pick my dog up in the evening, he is so worn out that he can hardly support himself on his three legs and is dragging himself around by his front legs. By the time I pick him up he can't bark because he has barked all day non-stop. Bark! Bark! Bark! (Gary Larson of *The Far Side* cracked the code to dog language once and for all. When a dog says, "Bark! Bark! Bark!" he means "Hey! Hey! Hey!")

My mother's own two dogs have kind of a weight problem, so she feeds them only about a cup of dog food a day apiece; if they're still hungry, they go up to the barnyard to chew on dead raccoons or chunks of manure. My dog too will chew on a chunk of donkey dung with great pleasure. When I say his name in a way that expresses my disgust (Oh, Re-bar!), he looks up with pride from what he is doing. In case you were wondering, I am not one of those people who kisses my dog on the mouth.

As I have mentioned before, at my mother's house the dog food is not plentiful, but the dogs get plenty to eat one way or another. My mother has the habit of tossing food to the dogs from her plate while she is eating. She usually eats at her desk with her feet up. Mom has some really tough meat in her freezer from a milk cow that Steve Kirklin the dairy farmer had to put down. Mom also has a removable dental bridge, which she takes out at night; it is made of wire and one prosthetic tooth. One day my mom was chomping on a particularly gristly piece of milk-cow meat and she gave up on it and tossed it to Re-bar, who caught it in his mouth and gulped it down without chewing.

Mom felt around in her mouth with her tongue and realized her re-movable bridge was missing. She looked at Re-bar, who had a stupid grin on his face and who awaited more meat.

My mother resolved not to tell me what had happened until a month was up, so that I would not feel obligated to follow him around and reclaim the device. I am grateful for this kindness of hers. If I come across it in the yard, though, I'll certainly offer it back to her.

Canine Films Currently in Production

[Brian Frazer]

Air Bud: Enough Already!

Air Bud gets tired of all the leaping and jumping and runs away. Also starring Mare Winningham as Mrs. Abernathy.

Dogs Gone Wild: Totally Off Leash!

These dogs are *totally* wild! Corgis who roll over without even being asked!!! Irish Setters who will lap up ANYTHING! Terriers who won't stop barking—even when there's nothing to bark at!!! They howl, they fight, they love, they hump chairs! They're completely out of control!!! Starring Forest Whitaker as the guy on a bullhorn trying to see if *anyone* knows how to sit!

Honey, I Shrunk the Mastiff!

Rick Moranis is back in this *dog*-sterical farce. This time the family's 184-pound Neapolitan Mastiff is accidentally shrunk to the size of a Pocket Puggle.

Cold 'N Tired

It's Erin Brockovich meets the Iditarod as a group of Siberian Huskies go on strike because they're sick of pulling sleds across the 34-degrees-below-zero (not factoring in the wind chill) tundra for some pointless race that should be held on snowmobiles.

Wes Craven's Microchipped!

A timid Goldendoodle (played by Sharon the Labradoodle) is off to the vet to get a tracking device injected between her shoulder blades in the master of horror's latest masterpiece. Little does the doctor know, this 'doodle's out for revenge: she's packing a nuclear warhead!

Really Really Really Old Yeller

Old Yeller's back! With the original cast! You're guaranteed to shed some tears during Old Yeller's walk to the mailbox in this 322-minute epic.

Watch Dogs

A group of Pugs fight back when their dog walker (Toni Collette) only takes them for a twenty-three-minute walk instead of the full-hour walk their owner paid for in advance. Directed by Jerry Bruckheimer.

The Shaggy Bailiff

A Doberman with hair extensions stars in this hilarious legal romp where justice is served without the kibble. Cameo by Kurt Russell as the court stenographer.

Non-opposites Attract

The touching story of a Basenji and an Akita who fall in love, consummate their marriage, and then start to bark like there's no tomorrow, perplexing their respective breeders. Costarring Crispin Glover as the dog-walker who introduces them.

Kennel Cough 3

Dustin Hoffman stars as a veterinary specialist trying to find out why none of the strays at the pound are responding to any antibiotic. Finally, Robert Downey Jr. puts it all together: a disgruntled volunteer has replaced all the drugs with placebos!

This Maltese Ain't No Falcon

A Maltese named Scooter tries to solve a jewelry-store heist with the bumbling duo of William Shatner and David Caruso.

Turner and Hooch and the 101 Dalmations vs. Cujo (In 3-D!)

In this tail-wagging adventure from the producers of *Wedding Crashers,* Tom Hanks and his 102 pals' joyful afternoon gets turned upside-down when Cujo shows up with Vince Vaughn and opens up eight dozen cans of whoop ass on our cuddly gang!

Ebony and Yellowy

A yellow Lab and a black Lab hook up and are immediately ostracized by their own families. Halle Berry tries to smooth things over, but will her pleas fall on deaf ears?

My Puppy Looks Weird!

A self-conscious Mexican Hairless teams up with Fabio on a nationwide search for a really good wig. Thanks to a determined Newfoundland, a surly groomer, and a little Epoxy, *MPLW* is a heartening tale of acceptance, friendships, and learning how to make the best of what you're stuck with.

The Poodle Wears Prada

No matter how expensive the designer sweater Penelope is forced to wear, this prissy pooch wants no part of it! Costarring Reggie as the Lhasa Apso who helps set her free.

In a Jam!

Teddy the Bloodhound searches for the misplaced raspberry jam in this BBC thriller.

Bling Bling Benji

Strange Bedfellows

[Kinky Friedman]

What happens in my bedroom after the lights go out?
On most nights a lot of purring, scratching, and howling—not to
mention heavy petting.

 I SLEEP IN an old ranch house in the Hill Country with a shotgun under my bed and a cat on my head. The cat's name is Lady Argyle, and she used to belong to my mother before Mom stepped on a rainbow. It is not a pleasant situation when you have a cat who insists on sleeping on your head like a hat and putting her whiskers in your left nostril all night long at intervals of about twenty-seven minutes. I haven't actually timed this behavioral pattern, but it wouldn't surprise me if the intervals were precisely twenty-seven minutes. This precarious set of affairs could have easily resulted in a hostage situation or a suicide pact, but as of this writing, neither has occurred. The two reasons are because I love Lady as much as a man is capable of loving a cat and Lady loves me as much as a cat is capable of loving a man. It is a blessing when an independent spirit like a cat loves you, and it's a common human failing to underestimate or trivialize such a bond. On the other hand, it's not a healthy thing to observe a man going to bed with a cat on his head like a hat. And, in the case of Lady and myself, there are observers.

The observers of this Van Gogh mental hospital scenario are four dogs, all of whom despise Lady—though not half as much as Lady despises them. The dogs sleep on the bed too, and they find it unnerving, not to say unpleasant, to be in the presence of a man who has a cat on his head. I've tried to discuss this with them on innumerable occasions, but it isn't easy to state your case to four dogs who are looking at you with pity in their eyes.

Mr. Magoo is five years old and highly skilled at how to be resigned to a sorry situation. He's a deadbeat dad, so his two sons, Brownie and Chumley, are with us as well. Brownie and Chumley were so named after my sister Marcie's two imaginary childhood friends and fairly recently have been left in my care, as she departed for Vietnam with the International Red Cross, an assignment she correctly deduced might be harmful to the health, education, and welfare of Brownie and Chumley. The animals divide their time between my place and the Utopia Animal Rescue Ranch, a sanctuary for abused and stray animals. (It's run by Nancy Parker and Tony Simons; my role is the Gandhi-like figure. For more information go to utopiarescue.com.)

If you've been spiritually deprived as a child and are not an animal lover, you may already be in a coma from reading this. That's good because I don't care a flea about people who don't love animals. I shall continue my impassioned tale, and I shall not stop until the last dog is sleeping.

The last dog is Hank. He looks like one of the flying monkeys in *The Wizard of Oz,* and he doesn't understand that the cat can and will hurt him and me and the entire Polish army if we get in her way. Lady is about eighteen years old and has lived in this house on this ranch almost all her life, and she doesn't need to be growled at by a little dog with a death wish.

So I've got the cat hanging down over one side of my face like a purring stalactite with her whiskers poking into my left nostril and Hank on the other side who completely fails to grasp the mortal danger he's placing both of us in by playfully provoking the cat. It's 3:09 in the morning, and suddenly a deafening cacophony of barking, hissing, and shrieking erupts, with Lady taking a murderous swat at Hank directly across my fluttering eyelids and Mr. Magoo stepping heavily on my slumbering scrotum as all of the animals bolt off the bed simultaneously. This invariably signals the arrival of Dilly, my pet armadillo.

Dilly has been showing up with the punctuality of a German train in my backyard for years. I feed him cat food, dog food, bacon grease, anything. He is a shy, crepuscular, oddly Christ-like creature whose arrival brings a measure of comfort to me at the same time it causes all of the dogs to go into attack mode. It is not really necessary to describe what effect this always has on Lady.

After I've slipped outside and fed Dilly, I gather the animals about me like little pieces of my soul. I explain to them once again that Dilly is an old, spiritual friend of mine who is cursed with living in a state full of loud, brash Texans, and we don't have to make things worse. Somewhere there is a planet, I tell them, inhabited principally by sentient armadillos who occasionally carve up dead humans and sell them as baskets by the roadside. Perhaps not surprisingly, the animals seem to relate to this peculiar vision. Then we all go back to bed and dream of fields full of slow-moving rabbits and mice and cowboys and Indians and imaginary childhood friends and tail fins on Cadillacs and girls in the summertime and everything else that time has taken away.

A dog's pathos is that his mouth is his hand. —Dan Liebert

Doggy Love

[Scott Bradfield]

Tall, Dark, and Furry

I find it quite awkward all this silly writing about myself, but here goes.

I am a reasonably attractive mixed-breed Setter and blond Lab (on my mother's side) seeking a companionable mate in the vicinity of Regent's Park, where my master takes me most afternoons between four and five-thirty. I am three years old and, while still a virgin, my genitalia remain fully intact, which has led to some rather embarrassing confrontations with my master's guests recently. Especially if they've been in contact with a female dog in the last, say, seven or eight hours.

I can't help myself. I'm quite amorous by nature.

I enjoy grooming (myself and others), television (with the sound off), and most of Haydn's late wind concertos, even though they are normally dismissed by the world's dull-as-dishwater Mozart enthusiasts. I'm not disparaging Mozart, understand. I just think there were a lot of equally talented eighteenth-century composers running around Europe, even if their lives weren't melodramatic enough to inspire an Oscar-winning film by Milos Forman.

My ideal partner would be a mixed breed like myself, since I don't want to get into a lot of weird social games about who pisses where. She should be attractive, with a nice rump, and enjoy the same things I do, such as catching flies, and illegally bathing in the duck pond. Also, it would help if her master got along with my master, kind of like in *101 Dalmatians*. My master, incidentally, is a very kind (and totally unattractive) human male who doesn't like living alone any more than I do. When he's not at work flogging surplus capital in the City, he lies around the house masturbating and watching Nazi documentaries on the History Channel.

No time wasters, please. Photo available on request.

This Lady's Not for Stroking

Dear TDF,

I joined this service as a trial member a few nights back when I came across your profile. You sound really nice and yes, I, too, live within the immediate vicinity of Regent's Park.

It feels sad joining a computer dating service, but I'm a middle-aged bitch who has never been on a proper date in her entire life, so I've got to start somewhere. I should mention right off that I'm not a virgin. This is due to an unfortunate week spent in the so-called "animal-friendly" Doggy-Do Kennels in West 14, when my mistress went to Barbados. It's an experience I'd just as soon not talk about right now.

I hate trying to describe myself, so I've attached a recent e-photo. Sorry my mistress is in it, but she butts into all my photos. And yes, I realize she is pretty unattractive, even for a human female. But she has a good heart and walks me twice a day. So I guess I probably love her.

As for my likes and dislikes, here goes.

I like long runs at the beach; raw meat (though I can get along fine on cereal); and lazy days lying at home on the shag carpet with a good video. I guess it's hard to describe my ideal mate, since it boils down to a matter of chemistry, but I value honesty and a good sense of humor above all else. And well, okay. A great-looking rump doesn't hurt.

On the other hand, I hate phoniness and cynicism and needless cruelty to trees.

Hope to hear from you soon,
Denise

Russian Princess Seeks American Prince

Zdrastvuyte from Mother Russia, where lonely Slavic princess find herself living with great-nippled Mamma and six beautiful lesbian sisters. I am being much fond of America and its peoples all the time, where I would like to visit shortly, preferring it be in company of tall handsome butch American so-and-so. Perhaps you may find yourself this hunky pup as described?

Perhaps we become pen pals and you help me with my troubled English?

Love,

Anastasia

P.S. My rump not so terrible for looking at neither. But why take my word for it? Check out my doggy action at wolfbitches.co.ru. And prepare yourself for hot humpy loving all night long!

Lovely

Dear Denise,

Thank you so much for your lovely photo. I had my doubts before, but perhaps this Internet dating service has its merits.

Time will tell, perhaps.

Please find attached a recent photo of myself on holiday last spring in the Lake District, a gorgeous country filled with so many brilliant smells you wouldn't believe it. I know I'm no Rin Tin Tin in the looks department, but that has never left me wanting for female admirers, since I possess many compelling natural odors that are not convertible into rich text format.

Of course, this innate attraction to the opposite sex has never paid off in what might be called carnal dividends. Sure, I'm allowed to race and frolic with the ladies of Regent's Park, but once the action gets serious? My master hits me on the nose with a rolled-up copy of *Private Eye*.

I loathe *Private Eye*. I don't know about you, but I genuinely loathe it.

Maybe we could meet sometime soon. My master and I usually arrive at Marylebone Green around four or four-thirty.

Is your mistress persuadable?

Your new friend,
Randall

Do You Yahoo?

Dear Randall,

I'm sorry I took so long getting back to you. My mistress was home sick and I couldn't get near the PC.

What a handsome doggy, Randall; I'm really impressed. You're definitely a lot better looking than you seem to realize. (Not that looks matter to me in the long run.) Actually, I still have my doubts about this dating service. With the obvious exception of yourself, Randall, the only people who ever write me seem like total creeps and weirdos. Russian pornographers, cosmetic surgeons, international loan brokers, and e-perverts of every species and description. It makes you wonder about the genetic imperative, doesn't it? Reproduce or die. Is that what it's all about?

Being a single female in the big city has made me a little cynical, I guess. As far as an assignation, I'll see what I can do. There are two ends to every leash, as my old mom used to say.

Love,
Denise

Doggy Doggy Doggy Doggy

Doggy doggy doggy me love doggy doggy are me favorite me like big doggy me like strong mean doggy doggy get mad and bite me doggy get mad and chase me down and bite me hard like big strong doggy bite me hard miaow sorry for that miaow sorry for that me a big doggy me a miaow sorry sorry big mean doggy paws are too big for master keyboard miaow love the big doggy love the big doggy doggy love me?

Please write back please send photo of big mean doggy growling hot angry all night long photo please jpg format please big doggy so hot and angry me want you so bad me a very big doggy me very strong doggy please love me please.

Your obedient doggy need discipline now,
Rosco the Very Big Doggy Definitely Not a Cat Miaow

A Perfect Day

Dear Denise,

What a lovely day in the park. Even if the best part did only last a few seconds. I love my master and remain devoted to him. But if he ever goes near you again with that rolled-up copy of *Private Eye,* I'll see to it personally that he spends the rest of his life learning to sit on one buttock.

Will write more later but I can already hear his feet on the pavement and smell his awful signature odor wafting through the kitchen window. I can't help myself.

I just start barking like crazy.

Will write more soon,
Randall

Counter-conditioning

Dearest Randall,

What can I say? I detected a pretty convincing whiff from our correspondence, but as soon as I smelled you coming across the children's playground I knew you in my bones, Randall. You make me feel like radar.

It was so perfect. The bits of sun shining through and the green grass and the dusty pollen everywhere. Racing and snapping at each other and then you caught me (just at the moment I let you) and please, don't blame your master for getting strict with that rolled-up rag. We both kind of deserved it.

That weird orange cat freaked me out, though. Slithering through the nasturtiums and purring and hissing and licking himself. What a creepy guy.

Do you think our respective masters hit it off? They hardly looked each other in the eye, which, considering their appalling features, is pretty understandable. And the smell!

How can they make love face to face?

Love,

Denise

Brainy Hunk Seeks Same or Better

As you can see from the attached photo, I'm a great-looking, well-exercised, full-blooded German Shepherd who believes in maintaining himself both in body and mind. As such, I spend large parts of the day contemplating life's inpenetrable mysteries, such as the meaning of existence, or the corporate destruction of animal life. Not to mention I once caught thirty-seven Frisbees in a row at the beach.

Do you ever wonder what's really going on inside the heads of our bizarre and often useless masters? Do you ever wonder how healthy, intelligent dogs such as ourselves kept in touch before this marvelous invention called the Internet? Do you feel it's time for a revolutionary change in the cause of animal rights? And I'm not just talking about the poor cows and pigs being chopped up for sandwiches. I'm talking about us dogs, who have been unfairly restricted from attending our nation's churches, schools, and government buildings for centuries.

When was the last time you saw a dog run for Congress or Parliament? And considering the woeful state of our Western democracies, who could it hurt?

If you ever stay awake nights worrying about these and other questions, please drop me a line. And don't forget to attach a photo of your hairy posterior, just so I know our chemistry is clicking.

Love,

Rex

So Long You've Been Gone

Denise? Honey?

Every day we go to the park and you're not there. I know it's hopeless in terms of a long-term relationship. I know our masters are too hideous to develop an attachment to each other. But I can only think about tomorrow, Denise. I need to see you.

Even if it's only for an hour or a minute.

Will I? Soon?

Love,
Randall

Someone to Share the Magic

Dear Randall,

Can't talk now. I've been doing a little research and you won't believe what I learned. I feel so ashamed for all those silly, cynical things I said about Internet dating services! Hold on, baby! We're almost home.

Love,
Denise

Oriental Beauty Seeks American Male for Much Loving

Do you often wish for lovely Oriental bitch with much loving for to give? Do you live in a warm climate with many electrical appliances for personal entertainment and comfort? Do you much desire small bundle of Chinese love to cuddle in your big soft doggy bed? Me would wish enjoy such cozy doggy bed much time soon.

Perhaps you consider marriage or cross-breeding or even cohabitation with little Chinese beauty of much loving to give.

Please send photo of esteemed doggy self along with photo of sunny backyard, photo of local trees and vegetation, photo of master(s) and/or mistress(es), and especially photo of cozy doggy bed.

Me looking forward often to hearing from you much time early.

Love,

Yinyang

First Contact

Dear Reginald of Regent's Park,

Please believe that I never evinced myself in this brash manner previously, but I was browsing the singles Web sites and consequently made visual contact with your photo and profile under the mutually intriguing title "Lonely but Loving." What a fortuitous circumstance of formidable complexity!

Perhaps you will not recall an incident of such inherent triviality, but we actually encountered one another in Regent's Park last week, or more accurately, our canine associates encountered one another in what might have developed into an unwholesome public display had you not intervened with your handy magazine, of which I am likewise fond on many occasions.

I have considered your scent often in the many weeks since our encounter and cannot get your attractive buttocks out of my mind. You will have to pardon my American bravado and vocabulary. I believe you refer to it as your "bum," and might consider it gauche for a strange bitch such as myself to speak of it openly in free correspondence.

Please excuse my American candor, however, and perhaps my resultant awkwardness in formal composition regarding these matters. But I felt I must write you since it has caused me much joy to contemplate our reencounter in a parklike setting of our mutual convenience.

Perhaps I might put this more bluntly. Could we perhaps meet sometime soon? Since you are the male aggressor in such matters, I will leave the time and place to your decision totally.

Might it not be pleasing to our canine associates to come along for the encounter? I am sure they have learned their lesson, and will not grow excessively amorous in any way disturbing to public decency, especially that of the English.

In case you are lachrymose in recalling my attractivity, I have enclosed an e-photo of my most compelling feature. Please use it as you see fit, say as a screen saver on your computer, which would remind you of my charms periodically and will arouse your semen-delivery mechanisms.

Being a female of shy and reticent demeanor I have surprised myself fully with this open display of honesty, and ask that you kindly not remind me of such displays in the future, as they might scare me away, or make me less receptive to the types of licking and sniffing I enjoy upon first greeting in an amorous style of behavior.

Please understand that I am not a "loose woman" whatsoever but have spent my entire life saving up my passions for someone who smells exactly like you.

Anticipating your reply,

Candy

Ready for Adventure

Dear Denise,

What a brilliant bitch. I can't tell you how proud I am.

Bonehead has been running around all day with his head in the clouds. He can't sit still for a minute. He even bought me a new collar with these green, gemlike studs in it. They're just colored glass, but I can't wait for you to see how it looks on me. My master did himself one better. He's had a haircut, a facial, a manicure, and even started using a moisturizer.

He smells as bad as Lysol air freshener, but he has a good heart and I hope your mistress appreciates all the time he's been putting into his appearance. (Not that she's any gift to nature herself, if you ask my opinion.)

I'm so excited I could piss all over the crummy linoleum. But I'm saving everything I have for you!

See you in the park, muchacha!

Love,

Randall

Satisfied Customer

Dear Doggylove.com,

My name is [name withheld] and I'm writing to thank you so much for your lovely dating service.

I guess I've always been cynical about these deals in the past, but that was before I met [name withheld] and found out how wonderful true love can be.

It seems like only weeks ago we were living in our separate domiciles, chewing our crunchy biscuits and moping, with nothing more exciting to look forward to than a scratch behind the ear from one of our sad, homely masters. Then we joined doggylove.com and our lives were transformed into a magical miracle of romance. Even our masters got in on the act, mated, engendered an offspring, and bought a house in the country, to which we will be transporting our doggy beds in a few short days. Not to mention have a litter of our own and raise them in open harmony with nature, much like in the concluding scenes of our favorite movie, *101 Dalmatians*.

Sometimes I turn to [name withheld] in the night and say to him, "Honey, bite me on the rump. I must be dreaming."

And [name withheld] always does exactly what I ask. Because, of course, he truly cares.

Yours sincerely,
Lost in Heaven

Editorial Reply

Dear Lost in Heaven,

Thanks so much for sharing your positive, life-affirming experiences with the rapidly expanding membership of doggylove.com, which has recently opened branches in Germany, the Netherlands, Saudi Arabia, and the Philippines. All over our exciting planet, canines are coming together to share their unique passions for giving and living. So go out there and get the love you need! Don't settle for second best! Or you'll find yourself lying alone someday in a smelly basement with nothing but a red rubber chew toy to keep you warm.

As our cofounder and senior board member Rosco the Big Mean Doggy likes to say: *Have faith in someone besides yourself, no matter what they tell you, no matter how they smell. . . .*

So until next week, happy sniffing to all you hunky dudes and bitches!

Miaow!

(Ooops, stupid keyboard. Let's run by that again.)

Woof woof.

And love don't come truer than that.

How to Raise and Train Your Mini-Berger-with-Cheese-Doodle

[Georgia Getz]

 So you're ready to commit to late-night whimpering and questionable bladder control. You've fenced your yard to prevent escapes and purchased bacon kibble! And while it's admirable that Grandma is coming to live with you, this brief guide concerns your decision to share your home with a Mini-Berger-with-Cheese-Doodle.

This noble breed is a refined combination: the perpetual motion of the Miniature Pinscher, the linebacker protectiveness of the Leonberger, the trembling timidity of the Whippet, the insouciant stubborness of the Chinese Crested, and the telepathic sensitivity of the Poodle: put it all together and that spells enzyme disinfectant. You've acquired the best of both worlds plus three more!

History of the Breed

According to canine artifacts and Vedic Sanskrit, the elegant Mini-Berger-with-Cheese-Doodle dates back over 2,000 years to Eastern Assyria. Originally bred to husk corn and stoke the early morning kiln, this pride of dedicated dog fanciers is now a common centerpiece in three-disposable-income families. Majestic, cowering, intelligent, imbecilic: you'll find yourself at a loss to find just the right laurel to describe your faithfully perfidious companion.

Is This the Right Dog for You?

Do you have the space for a couch potato with a springy gait who likes to chase his own tail stump? Do you have the wallet to deal with kneecap replacement surgery on spindly five-inch-high legs? Do you have the time to groom tufts of thick tawny hair while applying skin salve to large expanses of nude flesh?

This breed is not the right choice for everyone. Are you allergic to dog dander? Do you live in an apartment, work long hours, or live in a large house? Are you prepared for drool, compulsive barking, flatulence, epileptic fits, tooth decay, destructive chewing, ear infections, fear-biting, hot spots, submissive peeing, or premature bone disease? If so, you may want to consider other breeds such as a guinea pig or an iguana.

However, this breed is most certainly the right choice if you are looking for a rugged agile-footed pet who will diligently dig to Tanzania while towing a sled at breathtaking speed. And this partially hairless furball will love you to death. Literally. Just ask the nice folks over at the Schenectady Crime Lab.

Preparing Puppy's Nursery

Just as you need a place to disappear after the pup's new Citronella No-Barking Collar detonates during your cocktail party (giving an all-new meaning to martinis with a twist), so your new puppy needs an area to call his own. We suggest a dog crate. Your crate should be big enough for the dog to stand in and turn around—*but not a nanometer larger.* The confined space teaches bladder control because instinctively a pup hates to soil his bed. (Note: Soiling his bed is not the same as making doody in his bed, because the Chinese Crested in him won't give that a second thought.) In addition the crate will make your pup feel as though he has his very own dog den. A dog den complete with metal bars and a chew-resistant lock. (Note: The Klaxon door alarm and klieg lights are optional.)

Next: Toys. Lots of toys. We love this year's Manolo Blahnik Chew Pumps. You might also consider digestible sofa cushions, now available in a wide selection of colors to match every shedding opportunity! We're crazy about this season's popular Demodectic-Mange Yellow. You will also need a lead. (Note: This is not to be confused with a leash, which costs a lot less, is made of nylon, and will be of no use if your pup spots another furry critter. And trust us, everything looks like a furry critter through cataracts.)

Your Doodle's First Months

Your immediate objective as a doggie parent is to housetrain your Mini-Berger-with-Cheese-Doodle. This isn't rocket science. It's behavioral science coupled with gastroenterological science, yes, but it *isn't* rocket science. All you need is unflagging persistence and a rigorous schedule. And then a new schedule after your puppy tinkles all over the first one.

Most puppies need to relieve themselves fifteen minutes after eating; a sensible plan would include a trip to the "soiling spot" fifteen minutes after mealtime. Done! Of course, his Whippet side needs to defecate only five minutes after eating while the Leonberger side holds his poo for at least three hours. Therefore, you can safely assume that somewhere between five minutes and four hours your puppy will have the urge to relieve himself. Or not. Simple!

Puppy socialization should be another of your initial goals. A well-adjusted adult dog is a direct result of your commitment to expose your pup to the various situations and rogue elements he will encounter throughout his life. This is especially important for a Mini-Berger-with-Cheese-Doodle who has a propensity to fear the usual enemies including but not limited to strangers, same-sex canines, very young children, older children, convertibles, wood-burning fireplaces, veterinary assistants, sandwich baggies, and metal garbage cans.

Your Doodle's Kit and Caboodle

Nothing prepares your puppy to be a good canine citizen like obedience drills. A puppy is a sponge that willingly soaks up everything you teach it—and that's a wonderful coincidence because a Mini-Berger-with-Cheese-Doodle is a lot like a sponge that reeks of yesterday's tuna salad. Your puppy should learn the basic commands "sit," "stay," and "come," which, because of your dog's uniquely disproportionate musculature, he can accomplish simultaneously. (Note: The command "heel" does not mean eating the trainer's foot even if his Miniature Pinscher lineage dictates otherwise.)

It is important to maintain a definitive tone during your training sessions. Issue commands only once so that your dog never learns to turn a deaf ear. (That would be the deaf ear inherited from his Poodle forebears.) No matter the distraction, your dog should always focus directly on you. To that end, you might want to consider surgery to correct the inbred eyelid abnormality. What's another thousand, considering what you've already spent and what you're sure to incur over your pup's next ten to fifteen years?

Your Cheeseball and You

It is important to recognize that, as a dog, your Mini-Berger-with-Cheese-Doodle is foremost a pack animal. Canines respect a social hierarchy and you should be positioned at the top. (Note: The time you spend hiding from your dog in a very tall tree does not count.) It is imperative that you establish authority with a firm and consistent manner. Simply practice the three P's: Patience, Persistence, and Percocet.

In return, your Mini-Berger-with-Cheese-Doodle will reward you with what dog people call "unconditional love," which means everything is grand until the pet store is out of liver cookies. Your pup will be your constant companion, the friend who is always there in time of need, especially since all five of the distinctly different breeds in your dog's exotic makeup share one important character trait: Separation Anxiety.

Something Extremely Important

[Merrill Markoe]

 TODAY OUR FRIEND Paul came to the house in a near dissociative state of panic. Suddenly and without warning it appeared his marriage was unraveling.

He sat down on the big red couch in my living room, I offered him some vodka, and he cautiously began to detail his anguish.

"Up until yesterday if you had asked me if my marriage was a happy one, I would have said yes," he said, choking back tears, his voice quivering with emotion, "and then last night, out of the blue, my wife comes in and tells me she wants a divorce."

As Paul spoke, his voice full of shock and misery, our dog Puppyboy, a skinny brown and black Tijuana Shepherd, approached him. It appeared to be one of those moments of poignant intuitive empathy that people and animals sometimes share . . . right up until the moment I noticed that Puppyboy's mouth was full of a large, black, completely deflated soccer ball. To Puppyboy, a ball is still a ball whether or not it is currently filled with air. And any occasion, even one that involves tears, is as good as any other to begin a game of fetch. So he placed the flat wet piece of rubber gently on Paul's knee, where it balanced like a rock at Stonehenge, then sat down right in front of Paul to wait for the games to begin. Paul, however, was too upset to notice.

"She told me she wants to start seeing other men," Paul said, in a voice riddled with pain. When he began to sob, it was heartrending. At least it was to me, though apparently not to Puppyboy, who saw it as a cue to apply a little additional first-inning pressure. So he moved the deflated piece of rubber from the edge of Paul's knee to a new spot on Paul's thigh, thus relocating it just a teensy bit closer to Paul's hands, for his added convenience. And having rectified the problem, Puppyboy sat back down in front of Paul and resumed his ceaseless staring, confident that he was applying just the right amount of additional pressure to finally at long last kick off the start of the game. Unfortunately Paul had the bad manners to be completely preoccupied by his own tragedy.

"I have no idea what I am going to do," he said, as Puppyboy moved in a little closer, and began staring a little harder, his eyes going intently from the flat ball balancing on Paul's thigh . . . to Paul's face . . . and then back again, as if to create a sort of psychic Google map for Paul out of thin air, in case he was having trouble figuring out where exactly that flat ball might be located.

"It's been just emotionally devastating," Paul continued. "Everything I've worked for has fallen apart. And what happens to me now? Am I going to lose everything? My house? My cars? My life savings?"

The more gruesome and painful Paul's story became, the more convinced Puppyboy was that it was only seconds until start time. So he picked up the flat ball off Paul's thigh and moved it to the most conveniently located spot of all, the very center of Paul's lap. After which he sat back down in front of Paul and resumed staring, his face as bright with expectation as a pre-school-age child on Christmas morning. Secure in the knowledge that he had found the perfect leg spot at last, Puppyboy sat poised at the ready, confident that it was mere seconds until a frenzy of throwing activity would begin. . . .

I sat and watched in awe as Puppyboy continued to pursue his inappropriate quest for the whole two hours that Paul was at our house. Despite the fact that Paul never acknowledged him at all.

Later that night, after Paul had gone home to pick up the pieces of his shattered existence, I began to wonder what Puppyboy was saying to himself during this piece of behavior, which, looking back, seemed to be akin to trying to start a game of catch with a man whose entire body was trapped in the basement of a collapsed building. So I asked him.

Puppyboy Speaks:

Hello, new seated person. I am Puppyboy and I can see that you are very upset for some reason. But I have something on my mind.

It is an idea so big that I can hardly hold my head up from the enormous weight of it. It is *more* than an idea. It is an *urgent message.* I am going out on a limb here and telling you that it is *the most important thing I have ever had to say.* And it is this: *I have placed a thing on you that you must throw.*

If you look down now you will see it. It is that large flat thing that is balancing on your knee. It is stretchy and chewy and damp: everything a large flat thing should be. Please listen to me when I tell you *that this is an opportunity you cannot pass up.* The reason I feel I must tell you *that I have placed this large flat thing on the edge of your knee . . .* by the way, you *have noticed* that your knee has a big flat wet thing balancing on it, haven't you? Or are you so busy sobbing and weeping and talking about *yourself* that you are having trouble seeing it?

Here's a hint: I am staring at it right now. So if you can imagine a laser beam coming from my eyes and then follow it down to the spot on your leg where it is focused, it will lead you right to it. . . .

There.

Now either you see it or you need to get your eyes tested.

The only other possible explanation for your puzzling lack of interest is that you are purposefully ignoring me. And why would you do that? *That* doesn't make any sense.

Especially since you are really hurting yourself more than you are hurting me. Because let's face it . . . you're the one who is passing up a great opportunity. And by a great opportunity I am referring to the chance to have the kind of fun that everyone dreams of having. *I speak of the chance to throw a big flat stretchy wet thing.*

Think about it for a second.

It is a thing that can be chewed but does not really need to be swallowed.

It is at once like dinner and nothing like dinner at all.

It is tough and meat-like and moist like a dead thing, but, here's the kicker: It's *all of the fun* of a dead thing and none of the attendant trouble. It stinks like a dead thing, and you can roll on it, or take it with you to bed like a dead thing.

It can be stretched and laid upon and pulled apart like a dead thing. But it *can also be flung repeatedly, without coming apart in a million pieces and losing all its guts like a dead thing . . .* If you can believe your good luck.

AND guess where it is right now? *It is now right in your lap.* I can't believe you would be foolish enough to pass up this chance.

I don't want to be preachy, but in life there are certain moments that may never come again. This, I believe, is one of those moments for you. Throw it now or live a life of regret.

I mean I can't *stop you* if you'd rather just listen to yourself talk. Wife wife wife, she did this, she did that, really fascinating.

FOR CHRISSAKES LISTEN TO ME *YOU WHINY HEN-PECKED M****ER . . . JUST look into my eyes, and play along!*

Pick up the big flat wet thing.

Pick up the big flat wet thing.

Pick up the big flat wet thing. PICK IT UP. PICK IT UP. PICK UP THE BIG FLAT WET THING?

CAN YOU HEAR ME OKAY? PICK UP THE BIG FLAT WET THING. Are you even listening? You know, maybe if you had LISTENED A LITTLE BETTER DURING YOUR MARRIAGE your wife wouldn't want a divorce. DID you ever think of that? IT WOULDN'T SURPRISE ME IF YOU NEVER THREW THE THINGS THAT SHE BROUGHT YOU EITHER!

Okay. I admit that was hitting below the belt.

So that was not the only chance you will get. I am going to give you another chance right away as you will see, if you will but gaze legward.

I have *again* placed the flat wet thing on your thigh and now you will find it is even more conveniently located than it was before.

And listen, pal, if I were you, I wouldn't pass an incredible opportunity like this up again.

[Mongrels are God's folk art. —Dan Liebert]

13 Questions

No Matter How You Frame the Question,
There's Only One Answer

[Susan Miller]

LATELY, I'VE BEEN interviewing dogs.

One thing I've learned about dogs. They don't like to be interviewed.

I tried to frame my questions creatively. They were breed-specific, yet accommodating to mixed breeds. Sensitive, even. Yet, curiously enough, several of the dogs I spoke with gave the same answer to every one of my questions. Which I thought to be nuanced and well considered. Still, no matter what I asked, the response always came back: Squirrel.

Sometimes there was a different inflection. Eager: *Squirrel?* Or annoyed, even defiant: *Could you be more of a fool? Do I have to spell it out for you? Squirrel. End of discussion.*

I posed a series of questions that I began to fear might elicit nothing but "squirrel" as idée fixe. Still I pressed on.

What do you think about? Am I your world? Do you know more than you're saying? Why do you like humans?

Where did you learn to put your head on the bottom of the bed like that with your eyes like that? And the sigh?

What embarrasses you, other than the one who is your world but who has named you Fred or Gumdrop or Larry?

How come you will lick a Republican?

What smells so f**king good everywhere? I'm not smelling it.

———————

I know dogs don't talk. Please. I know that. But, they can tell you things. They have information. They can tell you things.

Our dog is a rescue. By that I mean we are rescued. She's our rescue. Our fifteen-year-old black Standard Poodle, Pepsee, had died a year earlier. Pizza came to and went from our apartment without incident. Or joy. We were getting far too comfortable not going out in the middle of the rain-soaked muddy ice storm of night. We were bereft of dog. But could we love another?

We named her Henree. Well, why shouldn't she have gender issues too? She was two and a half. We adopted her in February. We were just going to take the drive and meet her and her foster mom in the parking lot of the Short Hills Mall. That's all. We'd just meet her.

In the first weeks, she ate an entire bag of Reese's peanut butter cups and a chocolate cake; recently, it was a box of truffles we brought back from Paris. Then there was the letter from our upstairs neighbor. Did we know that when we left her alone, Henree ran from room to room, barking and howling without cease? We bought a digital recorder and taped her. She ran from room to room and barked and howled without cease. We hired a trainer. She learned in a minute.

We got her to see that we might go, but we always come back. We got her to believe that this is where she's going to live for as long as she lives. And then she almost died.

Once we knew she would survive, I took the opportunity to interview the animals in the waiting room.

Do you know what death is?

Squirrel.

Come on!

There came then a kind of buzz, a hum, an instant and communal agreement, this grand energy of desire to tell me.

We don't know. We have no idea. We don't think about it. We don't want you to think about it.

I turned my attention to the old dogs in my building: Do you know what's happening to you? How can we make it better? When our aging Poodle entered her last years, there was this brief moment of surprise that registered in her eyes as she reckoned with each new loss. *I can't get up on the chair. What's that about? Okay. I'll just lie down at the foot of it.* Then—*I can't get up from the foot of the chair.* Or: *The humans are in the house. Last time I looked they were out. How did they get past me? So, this is how it is. All right. All right, then.* Her sweet acceptance and reliance gave me a tenderness for old dogs, old people. Old me. For a while, I couldn't even look at a puppy.

But, back to the day we brought Henree home. She's a brown Standard, by the way. Thirty-three years ago I had a baby who died. When I was a young girl, I always had this feeling that I would adopt someone someday somehow. And so, a few months after we lost our baby, there came Jeremy, my son—adopted at two and a half days old. And so it was Jeremy who called from L.A. first thing each day to see how Henree was when she almost died.

One of the questions I posed to Bess, a Terrier who prayed for Henree even though she would sooner bite her than share the Earth with her, was this: If she pulls through, will it change things between the two of you?

Bess was noncommittal.

In the parking lot of the Short Hills Mall—remarkable for its lack of detritus—my partner and I stood contemplating the papers we were about to sign giving us this darling, goofy, big-nosed, brown-eyed gal who had jumped up to hug us like long-lost soul mates but who still wasn't, after all, our old gal—our beloved Pepsee. We looked at the papers, at each other, and then we noticed something on the otherwise pristine, well-manicured, clean green grass. It was an empty can. An empty can of Pepsi.

The last question I put to the dogs was something I know a lot of you were probably hoping I would have the courage to ask: What do you really do when we're out of the house?

And you are not going to believe this! They just sleep.

So, I had to know. Why do you need so much sleep?

But, to dream, of course. To dream of—

Us?

I was laughed at.

Then what? To dream of what?

Oh, don't. Don't say it.

. . . Squirrel.

Poodles look as though they'd be good at math. —Dan Liebert

My Fifteen Minutes

[Melissa Holbrook Pierson]

 THERE'S THE Nobel Peace Prize, the National Book Award, and the MacArthur "genius" grants. Watch us pat ourselves on the back for excellence. But we judge using such a paltry human scale. *Arf-woof!* snort the dogs. *Small beer.* Most people have no idea how finely practiced their dog arts, how great their glee when true brilliance in their own endeavors is attained. But I do. For some reason fate has picked me to know more than my share of Canine Behavior World Cup holders. They compete in several events, among them, Ha-Ha Fooled Ya, as well as Championship Food Snatching. The dogs I have known make Marley look like an untrained piker, which I gather he was, although I didn't read the book (which has never seemed to me like much of a prerequisite for criticism).

My sadly missed former dog was a champion among champions in many of the dog world's most meaningful challenges. One of her highlights, in a life of highlights that also included the theft of an all-butter chocolate-ganache birthday cake meant to serve thirty, occurred one day in the city. Just a routine walk in the morning. Past the bagel shop. Midsentence, muffin poised to aid in dramatic point-making, a fellow seated on a bench outside turned to look at his suddenly empty hand. My dog continued on, her stride unbroken, but I could see on the back of her head the muscles around her ears moving rhythmically.

—————

I often wonder if to one another they communicate telepathically: *Hey, watch this! Wanna see me make my old lady pee in her pants? It's really funny.* My new dog, a sort of chip off the old block in that she's size-wise a true fragment but also working toward an advanced degree in Hijinks, has been tutoring a pal of hers. Mine is a twenty-pound Border Collie–hellion mix, and her friend is a hundred-pound Labradoodle ("I didn't buy him!" his conscientious owner always offers quickly, aware of the political and ethical incorrectness of that act. "This is his third home!" as if she's not, maybe, giving away a bit too much about his character). But these dogs are in love, and like many in the first blush of oh-please-won't-you-put-your-whole-head-in-my-mouth, they want to do everything together, in exactly the same way.

So Nelly has been teaching Willy a crucial maneuver. Its first step consists of looking so happy, grateful even, that Mom has brought you on a hike in the woods. That causes her to let down her guard, see, because she now believes she did the right thing in letting you off-leash to enjoy yourself; the joy is so obvious, it makes her joyful to see it in you. So she gives you a really long, glorious walk, safe in the belief that gratitude makes doggies behave nicely. That's when you let it rip. It takes much practice to perfect the next step: a pause—well out of reach, naturally—and an expression on your face so clear to read that it might as well be the Times Square news zipper: "That car over there? You want me to *get in* it? Do you take me for a fool? Ha, I say. HA." You have to make sure you stand there for a good long while, because apparently moms are slow on the uptake. Then, and only then, do you take off.

Willy has been a supreme student. Nelly sometimes gets waylaid by the scent of rabbit in some brush, and while she's digging a hole that's meant to swallow her eventually, I can usually get in there and just reach her tail. This particular day, I had gotten her on-leash when Willy turned to look at us. "HA!" Then he turned and ran up the hill, away from the lovely waterfall and all the sticks and the nice path and most notably his owner, and proceeded across a busy county route. He was heading for a quaint little village filled with fancy eateries and French cookware and eight-dollar soaps; the shoppes backed onto a fabulous alley where one could get positively lost among the garbage cans, parked cars, and discarded furniture that was deemed a mite too vintage to be saleably antique.

My friend looked at me with despair. She had learned that Willy's perfection of the routine meant the addition of another couple miles to the chase if he even caught sight of her coming after him holding a leash. I volunteered to go get him; there was always the surprise factor, I thought (*Silly human!* I think he telegraphed to Nelly at this point).

It's not a really good escape unless it gives the mom an indigestible wad of fear in the gut. Making her look like a lunatic in need of some grooming is the icing on the cake. I had no idea where Willy was heading. But it might take him back across the road on which cars heedlessly attained 40 or 50 mph. Sweat began to wet my hairline. I started to run. Whenever Willy turned to see what effect his performance was having I abruptly pulled to a stop, in an interspecies game of Red Light Green Light. Now I unzipped my jacket, dog treats, used Kleenex, and Ricola drops trailing from the pockets. I gracefully jumped over one trash can on its side. Unfortunately this had prevented me from seeing the other one right next to it.

It is still a matter of some amazement that I had the time and inclination, while brushing cinders from the knees of my already filthy jeans, to look up at the car that had just pulled in behind the emporium next door. Hmmm. BMW station wagon—they *are* nice, aren't they? Willy apparently thought so, too, since he stopped just in front of the car. Someone was getting out, and Willy was interested in that too. Whoever it was liked dogs, because he instantly put his hand out, and what dog can resist an outstretched hand? "Grab that dog!" I shouted. Maybe it was more of a hysterical scream. Anyway, he looked up and saw this insane harridan coming closer, and probably figured he'd better do what I asked. I saw his hand close around the collar and hold fast.

As I hurried toward him I was already throwing out pathetic explanations: *Oh, thank you, I couldn't catch him and he's not really my dog, you saved my butt!* And when I got there, I hooked Willy to the leash and brushed my hair out of my face and looked into the transparent and rather stunned blue eyes of Aidan Quinn. The handsome movie actor Aidan Quinn. The handsome movie actor Aidan Quinn whom I'd always wanted to meet.

Willy's life had been saved by Aidan Quinn. Not just because he prevented Willy from running into the road. Because my friend could not kill Willy now that he had been captured by Aidan Quinn.

A couple of months later I was at a party. My hair was brushed and my pants were clean. Even "a little lipstick," as my mother always pleaded. I turned from the hors d'oeuvres and felt someone's eyes. There, across the room, was Aidan Quinn. His look clearly said, *I know you from somewhere.* I smiled, then turned away.

No, sir. Only in my dreams.

Many dogs have a sense of humor, but only Dachshunds make jokes.
—Dan Liebert

Joni Mitchell Never Lies

[Marc Spitz]

 HOMELESS PEOPLE WOULDN'T ask me for change. The campaigners on my corner assumed that I didn't care about the environment or gay rights, or the Democratic Party. Unless a tourist was so lost that it was a question of "ask the sour-looking tall man in the leather coat" or "end up in the Pine Barrens sucking ketchup packets like they did in that famous *Sopranos* episode," they'd find someone else to guide them toward the Marc Jacobs store. I was convinced that my instinctive mistrust of my neighbors had helped me survive half my entire adult life here in New York City. I'd never sign for packages for any neighbor who wasn't home, despite urging from the UPS man. What if there were drugs or kiddie porn in there? "People ain't no good," Nick Cave and the Bad Seeds once sang, and I was inclined to believe it. My resistance to mixing in, I was also quite certain, had helped me establish some kind of identity as a creative individual. I read *Against Nature,* and thought it was a self-help guide. This misanthropic disconnect probably has its roots in my adolescence. When my father, a self-described degenerate gambler, used to introduce me to his friends at the racetrack, he'd warn, "Keep your mouth shut. Mind your business, and stay out of trouble," and pat me on the head firmly. It seemed like sound, paternal advice. By my thirties, I had my high walls and knew they were good ones.

I never thought I'd be a dog owner. I grew up among dogs. Whenever one of my grandmother's white, high-strung, yipping Toy Poodles would pass away, she'd quickly replace it with a look-alike. All these look-alikes were named Pepe, just like the original dog (whose vintage my sister and I could never determine). Dog owners seemed strange to us. I did make an effort, when I was thirteen or fourteen (in the mid 1980s), to convince my father to buy me a dog of my own. We were in Lexington, Kentucky, where he was working as a salesman of equine products. I was visiting for the summer and according to him, I saw a mother with a litter of puppies at one of these horse farms and it triggered some kind of tantrum when I was told that both the dogs and I were too young. This must have been so painful that I've blocked it from my memory for twenty years. My father recently reminded me of this, and it made sense out of my subsequent pet-ownership: cats.

Emotionally distant. I could take or leave my cats, and they felt the same about me, and it worked. We liked it that way. We were cool. We were the cover of *Bringing It All Back Home* by Bob Dylan (if you don't know what I'm talking about here, Google Image it and you'll quickly see the scene and the attitude I was cultivating through the '90s and well into the new century). I was allergic to cats, of course, but I was even more averse to opening up my heart to any companions who required a bit more accountability. This included, for a similar length of time, women. But then, in the spring of my thirty-second year, I met a woman who changed me a little. And together, we purchased a dog who changed me a lot. Didn't alter her so much. She grew up in New Mexico and had horses and goats and dogs and cats and toads and turtles right there in her yard. When she moved to Manhattan after college, she went through some kind of nature-girl withdrawal.

We had each other but she yearned for animals. We started watching a lot of Animal Planet, but that only seemed to make things worse. Soon, I'd spy her downloading dog porn. In particular, a video of a Basset Hound stumbling across a lawn, its ears and cheeks flapping as it bounded. She'd watch this on a loop. We were living together in my former bachelor pad: a studio on Christopher Street. There wasn't enough space for two people, much less two people and a Basset Hound. And what kind of messed-up-looking dog was that anyway? But I gave in, because I loved her. Not because I wanted a dog . . . at all. I was a cat guy. I wasn't even a cat guy anymore. I was a cactus guy. I had one on the bathroom windowsill and that was enough nature for me. Even the name we gave our new Basset was somewhat noncommittal. I suggested that we name her Joni Mitchell. By the time I'd fallen completely in love with her crepe-like old-man belly and snowshoe-size paws she already knew her name. We couldn't change it.

She was stuck with an ironic name. I could not have felt more sincere in my devotion to her.

Once Joni was fully vaccinated, I'd take her out into the city, but I soon realized that nothing could inoculate me from an unexpected invasion of fellow New Yorkers. At first, whenever people would approach us, I'd respond to queries like "Can I pet your dog?" or "How old is your dog?" or "Is that a Beagle dog?" or "Is that the Hush Puppy dog?" or "Is that the Sherlock Holmes dog?" or "How old is your *Beagle*?" with a cold glare. Sometimes I'd jerk little Joni away when someone would try to squeeze her without asking. Or I'd shrug, "I don't know," as if I'd just dognapped her, or was a particularly disgruntled professional walker. I knew exactly how old she was, to the day. And I also knew that she was the Hush Puppy dog but she was certainly not a Beagle-dog. Beagles are more slender and not nearly as grand as Bassets. They're like economy cars. Once I said, "Mind your own business, man," but in my defense, it was seven in the morning and West Fourth Street was covered with ice. I understood why they couldn't help themselves, even at that hour. It's like that scene in Cronenberg's remake of *The Fly* where Geena Davis explains to Jeff Goldblum about why the computer wasn't understanding how to transport the plate of steak; it's like how old ladies want to squeeze babies' cheeks. It's the power of the flesh. And Bassets have a lot of loose and powerful flesh; even French ones like Joni Mitchell. Some English Bassets, I've since discovered, are so dangly that they have to undergo eye lifts in order to see properly.

What I didn't get is why it was suddenly okay for strangers to talk to me. I knew people my age, single people, who got dogs for this very reason: to attract other single people and have sex with them. One female friend used to sit in the park and wait with her dog in her lap, and angle for eligible men. Most of those who approached her ended up being gay, but she had a Papillon, so what did she expect? I wasn't on the make, however. I wasn't single, and everything about my physical energy—my stance, my look, my black clothes—said: keep back or I will do something bad to you. Or did it? Had growing to love Joni Mitchell made me soft? And if so, how was I supposed to defend her against all these unknown people with their grabby hands and their crooked mouths that say things like "So cute!" and "Oh, puppy, puppy!" How was I supposed to defend myself against them? I loved Joni, but she was embarrassing me. I fantasized about constructing an indoor kennel with a mile of running track. We would go on "trots" in our bubble and never have to encounter anyone else. I could walk her, pick up her poop, and still be cool. Nobody would have to know that I "trotted."

Nothing blows your cool worse than worrying about your loved ones. As I never really had loved ones, I found this out pretty late. Joni had kennel cough when we brought her home from the pet store, and has pretty much been in and out of the vet's office ever since. Basset Hounds require constant and expensive care. They are prone to ear infections because they drag their long ears on the dirty ground as they walk. This, I've been told, and have told others who've asked, is how they've historically stirred up the scent on the trail. It's also how they get cooties. I don't know if Joni Mitchell the Canadian rock legend and respected painter has a sensitive stomach or not (if I had to guess, I'd say "not," she looks like she's pretty tough), but Joni Mitchell the Basset Hound cannot keep down a can of reasonably priced dog food like Alpo or even IAMS. She can only digest three-dollar holistic food with oatmeal, organic lamb, and sweet potato in it; a full can a day, every day. About a year ago, our vet advised us to feed her boiled chicken and rice when her runs were particularly explosive. Now, she refuses her food unless there's hand-cooked chicken from the Whole Foods market and rice (cooked with no oil) mixed in as well; twice a day, every day. I've already boiled more chickens than my great-grandma Dora ever did, and she lived into her nineties.

Joni was never crated as many puppies are these days. She sleeps with us, and always has because she gets lonely or scared in the night. When she twitches and whimpers in her sleep, I tell myself that she's chasing rabbits or squirrels in some dreamscape Union Square park. I secretly worry that she's tormented by dark thoughts. I'll do whatever I have to do, spend whatever I have to spend, and boil whatever pricey fowl I have to boil in order to *make* those dreams about rabbits and squirrels; and I guess it's become something of a liability as far as my street smarts go. If she spits up, I shake and blubber and fret like a little girl. People on the street have apparently picked up on this shift toward the dangerously paternal as well. Once you've blubbered, even in private, you wear the mark forever. I'm just not tough anymore. Reminding myself that Mickey Rourke, with his Chihuahuas, is not nearly as tough as he used to be either is no great comfort.

New Yorkers adapt. We pride ourselves on our stubborn nature, but we are also quite fond of our ability to overcome troubling situations and events: economic crashes, the Knicks' post-Ewing seasons, blackouts, gas leaks, and, of course, September 11. We are a gritty breed (unlike the Basset). I decided that I was going to make do with this new situation pretty quickly. I told myself that I would give people a chance. I should learn to like them. My dog likes people, and she is wise. All you need to do is look into her eyes when she's awake and her sharp acumen is evident (when she's asleep, her eyes roll back into her head and go pink and white and it's creepy). My dog trusts human beings. She thinks we're all right. Joni Mitchell, the singer, was a lonely painter who lived in a box of paints, or so she sang. Joni Mitchell the dog lives to jump on people and beg for a treat or a pat. She loves children, the elderly, and for some reason, people who pull carts best; but she doesn't discriminate. She loves homeless people too. Homeless people have started asking me for handouts now that I've got her with me on the street. And I happily give to them, because people need second chances to figure out their place in the world. Although it's not going to get anyone off the streets, sometimes a smile and a nod of "good luck getting through" is better than all of us rolling on cold and frantic like spilled ball bearings.

Even as I wrote those last words, part of me is ashamed of myself. "People need second chances?" "Like spilled ball bearings?" What have I become? Sunny observations beget horrible similes. Joni Mitchell hasn't made me a bad writer (completely). I don't believe that in order to write well, one needs to be alone and angry and drunk like Bukowski. In order to be a good writer, one needs to come up with better lines, that's all.

I'm a rock journalist most of the time, and shortly after observing this change in myself, I started complaining about it to my interview subjects. I'd kvetch to the more misanthropic stars about how I'd lost my edge. This was, more often than not, preemptive, and all of them came after a truly awkward Nine Inch Nails interview I'd conducted in pre-Katrina New Orleans; early 2005. Trent Reznor related how he was enjoying his reintegration into accountable society now that he'd beaten his drug and alcohol demons. "Yeah, I know what you mean," I said. "It's like . . . not all about you anymore. Like you have a dog, and she needs to be walked whether you like it or not. If you're not ready to engage with your neighbors at eight A.M., tough shit, right?" Reznor nodded his head in agreement but I could see he was also trying to determine whether or not I was taking the piss from him. Howlin' Pelle Almqvist from the Hives understood my amazement when I told him that for some reason Joni (or "Yoni" as he called her in his Swedish accent) would always pull Steve Miller Band's *Book of Dreams* album from my vinyl pile, but he couldn't seem to work up much interest otherwise. Maybe he was just being polite about *Book of Dreams* too. The Swedes are very polite. Even their porn is polite. Only Chan Marshall of Cat Power, who once had a Basset named Franklin (he apparently got bit by a snake and his jowls froze in a Nicholson-as-the-Joker face for a time), really seemed to feel me when I went on and on about Joni the non-icon: how she had pulled the stuffing out of every plush toy we've ever given her, and then kept the gutted skins like Buffalo Bill.

How she had a dark side, but also a good soul. How I was trying for both but failing to get the balance right. Getting human-friendly had, ironically, made me a shitty rock star interviewer. It used to be so easy. I'd inhabit a Nick Kent or Lester Bangs-ian persona. Throw on some shades, put a cig in my mouth, and I could go head to head with any of them, even those with quicker wits than me, like Morrissey. When I interviewed Morrissey pre–Joni Mitchell (shortly after the release of his *You Are the Quarry* album) in L.A., I felt like a badass. When I interviewed him in Rome two years later, and post–Joni Mitchell, I talked about my dog, revealed my weakness, and was zinged. "You call your dog Joni Mitchell?" the great man asked. "And does she come?"

Talking to regular people was only slightly easier. When someone with a dog would approach us, I had an in. "Uh, what kind of dog is that?" Or "How old is your . . . what kind of dog *is* that?"

Sometimes Joni Mitchell would get twisted in the other dog's leash (my girlfriend calls it a "lead" but it's only ever been a leash to me) and I could only see it as another metaphor. I was becoming entwined with the other dog-owning New Yorkers. I started to like my role. I'd patrol the dog run like Robin Williams in . . . *Garp*, chasing down speed demons, keeping the run safe from the miscreants who'd walk in with their dogs and leave the door swinging off the latch. Those people might reinforce my mistrust if I let them, but I won't let them shake me. I would like to see them all jailed, or at least smacked in the back of the skull with a rolled up *New York Post*. The dog owners who *do* shake my faith in humanity are the ones who address only Joni when we're out in the street. Like she's out walking herself, or just happens to be attached to a man who is not permitted to speak and will only stare straight ahead like a palace guard.

"I'm reformed," I want to remind them, "and I'm here too. Look up. Acknowledge me. Didn't you see me at the run the other day chastising those assholes? I'm on your side! I'm good people!"

"How are you today, Joni?"

(I assume they know her name because my girlfriend walks her and she is much friendlier than I am, even with my new approach to man and hound pedestrian-ism.)

"Joni, you're a good doggy! Good good doggy!"

"What about me? Aren't I a good person?" I scream internally whenever this happens. And this happens at least twice a week as two culprits, whom I won't describe in detail, should they read about themselves in this anthology, are on both my walking schedule and our route. I've stopped doing drugs. I have a stuffed wooly mammoth, panda bear, Vans checkered sneaker, blue Chevy Impala, American buffalo, hedgehog, anteater, sock monkey, red squirrel, and Canadian goose in my living room, all crusty with slobber. I haven't started a rock journalist fistfight in a bar in two years. I don't even feel comfortable in this leather coat anymore. I'm thinking about tweed. Doesn't that at least merit a glance? A "Her coat's looking good. What shampoo do you use on her?" Aren't we supposed to bond? Dog owners? Human beings?

In this way, I'm no different from my friend who sat in the park with her Papillon on her booty calls. Except I don't want booty. I want human kindness, a sense of belonging and empathy. I want my existence acknowledged too. When I'm not with Joni and I see another dog owner who happens to be sans canine as well, we never, ever say hello. Remove the dog from the equation and we all become walled-up New Yorkers again, and that's just sad. Now that I share my life with an animal, I don't need an animal around all the time to make me more human. Or do I? "Say hello, or . . . hey," I tell myself. I never do.

My shrink says that Joni is prep for a real kid, like some of my friends have: a human baby. I can't see how it would be much different. Joni Mitchell is our kid. She's as much a part of our family as a kid would ever be. I guess I'm saying that now because I don't have one. The other day I held a baby for the first time. I'd been asked to become the godfather of a friend's newborn boy. This is their second child. Their first is four. I wasn't even a candidate back then. It felt weird holding a human baby. But I remember when it felt weird holding a puppy too. Four years ago, I probably would have told myself, "I don't see how getting a dog would change my life, except maybe I'd have to pick up a lot of shit," so who knows where this is going to lead. Maybe the shrink is right. Shrinks are sometimes. When I uttered that "shit" line by the way, I'd probably be wearing black sunglasses, and smoking too . . . and if you saw me coming, you'd most likely avoid all human contact. You're luckier now. And so am I. It's not all rabbits and squirrels yet . . . but it's getting there.

You never see dogs do their tricks for each other. —Dan Liebert

Carolina's in Heat and I'm Not

[Abigail Thomas]

 M Y H O U N D D O G Carolina is sitting in the car, and I'm in the drugstore standing in an aisle I haven't been down for fifteen years. Carolina is in heat. Such an archaic concept, heat. I'm looking for something to slip into the mesh pocket of a red Speedo-like contraption I've just bought for her. Who knew they made such things for dogs? I recall the flimsy little garter belts we girls got with our first box of sanitary napkins and the accompanying pamphlet regarding the human reproductive cycle. Light-years ago. I pick an item that comes wrapped in pink and says mini and then I hobble over to Aisle 4b, Pain Relievers, where I'm more at home. My back hurts. I grab aspirin, pay for everything, and head for the car. Carolina's nose is smeared against the window. Good dog, I say, good dog, and manage to get myself sitting down without screaming and I pat her big head and nuzzle her neck, and her tail thwacks against the passenger seat. Carolina is halfway through her first treatment for heartworm and going into heat seems grossly unfair. "Jesus, yet more trouble," as some martyr said when the executioner reached in to yank out his intestines. (I can't remember which saint this was, but my mother loved to quote him.) Before I start the car I line up the arrows, take off the cap, stab a pen through the foil seal and gobble down three aspirin.

This is my first experience with a dog in heat but the back pain arrived thirty years ago when I bent to pick a canned peach off the kitchen floor and couldn't straighten up. My new husband seemed familiar with the problem. "My god, what is this called?" I cried as he tried to help. "It's called my back is killing me," he said. This version of my back is killing me comes from wearing a pair of stylish new red shoes that pinch my left foot and make me walk lopsided. I don't know why I keep putting them on except they show off my ankles. At age sixty-three, ankles are my best feature unless you count cake.

When I get home I discover it's nearly impossible to put this thing on my dog. There is a place for her tail and Velcro fastenings that go over her haunches but try sticking a dog's long tail through the hole of a small slippery garment while the dog turns around and around in circles. It takes fifteen minutes and when I succeed, Carolina turns her baleful eyes on me and I want to apologize. She is a dog dressed like a monkey.

The next morning I can barely walk. My friend Claudette comes to the rescue. She puts Carolina on a leash lest a pack of hormone-addled canines show up in my yard, and later she drives me to her acupuncturist. I have never been to an acupuncturist but I'm ready for help here. The process is very interesting, all those needles tingling in my feet and legs and hands, and so relaxing that I would probably doze off were it not for the needle stuck right under my nose. I just can't stop thinking about that one. Nevertheless I do feel better until I hit the dairy case at the Hurley Ridge Market and reach for half a gallon of milk. On the way back through town we drive past the half-dressed youth of Woodstock lying on the village green. They are a beautiful sight, but what with my bad back and good memory I am glad not to be one of them. They have far too much future. Sometimes it is a relief to be over the hill.

Meanwhile, my fat Beagle Harry has found himself capable of leaping straight up into the air like Rudolf Nureyev. If Carolina doesn't notice, and she doesn't, he does it again. He is no longer capable of reproducing, but that doesn't dampen his spirit. Rosie too is affected by whatever hormones are flying. She engages in much vigorous grooming, attending obsessively to the nooks and crannies of both Harry and Carolina. She would have made an excellent mother. Now and then Carolina rouses herself long enough to emit a howl. Everybody's getting hot around here except me. I am just beginning to wonder where all the would-be suitors are when a big white dog materializes in the driveway. Ha! Carolina's first admirer. Harry and Rosie take up their positions on the back porch barking their heads off, and I call my sister and tell her proudly we've got an intact Huskie hanging around who probably never finished grammar school. "Now you know how Mom and Dad felt," she says. I go outside holding Carolina's leash in one hand, and a mop in the other. The mop doubles as cane and threat, and I shake it at the ruffian when he comes too close. He looks at Carolina and she looks back. Oh yeah, I remember that look. If this animal were human he'd be wearing jeans and a white T-shirt. He'd be lighting a cigarette. Forget my bad back, my advanced years. If this animal were human and I were in Carolina's shoes, let's face it, I'd be all over him like white on rice.

Beagles get drunk on their own voices. —Dan Liebert

Bone Alone

[Rob McKenzie]

with art by Graham Roumieu

WHAT YOUR DOG thinks about when you're gone:

2:47 P.M.: Yumyumyiamyiamyiam . . . brother this is good peanut butter . . . haven't tasted peanut butter like this since . . . oh damn.

2:48: Every time. Every frickin time. They get that hollow rubber ball with the holes in it, they jam it full of high-grade p.b. and I, I can't help it, I'm like a cat in a kibble shop, I lose my mind, I just have to fill my snout with peanut butter—and then I come up for air and they're gone, vamoosed, fast as squirrels. And I'm alone.

2:55: Maybe they meant to bring me along but just forgot. After all, I'm *the dog*—what kind of trip would it be without *the dog*? So maybe every now and then I ralph in the back-seat—who hasn't? Let he who is without sin cast the first tennis ball. Hey, did someone just say "tennis ball"?

3:01: It's no use. "Chase the ball" just doesn't work when you're alone. It's like solo synchronized swimming. I can sit here all day and drop the ball down the stairs, I can hear it

pa-dunk pa-dunk down the steps, I can
see it pinball all around the landing, but
it's not the same without someone to
bring it back to.

    3:03: I wonder what time it is. On
second thought, I wonder what time is.

    3:05: Zzzzzzz lamb chops zzzzzzz
all-beef wieners zzzzzzz Beagles in heat
zzzzzzzz.

3:28: It's been, what, six days now?
That's it. I'm doomed. They ain't never
coming back. I'm the Papillon of puppies
here. Dogman of Alcatraz. The Mutt in the
Mask. Bichapoo Caruso. Bone Alone, with
me in the Macaulay Culkin role. A three-
hour cruise . . .

    3:31: America Held Hostage: Day 38.

    3:33: Oh jeez. It's Sprinkles the idiot
Dalmatian and he's being walked right by my house. WOOF WOOF
OVER HERE A-HOLE! SEND FOR HELP YOU USELESS PIECE OF
CATNIP! WOOF! YES I MEAN YOU! And what does he do? He pisses
on the pansies. Last time I sniff his ass.

    3:35: Must . . . have . . . food. But
what idiot designed the tall box that
keeps the food cold? It's impossible to
open unless you have claws like the two-
legs do. Maybe if I stare at it for a while,
it'll, you know, miraculously open.

    3:36: Damn—I blinked. That thing
has a will of iron.

    3:40: Gotta go. Gotta go real bad.
Shouldn'ta drunk all that water. Gotta

go. Maybe if I let loose on that shaggy, ropey grassy stuff they have all over the living room, maybe it'll kind of disappear.

3:41: Or not.

3:45: Aye, a man gets lonely at sea, he does. A man has needs. Ever been to sea, laddie? True, it's you I'm talking to, Elmo. I know what you're all about. You sit there in the far end of the playroom, day after day, not moving, but I feel your big eyes on me. And Elmo, I am about to tickle you like you've never been tickled before. And be forewarned: We operate by the "What happens in Vegas" rule today, my friend.

3:46: YES! YES! LOOK OUT ELMO 'CAUSE I AM—

3:47: Coming up the driveway! They're coming up the driveway. Woohoo (repeat). Gotta jump up and down till I'm dizzy. Gotta wag the tail. Gotta lick 'em. Yes, I forgive you! I do! Elmo, I'm not so sure about.

Part Pooch, or: More Than an Act

[David Smilow]

 I DON'T HAVE a dog. I am one. At least in part. Call
me *Canis erectus*—the latest hybrid in the tradition of
Schnoodle and Cockapoo: a Humutt. I'd always suspected
I had bowzer in the bones. (Something about the way I wolfed my food
and cozied up to the funkiest of couches.) But confirmation came last summer when I was cast in a regional theater production as, yes, a dog.

"Not a cartoon dog, or a dog that talks," the director explained at the
audition, without a fleck of irony. "A dog." Which is where the irony *did*
come in. Straight dog made getting the part a cinch. All it took was one
scratch. Specifically, behind my left ear.

I'd "sat" alongside a production assistant who was playing my master in
an improvised scene. He looked down at me. I looked back, soulful with
love. So he smiled, said "Good boy," and reached to work that ear spot. A
little Norman Rockwellish, maybe. Still, the instant he made contact, my
whole body contorted in a rictus of pleasure. My head twisted and thrust
forward. My eyes glazed over. The corners of my mouth pulled back as far
as they could go. One foot drummed against the floor in helpless auto-
nomic rapture. I was prepared—like any dog in blissful seizure—to go on
like that, rigid yet thrashing, until I either died or the scratching stopped. It
didn't even matter to me which way it went. The ecstasy was all. And was
pretty much it: I got the gig. I was officially a show dog. Stage show, that is.

The director instructed that in the time before the play went into rehearsal, I was to study every dog I came across—really pay attention to how they sat and walked and reacted to things. She needn't have worried I'd show up unprepared. The dog in me began to assert itself almost immediately.

Take what happened a few days later. I was at the counter of a diner waiting for my short stack (no, no meat with that) when I realized I was tracking the waitress's every movement. Not unusual, in and of itself. I'm big on watching waitresses move. Only this time I wasn't following her with my eyes. I was swiveling my entire head, doggy style. This resulted in a) my keeping the waitress directly in front of me and blatantly focused on and b) the waitress sensing there was something off about her customer, something she couldn't quite put her finger on.

Then there was the Face/Sniff Thing. I'd started inching my face forward and sniffing to check out any change in my environment. Anything at all. Somebody would walk in the door. Face. Sniff. A plate of food would be carried past. Ditto. An ant would appear on a windowsill. Ditto ditto. I even did the Face/Sniff Thing with my own mail. (Hmm. [sniff] Seems like a phone bill. [sniff-sniff] Yup.) Meanwhile, in parallel developments, I'd taken to ostentatious lip-licking, sub-vocal "mffs" if unsettled, and—of course—cocking my head when someone called my name.

What struck me about all this wasn't how quickly I'd shifted to the Fido frequencies of the behavioral spectrum, but how natural it seemed. In fact, my sense is that if I'd been able to scratch that spot behind my ear with my foot, I might never have come back from my woof on the wild side. Clearly, I was ready to perform.

I arrived early the first day of rehearsal, yet, within an hour, had learned an important lesson: If you're a dog in a room full of humans who've only just met, the humans pay attention to each other, not you—unless you're vomiting, or preparing to vomit. For the read-through of the play I sat in a chair. (Human style. The torturous perching on block-like scenic elements wouldn't begin for another week.) And for hours at a clip simply, well, sat. Everyone else had jobs (director, dramaturge, actor) and a lot to say about how they were going to do them. I was just a dog. Not a cartoon dog or a talking dog. A dog. What was there to discuss?

The play—about the cross-country journey of a man and his long-in-the-tooth, terminally ill pet—was composed of long monologues delivered to the man by an assortment of oddball characters he meets along the way. Aside from the occasional script-mandated look in my direction or pat on the head (which I savored shamelessly), I was ignored that first day—a victim of phylum bias. Even when we moved to a rehearsal hall, I proved to be too doglike for my own good—so convincingly obedient, so resolutely looking to my master for cues, nay, for my very reason for being, that nobody gave me a second thought. When lunch break was called, the actors would scoot off to eat without a backward glance. And there I'd be, alone. Because, hey, I was just a dog.

I became despondent. I was isolated—stuck between two worlds. On the one hand, I was a human being (at least according to my driver's license) but on the other, I was now too doggy to *not* be a dog. I'd gone past the Pointer of no return.

I began to take long walks in the blazing heat during breaks to get my mind off my dilemma. But something would always bring it back. Usually something with four legs and a wet nose.

Perfect example: One day on walkabout, I saw a sun-wilted family far down the sidewalk trudging my way—a harried mom pushing a stroller, herding a clot of toddlers, and leading a Papillonoid mixed-breed on a leash. Suddenly, the dog's head snapped up. He stared at me for a second, then strained at the leash, pulling it taut as he struggled to close the gap between us, tail thrashing, tongue out. By the time we were ten feet apart, the dog's claws were scrabbling on the sidewalk and he was choking, so mighty was his effort to get to me. The expression on the woman's face was pure "What the hell . . . ?," but I knew what had happened. I'd been sniffed out from over fifty yards away.

I sighed and squatted down, addressing the dog. "Okay, come say hi." The little guy was on me in a flash, muzzle in my face, sniffing, licking, whimpering.

"He never does this," said the mom.

I smiled feebly. "Right." What I should have said was, "He thinks I'm his uncle."

Things began to look up after that, in part because actors run in packs too. They stick together and defend each other when confronted by their natural enemies. Like directors and stage managers. I might have just been a dog, but I was still a cast member. And since during times of duress (i.e., rehearsal) there's safety in numbers, I was welcomed into the actors' pack, making me a kind of double dog. But more and more, what soothed me was a phenomenon I began to experience onstage: the serenity of not being human. I got to untether myself from the prerequisites of man. Language, for instance. That was a biggie. I'd look up attentively at whoever was speaking (good boy that I was) but the words grew increasingly meaningless. Soon they were just sound. All that registered was tone and inflection. The *vibe*. I never had to answer anyone, or make so much as an effort to understand them. Oh yes, this was a part I could get into.

Indeed, by opening night, I was completely at home in my separate, ground-level reality. Despite the physical rigors of the role (I wore multiple layers of padding on my shins to make my protracted "sitting" bearable and, in curling my fingers under to convert my hands into paws, had actually developed calluses on the first knuckle joints where they made contact with the floor), being a dog meant liberation. The characters around me may have been churning with regret and loss and worry and confusion, but down on the floor, I was free to sniff things. And sit. And look over there. Then over there. And sniff something else. Then look over there again. Life had become so clear: it was *all* sniffing and looking. Time didn't even matter anymore. There was no future, no past. Only what turned up in front of my nose right now. Isolation had transformed to meditation.

The audiences knew right away I was fully commutted. When the lights came up at the beginning of the play to reveal me sitting next to my master, dutifully looking up at him between sniffs at what have you, a ripple would pass through the crowd. I could feel them thinking, *Oh my God. He's a dog.*

Not just any dog, though. *Their* dog. It's funny, I'd seen myself as being of strictly promiscuous provenance—a little idiosyncratic Terrier mixed with a lot of doleful Hound on a base of sweet, patient working dog—but I'd invariably hear of audience members who, during the show, had whispered to the person next to them with absolute certainty that I was a Portuguese Water Dog. Had to be. I was exactly like Farfel. Or Beeps the Springer. Or Otto the Mastiff. Or Hans. Zeke. Max. Lulu. Somehow in moving to a different species, I'd embodied its every breed. The transference went even further. Full circle, in fact. A close friend of mine got hysterical during the play because everything I did reminded her of her dog Chris. A few weeks later, she reported that everything Chris did now reminded her of me.

People would come up after the show giddily wanting to pet me, or wishing they could take me home (to meet Hans, Zeke, Max, Lulu) or, in one instance, weeping that the pooch in the play wasn't long for this dog's life. What they all had in common was a certain look in the eye: a tacit acknowledgment that they had seen a dog onstage—even if it had been, in the end, their own. I didn't mind. I was too busy lapping up the attention.

I did get my own jolt of recognition as to how deeply I'd delved into Dog. One night during Act One, I wheeled to follow my master off, and suddenly noticed my sharply etched shadow on the white-painted stage. "Look at me," I thought. "I'm a fifty-four-year-old man clambering around on all fours under a spotlight in front of total strangers." It wasn't the thought itself that jarred me. I *was* a fifty-four-year-old man clambering around on all fours under a spotlight in front of total strangers. No, it was the fact that thinking at all had become so alien, so intrusive. Fortunately, I was able to banish further cerebration with a quick sniff of my master's shoe.

And then the play closed. In one fell swoop, I lost both my stage family and my excuse to act like an animal who can lick its own privates. Behavior that had been deemed Spot-on was now regarded as bizarre, even borderline disturbing. I'd catch myself doing the Face/Sniff Thing on a date. Panting and whining at the Department of Motor Vehicles. For my own protection, I forced my inner pup back in.

But evolution doesn't go in reverse. Once mutations occur, they can't be undone. So while it's true I now walk upright, follow movement only with my eyes, and actually listen to people, the real story comes out when I visit my dog friends. They look up at me, quivering in that instant before the joyous orgy of licking and playing begins, and they *know:* I'm one of them.

Chased by a Saluki, a rabbit becomes an Egyptian hieroglyph. —Dan Liebert

Do You Take This Norwegian Elkhound?

[Alysia Gray Painter]

 THE DECORATIONS (balding tinsel strands and last year's Christmas ornaments, the round kind that become hairy when the fibers begin to fray) were hung with pomp. The reception buffet, complete with a variety of different tastes like beef, chicken, and beefy chicken, was elegantly displayed on a nearby rock chosen for its proximity to the altar, its largeness, its flatness, its surprising lack of sunning lizards and the fact that it was remarkably clean as far as rocks go.

Dressed for my role as wedding consultant/minister/flower girl/best man/maid of honor/mother of the bride/caterer/reception singer in a semi-damp bathing suit, flowery shorts and bare feet, I went to go check on the groom's progress. Conveniently, he was staying across the street from the ceremony, which was scheduled to commence under a small grove of palo verde trees promptly when I could round up all the napping participants. Not yet dressed, the groom looked meditative when I found him, his eyes mostly closed as he sprawled on the sunny pool deck, head lolling, his stocky legs splayed this way and that. After some gentle coaxing and pulling to get him on his feet, he lazily (nervously?) followed me to the First Church of My Front Yard, where I loosely arranged one of my father's favorite ties around his foldy neck.

After huffingly and puffingly positioning Lars, a handsome Norwegian

Elkhound, to sit (and stay! stay! stay!) under the Christmas decoration-laden branches, I ran inside my own home to collect the bride. I found her standing in the kitchen, quietly, solemnly even, staring at the garbage can, perhaps taking a moment to wonder if she had made the right choice by agreeing to enter into this eternal union. Or perhaps she was wondering whether it wouldn't be a grand idea to knock over the garbage can, hastily spread 98 percent of its contents around the room and snuzzle about for that luscious, liquidy bag that once held last night's pork chops.

There was no time for a pep talk or pork chop juice. I picked the bride up, opened the back door, and sprinted for the altar, where Lars was licking wetly at his tummy, my dad's tie now draped across a prickly pear cactus a few feet away. Setting Lucy, our mouthy mix of a Poodle-Terrier-Something, down next to him, I scurried away on my last errand—find a witness or two. The Labrador down the street? Staring from a window, in-conveniently locked inside while his family was out (his huge, moist eyes seemed to say, "Tell the bride I love her"). The mutts who loiter around down in the cul-de-sac? Either at the kennel or sleeping under some bed. I paused. I needed a nuptial witness who could sit and stay (and fast). Should I invite Greca, the Siberian Husky currently living with Lars? It was a thorny issue, one I'm not even sure Emily Post would want to address: Can the female—and a gorgeous female with a swishy tail and silvery coat of thick hair at that—who is currently living with the groom attend the wed-ding, or will there be a scene? Throwing etiquette to the warm Arizona wind, I located the Husky snoozing on some hot pebbles in her driveway and got her moving, slowly, slowly, come on, slowly, in the direction of my house.

Where was Lars? After a dash around the yard, I spotted the reluctant groom wandering over to greet the mailman. Lars! Larrrrrs! I helloed the mailman, grabbed the mail, got Lars, escorted him back to the palo verde grove, shooed the bride away from the buffet rock (where she had handily gulped down the entire reception feast during my witness search) and began. I was sweaty, out of breath, and barefoot, with a pile of catalogs and bills in one hand and a "don't-wander-off" arm around the groom, but a marriage was happening and that was something sacred and beautiful. Near the end of the forty-five-second-long ceremony, the bride began to bark, the groom began to doze, and the witness pulled the tie off the prickly pear cactus for some quality chewing action. And I now pronounce you husband and wife. You may now wander off in search of a rawhide treat or a lap to curl up in.

I spent the close of the 1970s presiding over the marriages of just about every dog to every other dog in the cactusy desert north of Tucson. Family dogs—and it seemed like just about every family had a dog—had more roaming privileges back then in the wilder nooks of the Catalina foothills, where car traffic was low and nature ran up to (and sometimes straight inside, thanks to the occasional curious tarantula) each home's doorstep. So procuring a groom and a bride, especially if I felt a certain dog had gotten married too many times in recent weeks (nearly an impossibility in my mind; the more "I dos" a dog had, the better), was never an issue. A potential nuptial candidate was likely to wander in from the desert at any time, and I knew just about every dog in the zip code, it seemed, so I always had a promising bride and groom in mind.

If you lived in that neighborhood at the time, and had a canine, I must admit to you now that it was extremely likely he or she got married a few times while you were at work or out running errands. Maybe that explains why one evening your pup arrived home with Christmas tinsel threaded around his tail, not hungry for dinner after having gorged on a reception buffet of bologna slices and Milk Bones. Mystery solved.

Even at the time, I recognized that one of my favorite summer pastimes was a bit absurd; dog weddings became one of my favorite ways to spend my time because I liked spending my time with dogs. Of course, I liked organizing my day, planning events, and making itineraries, still do, and if anything has a set-in-stone structure, it is a wedding. But if you had told me that, by the time I reached adulthood, people would be throwing lavish weddings for their darling woofers, but for real, like, complete with florists and an organist, I would have scrunched up my freckly little nose with a "nuh-uh, not even" look on my face. And they are indeed; entertainment channels and magazines frequently feature expensive ceremonies between two dogs soon to be bred; the groom has a tiny tux, with an embroidered hole for tail, while the bride licks demurely at her lacy veil. I make no bones about these over-the-top rituals between consenting (or, at least, tail-wagging, if that can be considered consent) canines; I send the happy couple every joy (and toy) along the way. What gives me pause is the too-late aspiration that perhaps, by limiting myself to dog weddings, I had not fully explored, through my pooch protégés, other adult rites of passage. Surely if dog weddings have become de rigueur, won't other major moments of our human lives soon go to the dogs?

Rather than placing the Norwegian Elkhound, the Husky, and the Poodle-Something in front of an altar and invoking the marital vows, I wish I would have thrown my own college graduation, complete with the formal handing out of diplomas (in this case, slices of turkey cut in squares and rolled up, parchment style). I'd then lecture the furry graduate about getting a decent job; he'd grow weary of my advice, and soon would waddle over to sniff the college president, who would in turn sniff him.

Or, I could have sat down behind a small boulder (my desk, in this case) and faced my canine client, who would likely scratch with boredom on the other side, while I did her taxes. I'd ask her if she had any write-offs to declare (one woof for "no"), then I'd ask her to "shake" before she put a dusty paw of approval on the crumbly piece of green construction paper that would serve as her W-2. My crayon signature would attest to the veracity of the document, and off to the government agent (the nearest Golden Retriever's mouth) it would go.

There could have been the DMV (line the dogs up for an interminable amount of time, only to tell them they had not brought the correct paperwork before letting them wander off). Or a job interview (the dogs would have to talk about goals and their best qualities, or at the very least not chase their tails during the salary negotiation phase).

In fact, the more I find myself going through the routines and procedures of adulthood, those thousands of tasks, meetings, and appointments we must participate in daily, the more I think how much better it would be if my dog could go in my place. He doesn't care about per diems or income brackets or signing on any dotted line. Rather than worried questions, the filling out of forms and the making of late payments, there'd probably be instead some languid ear scratching or rump scooting or foot smelling, all things I myself have never done during an important interview or conference (not that I wasn't tempted).

Somewhere right now, I hope, there's a little girl convening some neighborhood mutts under a thicket of trees, not for a wedding but rather to play traffic school or empowerment seminar. I'm not saying that in twenty or thirty years we'll actually see real dogs attending a real seminar called Extreme Goal Setting in Romance and/or Finance Now!, but the chances are seriously good.

Chihuahuas possess the jittery intensity of a dime dropped on a marble floor.
—Dan Liebert

Becky Has Two Daddies

[Robert Masello]

I T ' S B E C O M E an early-Sunday-morning ritual. I stumble out of bed, throw on a ratty robe, and wait for my apartment buzzer to go off.

It's Bill, Becky's other dad, come to take her for a seven-mile hike up into the wilderness trails of the Pacific Palisades and Malibu. Becky is my two-year-old black Lab. Bill, a steel-gray captain-of-industry type, is the capable, commanding, and alpha dad who gives Becky the exercise and discipline she desperately craves, while I am the lazy, good-for-nothing beta dad she's forced to live with all the rest of the time.

If it takes a village to raise a child, it takes two daddies to raise this dog.

My old dog, Sam, died earlier this year; Sam was a once-ferocious mutt who had calmed down over the years, so much so that I could read the paper while taking him for a slow mosey around the block. Becky, recently acquired from a down-on-his-luck screenwriter, is a fancy-shmancy dog, an AKC-registered hound with more papers than a *Mayflower* descendant. She's sleek and black and beautiful, like a well-oiled seal, and at 61 pounds, too strong and energetic for me to handle without a Haltie, a choke collar, a bridle, and a stun gun. (Just kidding about the stun gun.) Laurie, my wife, who's also in better shape than I am (let's face it, Dom DeLuise is in better shape than I am), is a mere slip of a thing, and prefers a genteel game of tennis to being dragged by a dog who's pulling with the power of a tow truck in pursuit of every squirrel, bird, butterfly, and blowing candy wrapper that crosses her path.

Which may be why Bill has volunteered to perform this unusual form of community service. Becky leaps up, yipping, at the first sight of his Ford Explorer, her paws scrabbling at the side door, her tongue hanging out, her neck straining at the Louis Vuitton collar and leash. (My wife's idea, may I add.) Bill gets out to let her in, and I cannot help but admire his taut abdomen, his well-muscled calves, his take-charge attitude; even though he's a few years older than I am, Bill hasn't let himself go. I, on the other hand, never really had a hold on myself in the first place.

While Becky and Bill are off hiking and running and romping in the hills, and Laurie's tearing up a tennis court somewhere, I go back to bed (on a well-timed pickup day, the blankets are still warm), then set another alarm to get up and throw together a sad excuse for a brunch. Some coffee, some grapefruit juice, some pricey (but good) muffins from the new City Bakery in the Brentwood Country Mart. It's the least I can do. Laurie tries to get home from her tennis match around the same time as Bill—often accompanied by his equally fit counterpart, Mimi—returns with Becky.

But sometimes they're all a bit late, and that's when I have too much time on my hands—time to think about how this all looks. My dog needs another man to give her what she requires, and everybody knows it. She needs the strong, sure hand I do not know how to provide.

When we first got Becky, we briefly hired an expensive trainer, a big woman with short-cropped red hair and baseball cap, who observed my dog-walking technique. For a block or two, I did my best to control Becky's wild and powerful lungings while at the same time trying to reason with her, to explain to her why she needed to stop pulling, or spit out the snail she'd just crunched between her perfect white incisors. "You're a man of words," the trainer finally said, fixing me with her gimlet eye. "Yes, I guess I am," I said, modestly, "I'm a writer." "Dogs don't understand many words," she said, taking the taut leash from my hands and effortlessly removing the squashed snail from Becky's slavering jaws, all with a magical gesture of some kind and a simple "Leave it." The dog looked up at me as though thinking, *Is that all you wanted? Why didn't you say so?*

Why indeed? Because, as this dog has brought home to me, I lack the dominant gene. I cannot impose my will on anything: I can barely retrieve a soda from a vending machine. Do Becky and Bill, I wonder, laugh about that, as they march over hill and dale? What do they say about me and my slothful habits? Does Becky implore Bill, her other dad, to—I can hardly contemplate this—adopt her, to give her the active, fun-filled life that I, with my sedentary habits and submissive nature, can never do?

Do they talk about my bald spot?

When the buzzer goes off again, and Becky bounds into the house, racing for her water bowl, everyone is all smiles. Bill says something nice like "Oh, Becky's home again, and wants to see her daddy." And Mimi exclaims over the muffins. My wife, in her tennis duds, crows about her latest victory, and I try to turn the topic to a book review or an inflammatory editorial—whatever I've managed to read in the fifteen minutes I've been up since the last alarm went off. But nobody's fooled, not even Becky. We're all wondering how long we have to keep up this charade, how long we have to go on pretending that Becky needs two daddies at all. I offer everyone more juice, and try to hold the pitcher—still pretty full and heavy—steady as I pour. But everyone, I fear, can see the tremor in my hand. Becky in particular doesn't miss a thing.

Can We Interest You in a Piece of Cheese?

[Alison Pace]

MORGAN, ADELAIDE, Mischief, Boswell, Maxwell, Winston, Brentwood, Sasha, Spanky, Maggie, Bailey, Jake. Those are, respectively, the names of the Saint Bernard, English Bulldog, French Poodle, English Mastiff, Irish Wolfhound–English Sheepdog mix, Scottish Terrier, Wheaten Terrier, Shar-Pei, Shar-Pei, Shar-Pei, Jack Russell Terrier, and Corgi with whom I shared my formative years.

The years I remember as the Shar-Pei years began when I was eleven with the acquisition of Sasha, a black version of the breed who had eyes only for my mother. Sasha was followed shortly after by Spanky, the fawn-colored great love of my life, and then later by Maggie, an apricot beauty who never quite grasped the concept of her name, or of coming to the person who called it, and who in later years we began to call Margaret.

At the height of the Shar-Pei years (years that also included Max, the Irish Wolfhound–English Sheepdog mix of exceptional intelligence, and Brentwood, a renegade Wheaten Terrier), visitors caused such great excitement in our house—some might even say hysteria. "Someone's here!" someone inside the house would say (the exclamation point always heavily implied) even though such a statement wasn't exactly necessary. The dogs, clearly brilliant sages, always knew someone was approaching our house long before a car ever turned into the driveway, and would announce it vigilantly. (Except for Brentwood, the renegade Wheaten Terrier, who often saw the mayhem caused by a knock on the door or a press of the doorbell as an opportunity to head straight upstairs into my parents' bedroom and pee on their pillows. And once, in an especially unfortunate episode, he used this time to have his way with my stuffed bear, Esme.)

The first step to answering the door, and an extremely important one (though really each of the steps could be categorized as crucial), was to herd the dogs away from the front door, down the hall, through the kitchen, out the kitchen door, and into the yard.

"Outside! Outside!" we would yell, and this worked well. "Well" in this case is defined as Sasha (the black Shar-Pei), Spanky (the fawn Shar-Pei), and Max (the Irish Wolfhound–English Sheepdog mix) heading outside in a mass of fur and energy and excitement. Maggie, the apricot Shar-Pei, would often become confused and disoriented and, in most scenarios, run into the den.

"That's okay," we'd say, the reasoning being that surely whoever had come a-calling on that particular day would be fine with *just the one* dog. Only the one dog was a crazed, foaming-at-the-mouth, somewhat-close-to-marauding Shar-Pei. And while a Shar-Pei puppy is all wrinkles and cuteness and all sorts of cuddly, that same grown Shar-Pei can indeed look aggressive. "Threatening," "fierce," "frightening," "downright horrifying" are among the words I often heard being bandied about in the vicinity of our claw-marked front door.

There were narrow, vertical leaded-glass windows on either side of the door. Whoever was not already in the kitchen would knock on the glass and hold up a finger, *One minute,* we'd suggest to our guests, before heading to the kitchen to get the cheese.

"Has anyone seen Brentwood?" someone might ask along the way.

As Maggie stood on the back of the sofa in the den, barking ferociously, flinging herself against the window and smearing copious amounts of drool in a variety of places, Brentwood remained stealth on his covert mission upstairs, and the three dogs outside took advantage of the space provided by the backyard to get a good running start. All the better to build up some speed and make a much more impressive thudding sound when flailing against the kitchen door.

Now, the second step, equally important, was to get the cheese. Often, this was my job, and with a great sense of importance I would head into the laundry room (our laundry room was also the room of the refrigerator) to take a cellophane-wrapped slice of Kraft American cheese from its place on the inside of the refrigerator door. Mission accomplished, I'd usually hand the cheese off to a parent or someone else in a position of authority, which as the youngest, was anyone but me. At this point in the process—fueled by the barking and the lunging, egged on by the drooling and the knowledge of what Brentwood was up to upstairs and how helpless we were to stop it—inevitably, two or more family members would turn on each other. Then, about a full five minutes after the arrival of our guest, we'd open the front door.

"Hi," we'd say, and maybe, "Welcome," although clearly that had been implied. Maggie would now have left the den and joined us at the front door. She'd begin to lunge with a great deal of zeal in the direction of the guest. On good days we could corral her into the kitchen, and on days not so good she could conservatively be called a preview of things to come.

"Here," we'd say to our guests as we led them into the kitchen, the thump, thump, thud, of Shar-Pei, Shar-Pei, and Irish Wolfhound–English Sheepdog mix making impact with the door providing both acoustic accompaniment and rhythmic greeting.

"Just take this piece of cheese," we'd explain encouragingly, soothingly. Perhaps in our voices there was just the slightest bit of underlying tension, a tension we hoped clearly relayed the sentiment of *What you should really do is absolutely take this cheese. Really, take it, please.*

"And take a seat in this chair here," we'd helpfully suggest as one of the white wood and not-all-that-sturdy chairs was pulled from the kitchen table, and placed, vulnerable and exposed, in the center of the kitchen. And finally, we'd unwrap the cheese and hand it over.

When I think about it now, I'm not really sure why it seemed preferable to our guests to sit in that chair with a slice of American cheese in hand and face what was on the other side of the kitchen door as opposed to simply saying, "I think you people, every last one of you, along with your dogs, are insane." Yet we all make our choices and somehow, most of our guests chose to stay. They would sit down in the chair—two chairs if there were two people, and then they'd each get their own pieces of cheese. We'd open the door, the dogs would come in and bark and lunge and bark a lot more. Max, in what he surely must have seen as a gesture of great affection and welcome, was very partial to pressing his nose into our guest's lap, causing both the chair and the guest to slide across the kitchen floor.

Eventually the barking would stop and the intensity of the lunges would diminish until they could almost be described, were you so inclined, as affectionate nudges. One of the dogs (usually Spanky, as food-driven as he was loving) had noticed the cheese. And though at times we might have forgotten to mention it in all of the excitement, the very, *very* important part was our helpful suggestion that the cheese be broken into separate pieces, one for each of the dogs.

The dogs would take the cheese and disperse, and it all suddenly seemed so simple. Someone might say, "Well, that was that." Someone else might wonder, "Has anyone seen Brentwood?" In retrospect, it all seemed a relatively small price to pay for the endless joy and happiness that came from living with a minimum of four dogs at any given time.

At some point, and I've never been completely clear on why, the location of the greeting ritual moved from the kitchen to the den. Anything that was gained in terms of proximity to the front door and immovable qualities of the couch was perhaps lost in the fact that said couch now provided the dogs with the opportunity to jump up on it and be at eye level with the guest during the bark-and-lunge phase. On the plus side, if you situated yourself on the stairway once the cheese was handed out and the kitchen door was opened, you were able to watch as the dogs rounded the corner and occasionally, just for an instant, lost their footing. No one ever got hurt or even fell, but there was this fantastic, exhilarating moment as eighty toenails scrambled for purchase on the hardwood floors. It had a wonderful cartoonlike quality to it, magical, really, if you looked at it the right way.

As the Shar-Pei years stretched out across the landscape of my childhood, I became hostile and belligerent or, rather, adolescent. Eventually, I lost the sense of camaraderie I felt with the Shar-Peis at the prospect of visitors. I literally became the person on the outside of the front door: a junior in high school and then a senior who knew she'd never be able to linger undetected in a car in the driveway, who knew there'd never be a way to sneak in or out of the house after curfew. Because there was a workforce inside—at the ready, ever vigilant, *cheeseless*—ruining, I was sure of it, my time. But as I got older, almost immediately after it was a thing of the past, I forgot the exact details of the hostile and surly ways of my adolescence (as I imagine people do) and now I'm always able to remember the Shar-Pei years so fondly.

There is a very handsome Shar-Pei named Wally who lives on my block, and whenever I see him walk by, he always reminds me. But then, I don't really have to wait for Wally. Merely a glimpse of any dairy aisle in any supermarket will remind me exactly of that feeling I had when we unwrapped a slice of American cheese and handed it to someone: that it was us and our dogs, and that was all that mattered. And that clearly, we made sense.

The Shar-Pei's face looks as though a child left the project unfinished.
—Dan Liebert

One-on-One with Triumph the Insult Comic Dog

[Catie Lazarus]

 MOST MALES FANTASIZE about being with a babe, but only one stud has managed to get up close and personal with so many hot stars, including Beyoncé, Lindsay Lohan, Heather Locklear, and J. Lo. Sure, he's a celebrity in his own right, with a Grammy-nominated CD, best-selling DVD, and a cult following that has only skyrocketed since his debut on *Late Night with Conan O'Brien* in 1997. That said, this biting and brilliant insult comic admits he is a bastard. In fact, Triumph the Insult Comic Dog is a short-haired, black-and-brown compact dog made out of felt and plastic.

The irascible hand puppet deftly pokes fun at celebrities who are making headlines. But the comic genius behind Triumph, Robert Smigel, also manages to pay tribute to old-school borscht-belt stand-up comedians by wearing a sparkly gold bow tie, chomping on a cigar, and peppering his jokes with a staple punch line, "for me to poop on," and tag line, "I keed."

CATIE LAZARUS: Your Grammy-nominated CD, *Come Poop with Me: Best of Triumph the Insult Comic Dog,* was such a success. Can your fans expect another CD or DVD?

TRIUMPH THE INSULT COMIC DOG: No, there's no new DVD on the horizon because the first one was the best ever. It has more laughs than

Air Bud or *Snow Dogs* and also way more graphic sex. Seriously, it's the most entertaining, life-affirming DVD since *Backdoor Beagles Volume 3*.

CL: Your comic sensibility seems to be influenced by insult comic Don Rickles, who was himself influenced by the late Jack E. Leonard. Do you have a protégé?

TICD: Rickles is my idol, I worship the ground he poops on. As for protégés, yes, I have one—Lisa Lampanelli. As you can see, the species keeps getting lower. I've taught her about timing and crafting one-liners but she's not housebroken yet. She still poops on the carpet.

CL: When you first started appearing on *Late Night with Conan O'Brien* in 1997, you were identified as a Yugoslavian Mountain Hound. How old are you in dog years?

TICD: I don't talk about my age, just my pink thing. It's one foot, in dog inches.

CL: You slammed former D.C. mayor Marion Barry, and went head-to-head with Eminem at the MTV Music Awards—are you particularly proud of insulting anyone else?

TICD: I got that Fox guy everyone bitches about, O'Reilly. I was on his show, but he cut all my punch lines. "No Spin Zone?" Who's he kidding? The only time I spin like that is when I'm crapping out a chicken bone. I told him, they call *me* a puppet—you're the one with Rupert Murdoch's hand up yours.

CL: If you were roasted—by The Friars Club or Comedy Central—who would you want on the dais?

TICD: You'd have to start with the great Freddie Roman, because there's no way I won't be able to top him. The last time Freddie Roman said something funny, mankind had just domesticated dogs. And I'd want Louie Anderson up there, so that for once, no one would blame me for the farting.

CL: Tell us about your upbringing. It sounds like you have an Eastern European accent. And tell us about your family.

TICD: It's called a dog accent, moron. That's how all dogs talk! My whole family has a musical background. My papa was a tummler. He did a little bit of everything: sing, dance, tell jokes, lick crotches. My mama is an Afghan who looks just like Celine Dion. My sister isn't musical, but she smells like Christina Aguilera.

CL: You have a cult following. What does it feel like to have all these adult fans who spend their time discussing you on message boards?

TICD: They're wasting their time. They could be on YouTube—there's three pages' worth of Lassie's nip slips. And don't tell me it's because she has so many. You never saw the early Lassies flash them like that.

CL: You have poked fun of popular dogs like Lassie and Benji; are there any celebrity dogs you like or admire?

TICD: Okay, you're setting up an obvious joke here, so let's just agree that Courtney Love is unattractive and move on.

CL: Have you met a lot of celebrity dogs—are they just like ordinary dogs?

TICD: In all seriousness, these Hollywood dogs, they're all freaks and pervs. Old Yeller got that nickname because he liked to get peed on. Air Bud went that way too. They didn't call him "Golden Receiver" for nothing.

CL: In interviews you have referred to your illegitimate children. How do you feel about dogs being spayed and neutered?

TICD: I've got about 200 paternity lawsuits that I'd like to clear up. There's a Schnauzer in Ohio who claims her puppies are mine, but how can she prove I'm the father when she was with Vince Neil and Fred Durst the same night?

To know how I feel about neutering, all you need to do is to buy my CD, *Come Poop with Me,* and check out "Bob Barker," my duet with Jack Black. Seriously, where does Barker come off telling people what to do with my balls? The guy's so old—he looks like a chew toy I threw out last year. At least when I go for a walk, I can find my way back.

CL: Humans tend to anthropomorphize dogs, rather than the animals they eat (such as chickens and cows). Do you think "dogs are people" too?

TICD: You know, it's best to keep in reality, though it's easy to let your imagination go. Sometimes I anthropomorphize Tony Danza.

A Gentleman's Ideal Companion

[Dave Barry]

I'M TRYING TO convince my wife that we need a dog. I grew up with dogs and am comfortable with their ways. If we're visiting someone's home, and I suddenly experience a sensation of humid warmth, and I look down and see that my right arm has disappeared up to the elbow inside the mouth of a dog the size of a medium horse, I am not alarmed. I know that this is simply how a large, friendly dog says: "Greetings! You have a pleasing salty taste!"

I respond by telling the dog that he is a good boy and pounding him with hearty blows, blows that would flatten a cat like a hairy pancake but that make the dog only like me more. He likes me so much that he goes and gets his Special Toy.

This is something that used to be a recognizable object—a stuffed animal, a basketball, a Federal Express driver—but has long since been converted, through countless hours of hard work on the dog's part, into a random wad of filth held together by 73 gallons of congealed dog spit.

"Give me that!" I shout, grabbing an end of the Special Toy. This pleases the dog: it confirms his belief that his Special Toy is the most desirable item in the universe, more desirable even than the corpse of a squirrel. For several seconds we fight for this prize, the dog whipping his head side to side like a crazed windshield wiper. Finally I yank the Special Toy free and hold it triumphantly aloft. The dog watches it with laser-beam concentration, his entire body vibrating with excitement, waiting for me to throw it . . . waiting . . . waiting . . . until finally I cock my arm, and, with a quick motion, I . . . fake a throw. I'm still holding the Special Toy. But, whooosh, the dog has launched himself across the room, an unguided pursuit missile, reaching a velocity of 75 mph before, wham, he slams headfirst into the wall at the far end of the room.

This stimulates the M&M-sized clump of nerve cells that serves as a dog's brain to form a thought: The Special Toy is not here! Where is the Special Toy?? The dog whirls, sees the toy in my hand and races back across the room. Just as he reaches me, I cock my arm and . . . fake another throw. Whooosh! Wham! The fake works again! It will always work. I can keep faking throws until the dog has punched a dog-shaped hole completely through the far wall, and the dog will still sprint back to me, sincerely believing that this time, I'm going to throw the toy. This is one reason why I love dogs.

My wife, who would not touch a Special Toy with a barge pole, is less impressed. She fails to see the appeal of an animal who appears to be less intelligent than its own parasites. Oh, I've tried to explain the advantages of having a dog. For example:

A dog is always ready: It doesn't matter for what—dogs are just ready. If you leave your car window open, the dog will leap into the car and sit there for hours. It will sit there for days, if you let it. Because the dog knows that sometimes the car just starts moving, and you have to be ready! Usually the dog will sit in the driver's seat, in case (you never know!) the dog is called upon to steer.

A dog is vigilant: One time, on a movie set, I watched a small dog walk past a line of six metal light stands. When the dog came to the sixth light stand—which was exactly the same as the other five light stands—the dog stopped and began barking furiously at it. The dog would not stop. The owner finally had to drag the dog away, with the dog yanking wildly at its leash, still enraged by the light stand. Clearly the dog had detected some hostile intent in this particular light stand, something that we humans, with our inferior senses, were not aware of. We humans were thinking, "What's wrong with that dog?" Whereas the light stand was thinking, "Whew! That was close!"

These are just a couple of examples of the practical benefits provided by dogs. There are many more, and I have tried pointing them out to my wife, but she doesn't see it. This is why, in our house, we have fish. They're nice fish, but they're not a whole lot of fun. Although they are excellent drivers.

Excerpts from Great Books in the Canine Canon

[Francis Heaney]

From *The Catcher of the Stick*

by Sal

If you really want to hear about it, the first thing you'll probably want to know is what breed I am, and if I was a cute puppy, and whether or not I know any tricks, and all that Rin Tin Tin kind of crap, but I don't feel like going into it, if you want to know the truth. I'm not going to tell you my whole razzafrazzin' pedigree or anything. I'll just tell you about this stray-dog stuff that happened to me around last Christmas. I mean that's all I told Magic about, and he's my littermate and all. He's in Hollywood. He used to just be a regular dog, when he was home. I remember he dug this hole that must have been four feet deep, just for the hell of it. He stood there and barked all night if anyone got near it. It killed me. Now he's out in Hollywood, Magic, shilling for a clothing store. If there's one thing I hate, it's clothes. Don't even mention them to me.

Where I want to start telling is the day I ran away from Pencey Obedience School. You've probably seen the ads for it. They advertise in tons of magazines—you know, *Dog Fancy*, that kind of crap—always showing some puffball Poodle wearing a ribbon jumping through a hoop for a piece of steak. Like as if all they ever did at Pencey was feed us steak all the time. I never even once saw even a package of ground beef anywhere near the place. Biscuits, that was it. You ever try to jump through a hoop for a biscuit? It's hard to get excited about it, let me tell you. Anyway, it was the Saturday of the obstacle course race with Saxon Kennel. It was supposed to be a very big deal. I remember I was way the hell up on the hill behind the school. The reason I was up there, instead of down at the race, was because I'd gone chasing a stick right in the middle of a race. I was halfway across the phony pool they called a river, and I just turned and ran. I guess it was a crummy thing to do. But it wasn't all my fault. Some kid had to keep tossing sticks around. Just tossing them.

See, what I have to do is, I have to play with everybody if they start to go throwing a stick—I mean, if they throw one and they don't care where it's going I have to come out from somewhere and *catch* it. I'd do it all day. I'd just be the catcher of the stick and all. I know it's crazy, but that's the only thing I'd really like to be. I know it's crazy.

From *Walkin'*

by Thor

When I wrote the following pages, or rather the bulk of them, I lived with a family, in the suburbs, twenty yards from every neighbor, in a doghouse that my master built himself with an Allen wrench, on the corner of Walden and Magnolia, in Concord, Massachusetts, and earned my living by the goodwill of my keepers only. I lived there two years and two months. At present I am chasing chipmunks in the woods again. The mass of dogs lead lives of constant deprivation. What is called emancipation is confirmed deprivation. From the rainy meadow you run into the barren woodland, and have to console yourself with the gristle of skunks and muskrats. When we consider what is the chief end of *Canis familiaris,* and what are the true necessaries and means of life, it appears as if dogs had deliberately chosen the feral mode of living because they preferred it to any other, yet it is never too late to give up our bestialness. But to make haste to my own experiment.

Near the end of March 1995, I went down to the playground by Walden Street, nearest to where I intended to find a house, and began to look longingly at some small schoolchildren, still in their youth and thus most vulnerable to emotional suasion. I stayed there for more than a quarter of an hour, just long enough to be chased away by a teacher, providing me a sympathetic, victimized aspect. So I went on for some weeks, loitering and begging tidbits. My days in the playground were not very long ones; yet I usually managed a dinner of baloney and cookies. Before I was done each thought I was his dog, or should be.

By the middle of April, my doghouse was bought and ready for the building. I was to be the pet of James Collins, a popular boy whose father worked on the commuter rail. James Collins's yard was considered an uncommonly fine one. I walked about its border, sniffing. I thought, a dog could spend a happy life sniffing all there is to sniff in a single yard, if he took the time to wholly appreciate each scent. Sadly, I was not to spend my life there, after an incident involving a handmade pillow and some meat drippings, but I learned much in those twenty-six months on the joys of civil obedience, and how, if a dog prefers walking on a leash to keeping pace with his wild companions, perhaps it is because he hears the whirr of an electric can opener.

From *Food and Leashes in Las Vegas*

by Hunter

We were somewhere around Barstow on the edge of the desert when the window began to roll down. I remember saying something like "ARF ARF ARF ARF ARF ARF ARF ARF ARF" and suddenly there was a tremendous wind all around me and my ears were flapping and flipping and waving around my head, which was sticking out of a car going just over 65 miles an hour with my family to Las Vegas. And a voice was screaming, "Hunter! You're stepping on my frozen yogurt!"

Then it was quiet again. My master had picked me up and stuck me in the backseat. It was almost noon, and we still had more than a hundred miles to go. They would be tough miles. Very soon, I knew, I was going to have to start chewing on something, possibly an armrest. But there was no going back, and no time for walkies. We would have to ride it out. Check-in for the Black Mountain Kennel Club dog show was already under way, and we had to get there by four or some standby Terrier would take my place. Grrrrrrrroowrrrrrrrrr.

The trunk of the car looked like a mobile pet store. We had two squeaky hot dogs, six bags of chew sticks, three tug-of-war ropes, twenty cans of premium wet food, one Frisbee, three hair clippers, twenty-five packs of batteries for the hair clippers, my fuzzy blanket, seven collars, four leashes, and a Tupperware container filled with eighty dog biscuits (minus the half-chewed one sticking out from under the passenger seat).

The only thing that really worried me was the Frisbee. There is nothing in the world more obsessed and uncontrollable than a dog in the depths of a Frisbee binge. But this wasn't that kind of dog show. This wasn't California, on a beach, jumping and catching and running. This was sitting still, playing nice. Not my scene. But I had to hold it together. I had to OH MY GOD BIRDS ARF ARF ARF ARF ARF ARF ARF ARF ARF.

From *The Great Cat Pee*

by Scotty

When I was a pup my sire gave me some advice that I've been nosing around ever since. "Whenever you feel like chasing a cat," he told me, "just remember that all the animals don't have the advantages that dogs have."

He didn't say any more because he was seized with an urge to scratch himself that lasted for quite some time, and I understood that he meant a great deal more than that. In consequence I'm inclined to let cats be, a habit that has opened up many aloof felines to me and also made me the victim of not a few novelty photographs.

And, after boasting this way of my tolerance, I come to the admission that it has a limit. Cats may sleep in the sink or the double-poster bed or on the back stoop but after a certain point I don't care where they decide to plunk themselves. When I came back from the kennel last autumn I wanted the house to be uniform and tidy and free from tracked-around bits of cat litter forever; I wanted no more rambunctious kittenish runs up the side of the bookcase, knocking the golf trophies into the spider plant. Only cat pee, the liquid that gives its name to this book, was exempt from my reaction. If smell is an ineffable sequence of aromatic explosions, then there was something combustible about it, some impossible whiff of gunpowder that fired the pleasure synapses in my helpless brain, as if I were a bomb-sniffing dog who wanted to throw himself into the very fire he was entrusted with preventing.

So it happened that on a warm autumn evening I walked into the hallway to see a puddle of cat pee where it should not have been at all. The silhouette of a moving cat flickered across the bathroom window, and turning my head to watch it I smelled the heavenly scent. I decided to roll in it.

But I was not alone. A figure emerged from the shadow of the kitchen doorway and was standing with a stack of napkins bunched in her hands. Something in her purposeful movements and the steady stride of her feet rattled me, and involuntarily I glanced away as she stretched out her arms to the amber water in a curious way. When I looked once more for the cat pee it had vanished, and I was alone again in the still faintly redolent hallway.

From *The Petamorphosis*

by Franny

One morning, when Gregor Samsa woke from troubled dreams about chasing rabbits, he found himself transformed in his bed into a Golden Retriever. He thought about it for a minute and decided he was fine with that, and went back to sleep.

One Step Out of the Dog House

[Frank Gannon]

THE CITADEL, the military college in Charleston, South Carolina, which only recently admitted female cadets, faces another crossroads this September when it officially admits a dog as an incoming freshman.

"This recognition of Canine Americans has been too long in coming," said a prominent authority from the Midwest who prefers only to be known as a dog whisperer from the Midwest. "CAs should never have been seen as 'second-class' citizens—now they're in the *same* classes as humans."

In the best-forgotten past, "dogs" were not even allowed on the Citadel campus. Even friendships between cadets and CAs were rarely acknowledged.

"I had a dog, Otto, and we were close," says Joe Forbear, a mid-60's Citadel graduate. "And I know he was interested in a military career. In those days 'K-9' was as good as you could hope for if you were a military-minded CA. I knew in my heart that Otto was better than most cadets—maybe even better than me. But I never felt comfortable talking about our relationship. We always arranged our meetings in secret."

Forbear gets emotional when he recalls those days.

"I guess I'm a little ashamed," he says. "Ashamed about myself, but also ashamed about the system. Goddamn the system! Oh, goddamn the system." He breaks down.

Today opportunities for CAs are obviously better, but how much better? No doubt, Citadel's first freshman CA will have a less-than-smooth path. But those who know the "first dog" say they have chosen a very good bellwether in Sparky.

Herb Finan, who has been feeding Sparky for years, has a lot to say about him—almost all of it laudatory.

"He has an air of maturity far beyond his three years—those are human years. So he's like twenty-one in dog years. He's very perky, but if you tell him to sit, he will. He rides in a car really well. He used to sort of loll his tongue out the open window; he liked to feel it flopping in the breeze. But he cut that out. Therapy helped. Now he rides with the window up, just like a statesman."

Many things set Sparky apart in his quest to be "the first." Admissions director Ted Tendon tells of being struck by the dog's application: "I had to check to make sure that it was, indeed, a dog who had sent it in. Sparky is clearly an admirable dog who would find success in any pursuit. He's clearly not limited to traditional Canine-American fields. When his military career is over, I wouldn't be surprised if he found himself in politics. Throughout his application, you could almost FEEL his leadership qualities. His singularity of purpose was striking, but it was Sparky's maturity that was the deciding factor. He looks at things the way a much older dog would. Maybe five. And he shows both canine and noncanine influences. Take his analysis of something as simple as 'retrieving': anybody can retrieve; Sparky understands WHY the act of retrieving is beneficial to us all."

However, in the military world, it seems that, eventually, you will hear something negative about every cadet. Andrew DiMaio, who lived next door to Sparky, paints a darker picture of the CA.

"Oh, he's very good, for a dog. Every few years it seems there's another highly touted dog. But my experience has been that when things get tough, the real dog in these individuals shows through. He's flashy; I'll grant you that. But he's got some bad habits, like chewing stuff. He actually shredded half of his own application. I came in the room and he was CHEWING

UP his transcript. How much trust can you put in an individual who has official documents sticking out of his mouth? How can you trust someone with your life when he slobbers—and not just a little bit? It's major slobber."

DiMaio paints a grim picture. But, in all fairness, this writer couldn't find anybody who would say anything good about that crabby bastard, as DiMaio is known to his associates. DiMaio, it has been revealed, is also a dues-paying member of the anti-dog organization Canines: NO!

DiMaio downplays the allegations. "I used to belong to lots of organizations back when I was a kid. I was a product of the times, and there was a lot of anti-dog sentiment back then. It had just been revealed that there were actually *multiple* Lassies on that TV show. You can't hold a man responsible for things he did as a kid."

But even beyond DiMaio's voice, questions persist regarding Sparky's background. On the surface, his family is not an atypical CA family: he has eight brothers and nineteen sisters. But at least one of his siblings is the product of an incestuous relationship, and there is evidence of as many as 150 half-brothers and -sisters. One brother was hit by a bread truck last summer, and alcohol may have been involved. Also, rumors continue to suggest that Sparky experimented with group sex when he was younger. (Some allege that photos may yet surface.) One of his brothers, Bobo, had sex with a Basset Hound and apparently fled the state. Sparky made no mention of Bobo—or the alleged group sex—on his Citadel application.

Sparky is, at present, residing in his backyard in Pennsauken, New Jersey. When his lawyers brought him mention about his acceptance at the Citadel, onlookers described him as "happy but guarded."

Sir Edmund Hillary, Roger Bannister—history books are filled with names that are famous chiefly for the reason that they were in fact "the first" in one avenue or another of near-human behavior. Sparky stands at the threshold of another "first." Perhaps he will be the great success who opens the door to other Canine-Americans across the world. Perhaps he will pee on somebody important or chew up more vital documents and ruin everything. Only time will tell.

Seven Days of Finny

[Ann Brashares]

with art by Jacob Collins

DAY ONE: Finny visits farm. Fails to notice plate glass door. Finny leaps through plate glass door, cutting self, demolishing door. Finny's family not invited back.

DAY TWO: Finny swims in Great South Bay. Finny punctures buoys marking channel. Finny swims far out and greets/terrifies water-skiers. Finny brought home by perplexed speedboat captain. Finny earns parents several summonses.

DAY THREE: Finny humps small children at birthday party. Finny scolded. Finny humps more small children at birthday party. Finny called "pervert" by irritated parent.

DAY FOUR: Finny leaves home while new refrigerator delivered. Picked up by kind stranger fifteen feet from home. Finny goes home with stranger. Happy Finny eats stranger's pricey dog toys. Stranger receives large reward from parents.

DAY FIVE: Finny finds four-foot-long stick/log on beach. Finny runs and plays, takes out knees, clears beach. Finny's parents make enemies, incur heavy fines.

DAY SIX: Finny prances around park with balls intact. Finny bitten by another dog. Finny keeps balls, discontinues prancing.

DAY SEVEN: Finny eats seven pounds of raw pork and ball of tinfoil. Finny vomits repeatedly during long family car trip. Finny loved anyway.

Newman

[Thomas Cooney]

 THERE WAS ONCE a slogan that implored us all to "make it a Blockbuster night," and this is the story of how my dog Newman and I did just that.

It was late on a Saturday night and I had no idea what I wanted to rent, no clue. I knew only that I wanted to lose myself in cinema and get away from the computer that was still grazing on the appetizer that had for months been Chapter One of a slow-developing novel.

We perused the New Arrivals, disappointed by the dregs left behind by those organized masses who had clearly chosen that morning to make it a Blockbuster night. I headed toward the foreign films section, hoping that a quietly intense bout of foreign cinema would inspire my own work, when all of a sudden, the plate glass windows began to roll in that way that stops all native Californians in our tracks as we quickly deduce: *Did a truck speed by? Is some NASA craft exiting or entering the atmosphere? Is this the Big One? Should I have had that second serving of cabbage?* My heart raced and Newman's back legs started to buckle, his tail withering between them.

The commotion was quickly explained when a Blockbuster employee who couldn't have been older than fifteen whipped out from behind the cash wrap and onto the street, where he found three guys pressing against the floor-to-ceiling windows. Everyone inside the store could hear him as he demanded that they *back their shit up.* Two of the guys apologized, hands up, palms out, while the third pointed through the window directly at us. The employee, who clearly couldn't have handled these kids should they have decided to take things further, motioned for them to go inside if they wanted. They followed him, this trio of nations did—one of the kids was Filipino, the other was black, and the third was too blond to be from anywhere in this country (even Utah) and so he must have been Swedish or Danish or some other fish-for-breakfast type—and they immediately headed straight for me. The Filipino kid slid his hood off his head, patted his hair down, and said: "Dude, your dog was talking to us through the window."

Before I could muster a response, before I could ask what Newman was saying to them, a girl three aisles over led her boyfriend by the hand toward us and said, "Oh my God, look, it's a Disney dog!" She then squeezed her boyfriend's hand before kissing him on the cheek.

"Say something," the Swede demanded of my dog.

"Oh my God!" the girlfriend squealed in delight.

"Dude," the Filipino said to me, "your dog rocks!" And it was from this last word that I recognized that distinct smell from my teenage years spent hanging around my brother and his crew: cannabis. So I looked closer at all three of them and realized that they were way gone, flying high, stoned out of their minds.

The two guys who had spoken began a bizarre game of punching each other on the shoulder and laughing, and then looking at Newman and then looking at each other again before repeating the same behavior. Newman, surprisingly, remained calm and seated through all of this, loving the Disney girl's fingernails atop his head and behind his ears to the point that *he* looked stoned.

The third guy, the black kid, the slightest of the three, had at some point sat down Indian-style in front of Newman. Finally, as if arriving at a decision, he said, "I f★★kin' hate dogs, but can we borrow him?"

The "yes" that followed from his buddies was like that "yes" one hears in a room of guys when an impossible catch is made in a football game. It was a "yes" that spoke of the brilliance of such a suggestion, leading the Filipino to say, "We'll give him pizza, and what? F★★king pretzels, and, dude, like, like, like—"

"We'll give him ramen," the Swede said. "*Top* Ramen." This sent them over the edge. The black kid sprang to his feet and they all fell into one another as if huddling.

As I pulled Newman away and continued my search for a rental, I couldn't help but wonder what they'd seen in him through the plate glass windows. What clarity had come to them in their stoned state?

Though I occasionally like a good five gin-and-tonics and have been known to single-handedly polish off entire bottles of Champagne, I rarely engage in any sort of illicit hedonism. I prefer to live dangerously in other ways: going onto the street in my bathrobe to get the mail or arguing with RadioShack employees about restocking fees. In fact—as most of my friends know—somewhere in my Reagan-Again-in-'84 younger days, I made a vow to Just Say No. And though only a year after Reagan's reelection, I left all those ridiculous morals behind, I somehow still clung to the no-drugs approach—something of a novelty in California.

I wondered if these kids had detected something in Newman that I'd missed. What if they were on his level? Communicating? And, what was he telling them about me? Did he tell them that one gin-infused evening I lifted his velvety earflap and put my ear against his, convinced that all his internal dialogue was in French? Did he tell them about the year I watched the Super Bowl in the aforementioned bathrobe, eating only soupy things straight from the microwave—oatmeal during the pre-show, cheddar cheese soup at the kickoff, chili con carne at halftime, baked beans for the second half? Or did he tell them that he knew he hadn't been the dog I'd come for that day four years earlier? That he was an accidental discovery?

It was spring and I had been in a deep depression, spending weeks on end with Churchill's black dogs. If it weren't for my job teaching at a local college, I might never have gotten out of bed from February to April. My friend, Denise, kept sending me endless e-mails with links to dog rescue sites, certain that I needed a real canine to chase the black ones away. The subject headings on those e-mails were hard to ignore: "Hey Little Puddin', Isn't There Room in Your Heart for Him?" or "You Buy the Collar, I'll Buy the Leash." One day, she finally beat me into submission, and we went to the local SPCA.

"I'm here to see about a dog named Tuffy," I said, loud above the din of the homeless canines. We were thanked for coming in and asked to follow the woman in charge. She fingered her way through key after key after key before finding the one for Tuffy. She put a temporary leash around his neck and led us to the fenced-in play area where we could take him for a "test drive."

He was a smallish dog, perhaps thirty pounds. I let him off the leash and put my sunglasses on to shade the glare that angled into the area. He ran to one end of the yard, stopped, turned around to look at me, and then took off full speed for a good twenty-five feet before leaping at me and, as if with opposable thumbs, ripping the sunglasses off my face and then barking in my nose as though I were the one who brought him into this dark cursed world to begin with. I stood up, rescued my sunglasses, and took him back inside.

"He's a bit of an asshole," I told the woman, my two-month depression affording me such behavior.

"Well," the attendant said slowly, "we can look at others."

And so we did. By then, however, I was in no mood for test drives. I had to be seduced; it had to be love at first sight or nothing at all. We looked and looked, Denise asked about this one or that one. Didn't I think he'd be great with her dog, Seamus? Didn't I think this girl over here would be a nice lady friend for Seamus? But it was No, No, and hold on . . . No.

"Well, that's it. You can always come another day," the attendant said as she struggled with the gate to the last kennel she had opened. The latch wasn't clicking shut. She cursed it. Finally, she swung the door out wide and slammed it shut. The whole building shook. "Sorry about that," she said meekly. But it had been so loud that it woke up a youngster, who stood on hind legs to see what the *&#@! was going on. And right then and there my eyes landed on the most fantastic set of dog-eared dog ears I had ever seen. Those ears capped two deep brown eyes as big as malt balls. Below those eyes was a beard as hysterical on a ten-month-old dog as it would be on a five-year-old child, but this dog wore it as if part of his rogue identity. It was almost a goatee and almost a Vandyke, and it certainly made him look up to no good. I took him home.

Now, at Blockbuster, he had worked this same charm on the miscreants and the Disney girl. He was in his element, ready to be loaned out to three stoned nineteen-year-olds, who were now taking turns kneeling next to him in order to be captured on cell-phone cameras. The Swede panted with his tongue out as he sat next to Newman. The Filipino posed with his back to Newman's flank, his arms poised gangsta style, and the black kid reclined in a manner that, with his elbows propped, put the top of his head just under Newman's chin. Newman was then photographed standing between the Disney girl and her silent but adoring boyfriend, for perhaps their Christmas card or wedding announcement.

Soon enough, however, they grew bored, or just hungry, the "munchies" kicking in. We had been in that store for over half an hour and there was clearly nothing to rent. I finally resigned myself to a night of TiVo'd episodes of *Judge Judy,* and we left. I think I detected a bow from Newman as he departed to a round of thunderous applause.

Later that night I thought about life and experience and how, just maybe, I would take the leap and try to get stoned so that I could find a new connection with this dog. So what if to do such a thing, to engage in such fetid sport as getting stoned, meant that I ran the risk of ending up using a hookah instead of a bong?

At the very least couldn't I bake a batch of "magic" brownies? I called a friend and ran this by him. "Thomas," Evan said, "pull yourself together. You know, one of the few charms about you is this stance against pot. It's so ridiculous. Besides, Newman looks like Woody Allen to me when I'm sober, so of course he's going to freak out a bunch of faded dudes on a Saturday night. You'll get nothing from this."

I looked down at Newman and could swear just then that he locked his eyes on to mine, and they said: *"Même si je pouvais te parler, ce serait tout en français."*

Dogma

[Neva Chonin]

"He has a look that pierces the soul."
—KAREN BRUNEAU OF HER GREAT PYRENEES, FAME,
AT WESTMINSTER.

I HAD SWORN to avoid the 129th Annual Westminster Kennel Club Dog Show.

Please understand. For the likes of me—a woman who stalks dogs to the point of illegality—watching two nights of television filled with 2,581 wagging tails is the equivalent of a junkie playing guest of honor at an opium harvest. This is crazymaking stuff, people. A one-way road to lunacy and lithium.

So I tried to watch the Grammy Awards, instead. By the time Jennifer Lopez and Marc Anthony hit the stage, however, I began tasting vomit in the back of my mouth. Am I imagining it, or is la Lopez literally sucking the life out of the former salsa king? With every appearance, she grows more robust; he withers. Ach. If this is the pinnacle of human achievement, I'll go with the dogs.

And that's just what I did: Both nights of the Westminster wagathon found me planted in front of my television, soothed by the company of my pale friend M. Pinot Gris. (OK, took an hour off to watch Detective Stabler remove his shirt on *Law & Order: SVU;* I'm still human, after all.) In truth, I had more company than I realized. Dog shows have grown trendy since Christopher Guest chronicled their special brand of psychosis in the 2000 film *Best in Show*, and Westminster sold out for the first time this year, packing in more than 18,000 spectators to watch thousands of placid dogs and their wild-eyed owners compete for puppydom's Holy Grail.

No beauty contest, this, but a sanctified ritual, each dog a pilgrim seeking perfection of spirit and form. I, for one, was on a spiritual high. By the time a waddling Pekingese named Jeffrey won in the toy group, I was besotted (hey there, M. Pinot Gris!), drooling, and speaking in tongues—a kind of cooing gibberish that roughly translated into, "Who's a fat little dog? Who? Who's my wheezy little sweetheart? Whose toes need to be kissed? Who's your mommy? Who?"

Ah! Rapture. How I raved at the sight of the Neapolitan Mastiff named Sirius Black. The nobility. The expression of prescient sorrow. The bags and wrinkles. ("Whose face needs to be stretched? Whose?") How I genuflected before the vision of a French Bulldog trotting across the ring, bat ears at alert, and a Brussels Griffon doing that inevitable Ewok imitation. In the end, a German Shorthaired Pointer named Carlee won best in show. I dutifully worshiped this triumph, but must admit I was rooting for Coco, a Norfolk Terrier who took time off last year to raise three puppies named Tom, Dick, and Harry. I like the little dogs. They're fierce.

Dog shows are a blessing and an addiction, no doubt. But in truth, every dog is a good dog simply by virtue of his dogginess. Anyone who's ever noted the uncanny resemblance between the eyes of Jesus and those of a Golden Retriever knows there's an air of the holy, of the uncanny and blessed, that hovers over the canine world. Go. Look into your dog's eyes, and it's there. It says, "I forgive you. I forgive you everything you've ever done and will ever do. I forgive you my empty water bowl and the night you went home with that accountant instead of coming back here and walking me. I forgive you for failing the bar exam the first time around. I forgive you your crooked teeth. I am your dog, and my love is unconditional, man."

It's no coincidence that "God" spelled backward is "dog." And now a final confession: Westminster was grand, and I love me a good Shar-Pei. But

I believe the holiest of dogs is, beyond a doubt, the mutt. Preferably a mutt with lopsided ears, a missing eye, and one gimpy leg. Sui generis muttology rules! When will we have a dog show celebrating the wonders of the wholly unique? (Cut to: Neva weeping while a Dachshund/Terrier mix grants absolution.)

As you've doubtlessly guessed from the depth of my obsession, I am currently dogless. I do have resources to feed my habit, however. I will now share my favorite with you, because canine evangelism is a good thing. Go to virtualpetadoption.com and admire the gallery of four-footed wonders. Marvel at Tutti Frutti, the grinning quasi–Pit Bull. Do a Snoopy dance over Carson, the Basset Hound/Retriever mix. Coo at Maddie, equal parts Chihuahua, Dachshund, and Terrier. Scrutinize Ponzo, who is listed as a black Lab but looks more like an amalgam of seal and Martian. Revel in the pleasures of all things dog and, if the mood takes you and circumstances permit, adopt one or more of these glorious specimens. Remember: all dogs go to heaven, and if you work it right, they might take you with them.

Now, if you're prepared, the ultimate in muttology and species fusion: www.humandescent.com. I lack the adjectives to describe this site, operated out of Sussex, England, by a guy named Martin. Let's just say Martin likes beer, salted nuts, potato chips, and creating animal images that are . . . well, they're . . . hmmm. Let's just say opposable thumbs aren't all they're cracked up to be, and leave it at that.

Let the Heeling Begin

[Bill Scheft]

ENOUGH.

I was about to enter my third decade of psychotherapy when my nutritionist gave me a cheap calculator for Hanukkah. I began crunching the numbers. Conservatively: 45 sessions a year at an average of $80 per session over 20 years. Adjusting for inflation and global warming, I came up with a figure that contained more zeroes than the house on *Big Brother*.

Freud once said, "The best therapist is the one inside ourselves." Spoken like a guy with a lousy HMO. But the man was not wrong. That's why I decided to rid myself of all the couch jockeys and start seeing someone who would only listen, not judge, and always be happy to see me. My neighbor's dog, Trotsky.

So, for the last six months, once a week, faithful as the Latin I definition of "Fido," I let myself in to Norman Spiegel's junior-4, sit opposite Trotsky, and speak my conscious mind for fifty minutes. Trotsky's technique, while unorthodox, has yielded unquestionable results. I feel the need to share excerpts from my postsession journals in the hope that others will benefit, and, as I have, be able to reintegrate themselves into society. A humane society.

18 January 07

My first session went incredibly fast—at least for me. I spoke mostly of my privileged upbringing and I was afraid Trotsky, part Border Collie, part Harrier, would not be able to relate, being the product of a decidedly working-class background. But I mistook his docility for confusion. Hardly! He was especially attentive when I spoke of my half-year at Park Country Day, a school for bronchially challenged boys. In fact, every time I mentioned "Park," or used the phrase "coughing boys," Trotsky excitedly jumped to his feet. I was only at Park for four months, but it is suddenly clear to me that this is an emotional field that has lain fallow too long.

1 February 07

I think I was given my first test today, and I'm afraid I failed. For over half the session, Trotsky stared at me, while a clump of something that looked like potting soil and Russian dressing hung from his usually kempt white goatee. I said nothing, so desperate for his approval that I would risk the uncomfortable silence. Finally, Trotsky got up and walked out of the room. Just walked out. I looked at my watch. Only thirty-six minutes. I sat for the remaining fourteen minutes, then left. I said nothing. I did not call out. I did not yell. I did not complain. I did not stand up for myself. Again.

8 February 07

Session cut short when Trotsky got sick on the kitchen floor. Took exactly fifty minutes to clean up, so I guess that counts as free association. Only theme we picked up on from last week was when I wiped up under the oven and found an empty bottle of Russian dressing.

8 March 07

Steady progress, which I attribute to one of two things: My growing sense of trust in Trotsky, and the realization that my abandonment issues have more to do with *me* leaving *people* than with *people* leaving *me*. It's either that, or the dried pig's ear I bring every week and lay at my feet, which takes Trotsky over an hour to chew through.

Of course! *I need to chew on the tough issues!* Even after my fifty minutes are up! Such understated blatancy.

(Note: Bring dipping sauce for pig's ear next week. Russian dressing?)

17 April 07
Okay, I'll say it. Trotsky is wise beyond his eighty-four years. In the past, I thought his constant fang-splayed yawns were rude rather than constructive, and his herding me into the less comfortable straight-backed chair was gratuitously obstinate rather than what it was, a practical demonstration of boundary setting. (One Collie's border is another man's boundary.) But today, he outdid himself. When I started in on how I found it irksome that my super is letting himself into my apartment every afternoon to take naps, Trotsky kicked a tennis ball at me. When I tried to pick it up, he grabbed it in his mouth. We struggled off and on for the next twenty minutes, until I began mimicking the sound he kept making. *Grrrrr. Grrrr. Grrrrr.* Suddenly, the ball was gone, but I was still making the sound. And I have not stopped, even as I write this.

I am NOT irked. I am NOT miffed. I am NOT not thrilled. I AM angry. I need to experience my anger. And I need to buy a tennis ball.

1 May 07
Well, it finally happened. Trotsky fell asleep in the middle of the session. Did I say middle? Ten minutes in, Trotsky's breathing got noticeably heavier, and his extra-dry cappuccino ears flopped over his eyes like a night mask. He was out. Twice, I woke him with a sharp yelp of "Kitty!" (My new attempts to experience anger can lapse into cruelty.) Both times Trotsky's eyes only stayed open for the amount of time it took to adjust his squirrel-chasing-toned torso. I then tried rousing him by doing an impression of an electric can opener, which was not only unconvincing, but aggravated a canker. The whole process exhausted me, which I know now was the point. Trotsky was encouraging me to probe my subconscious in his presence. I dropped off deeply for a solid half hour, and when he subtly buried his snout into my groin to nudge me awake, we still had a bit of time left for

me to tell him the dream I had while under. I'm sure we'll delve further next week, so I'll just give broad strokes now: It's me, in a lingerie store, trying to buy a bowl of soup, when Trotsky walks in on his hind legs, tail cinched at his waist, blond highlights in his ears, leading former Attorney General John Ashcroft around on a leash.

22 May 07

Trotsky met me at the door, as always, but immediately ran into the hall and ducked into the elevator just before it closed. I ran down the stairs and beat him into the lobby, where he raced past me out onto Fifty-sixth Street, squatted, and left a rather large package in front of where Benihana used to be. I gave the super $10 and said if he cleaned it up I wouldn't have his ass fired for taking naps in my bed.

When I walked back into the lobby, Trotsky was holding the elevator for me. He jumped up and hit the button for our floor. As I got off and waited for him, Trotsky looked up from orally scrubbing the loading dock of his digestive system and sighed. I let the elevator doors close. I knew.

My neighbor Norman Spiegel goes away every Memorial Day weekend to Brighton Beach. He takes Trotsky with him.

I don't know when they'll be back.

I don't know when I'll be back. We never made another appointment.

Hey, maybe I'm cured. If that's the case, from now on, when I see him, it'll be clear that our relationship is purely social. I'll say, "Hey, it's Trotsky!" and he'll go back to licking me unconditionally.

Come to think of it, he never did respond when I called him "doctor."

Recently Retired Federal Reserve Chairman Alan Greenspan Warns His New Puppy Against "Irrational Exuberance"

[Michael Ward]

MEMORANDUM

TO: Roark

FROM: Your buddy Al

DATE: October 21, 2006

RE: The Challenge of Stabilizing Your Exuberance Level Throughout Your Continuing Development

In the two months since I obtained you from the shelter, I have had ample opportunity to collect data on your behavior, and I have to report that I am, for the most part, quite pleased so far.

Although you initially had numerous problems with excessive liquidity, you have done an impressive job of developing internal controls, as well as external communications to provide others enough warning to take preventive action.

Your early problems of insufficient consumption also proved to be transitory. In fact, your consumption has grown so fast that we may need to switch to a stance of tightening our policy so you can avoid excess weight that might put unnecessary drag

upon you. Another area where you have made admirable
progress is your risk profile. Initially, I was worried that you
had a distinct tendency to underweight situational risk.
Whether it was wandering casually toward the freeway or nip-
ping at the tail of a 120-pound Pit Bull, you displayed a distinct
inability to assess potential threats. Fortunately, you seem to
have made measurable progress in this area, even if it did take
the claws of a large tabby to focus your attention on this matter.

All in all, I must applaud the upward trend of most relevant
indicators for your development from puppyhood to maturity.

There is, however, one aspect of your behavior that does por-
tend some trouble, and that is your continuing irrational exuberance. While it is understandable that immediately after
your arrival you would find everything to cause the most
extreme excitement, it seems like a threshold may have been
crossed where your excitement must stabilize.

So that you do not think I am issuing this warning without
cause, let me enumerate a few examples. When you enter a
room, your current practice involves sprinting full speed to
each person in the room in turn, jumping onto him or her, and
then proceeding to the next one. Although this was laudable
behavior in your earlier days, it is time to consider a more
restrained entrance and greeting policy.

Another case where your exuberance occasionally crosses into
irrationality involves flying objects. While there are many
cases where flying objects in your vicinity are intended for
your pursuit, this is not always the case. A less exuberant
stance toward flying objects would allow you to discern more
accurately which objects were not intended for your pursuit.

The final example involves ingestion. The enthusiasm you display upon finding any biodegradable substance within reach of your mouth creates a potential health hazard. Your current protocol of treating any substance that can be devoured as one that must be devoured exuberantly is unsustainable and should be revisited without delay.

Although I offer these examples and this gentle warning, it is not my intention to move you "dogmatically" to an entirely nonexuberant posture. Quite the contrary. Exuberance in a dog is frequently the appropriate demeanor. My warning applies only to situations where such exuberance is irrational.

I suppose that you could argue that my logic is untenable due to the incessant problem in economics of defining "rationality" and "irrationality." You could claim that a strong definition of rationality requires that I make improper assumptions about preferences, and that a weak definition forces me into the tautology of declaring that all choices must be rational because they were chosen. You could make these arguments, but I do not believe you will, because you are a puppy.

Since corrective action is always less difficult and less complicated when taken early, I am offering you this mild warning to assist you in planning appropriate steps. Now let's play fetch.

Kill Jerry

[Anthony Head]

 MY DOG DIED last night. I knew it would happen, and I talked with him all about it beforehand. I even trained him for it. But we really didn't know what it would be like until we both arrived at the preapproved location, a miniature-golf course.

As we walked through the magic castle arcade, which led to the tiny putting greens, someone asked, "Oh, is that Ruthy?" I said it was, even though my Beagle's name is Jerry.

I noticed that the man wore a telephone headset as he bent over to scratch Jerry behind the ears. "We buried you the other day," he cooed in that cutesy voice people use when speaking to dogs. "Tom," he barked into the mouthpiece, "the dog's here. Can you read me?" Then he turns to me and says, "Okay. Time to die." Jerry smiled—he does that—and flipped his tail in the air like he was tracing his name in the sky.

I was a little confused. I knew we were all here to kill Jerry—Ruthy, that is—but I wasn't aware that he'd already been buried. I guess that's Hollywood.

You see, I live in Los Angeles and my dog was discovered this year. It happened just like in the movies, when some young hopeful starlet is discovered in a diner. Only in our case, the diner was a sidewalk and none of us have Lana Turner's legs. We were walking in our neighborhood when a guy approached and chatted me up about the dogs. (I was also with Clark, my Weimaraner, who plays no significant role in this story.)

He starts sizing up Jerry, literally measuring him with his hands and squeezing his belly like he's figuring out if my dog's ripe. He says that he's working on a film and needs a Beagle.

When I ask if Jerry needs to be trained, I'm informed that if he can lie down, he'll do just fine. What luck! Apart from eating and pooping, lying down is my dog's raison d'être. I start envisioning a great future for Jerry: a double-wide trailer on the set, walks up and down the red carpet before the Academy Awards, maybe even first-class tickets to Cannes. I tell the guy that I'll throw in the Weimaraner at no extra charge. The guy says no thanks and tells me that Jerry won't be paid for his time, so it doesn't matter anyway.

A few weeks later when we get to the first set location, which is a house, the atmosphere is electric. Everyone is wearing headsets—it's like we're at NASA. There are miles of thick black cable lying everywhere. Three trucks of equipment hold a gazillion lights and a wardrobe collection. I actually hear "Quiet on the set" and "Rolling" somewhere in the distance. Jerry, though, is only interested in the table crammed with peanut butter crackers, Cup-o-Noodles, muffins, and bottled water. (It's good to see that stardom hasn't changed him.)

We then learn that Jerry is playing a female dog named Ruthy. To cover up Jerry's . . . uh, maleness . . . we take a trip to the wardrobe trailer and try on his new doggie pajamas. He comes out wearing a onesy with holes in it for his front and back legs and his tail. It is sunshine yellow with white baby ducks all over.

Jerry sets his chestnut brown eyes on me with true disdain, but he's such a professional that he marches right onto the set undeterred. The director and the actors light up when he enters, all decked out in his baby-duck PJs. When the sound engineer wants to get Jerry's voice—his lines, if you will—down on tape before the cameras roll, Jerry improvises some fantastic barks and howls. Really inspired stuff. Then he tries to sneak back to the buffet table.

This is where it gets tricky, because contrary to what I was told earlier, Jerry does not just have to lie down. He must lie down, then stand up. It sounds simple, but if you're familiar with the axiom "An object at rest tends to stay at rest," then you'll understand Jerry's philosophy of life. It doesn't help matters that he has scarfed down two or three muffins on the sly and has begun to lapse into a carbohydrate-induced coma. But since there are endless delays on a movie set, I have time to run through a quick training session covering how to stand up on cue.

And it works. Jerry nails it the very first time. And then he does it again. After each take the director says "Perfect"—and we have to do it all over again. After a few more flawless tries, the director yells "Cut" and says we can go home. We've been on location for four hours, and were on the set for forty-five minutes. By my best guess, the scene will last about eleven seconds on film.

The director comes over and says Jerry was better than he expected. "So, we'll all get together again real soon when we need to kill him," he says with a wink.

Jerry displays a flawless "play dead" at my feet, then lets out a huge, exhausted snore.

Which brings us to our second day of shooting. It was a night that would culminate with Ruthy's (Jerry's) death scene, and he was ready for action. On the drive out to the miniature-golf facility, where the scene was to be shot, Jerry rehearsed playing dead in the backseat, though he sometimes broke character with a loud snore.

We arrive at midnight and he perks right up when the scent of toaster waffles from the set's buffet table wafts into the car. We both head through the medieval castle arcade to find the crew. At first, we're told that the director is ready for us, but then there is one of many delays on the set. So we head off to the putting greens, where Jerry burns off some of his nervousness by chasing a squirrel through the windmill and down past the candy house before ultimately losing the pursuit after it scampers into the clown's head.

To kill some more time, Jerry and I rehearse. I had read the script beforehand, so I knew that Ruthy was to be hit by a car. We spend some time going over what I had taught him already. Jerry was to roll onto his side and simply put his head down for this trick. Even though he refused to stop breathing, he would lie still for a few seconds, looking like a miniature beached whale, before popping up to see if there were still some Rice Krispies treats left at the buffet.

Then we were called to the set. The night air was thick with movie magic. There was to be an establishing shot, in which one of the actors would hide in a wooden barrel with Ruthy. At some point, Jerry is supposed to pop his head out of the barrel and look cute. We hadn't known about this scene beforehand, and I admit I was a bit worried. Sure, Jerry has proven that he's got great range—what with the standing up on cue and all—but coming into a scene like this so unprepared would unsettle any performer.

The actor, who was wearing a pith helmet, climbed into the barrel and then I carefully lowered Jerry inside. Confused, he looked up at me, his floppy ears pinned anxiously against his head. In his six long years of life, clearly this was his first time squatting inside a barrel with a total stranger wearing a funny hat.

But when the director yelled "Action," Jerry's inner thespian took over. The actor spoke a few lines of dialogue, which was my cue. Standing offstage, I then called to Jerry, who popped his head up out of the barrel and stared right into the camera with a bleary-eyed expression normally found on pet-store puppies.

It was golden. The audience was going to eat it up, I thought. It was so perfect that they only asked for six more takes before, I supposed, we would be moving on to the death scene.

But then something curious and a bit sad happened. I was told that Ruthy's demise would not take place as planned. It had been decided that there would be a shot of a car crashing into the barrel, followed by a close-up of Ruthy's red leash lying among the wreckage. Her death was to be implied rather than shown for a greater emotional payoff.

No on-camera death? This was to be Jerry's career-making scene—the very onset of his fifteen minutes of fame (which, in dog years, equals an hour and forty-five minutes, by the way). I wanted to call Jerry's manager or his agent, but he had neither. I wanted to scream, "But this is when you're supposed to kill Jerry!"

But it was futile. So we just grabbed some cookies and left. As we reached our car, I heard a screech of tires and a sudden crash. "Well, I guess you're dead," I whispered. Jerry just smiled—he does that.

During the drive back home through the blossoming Los Angeles morning, Jerry continued to dazzle me with his "death" pose in the backseat. It was brilliant, until he broke wind. But even without that fatal scene, my dog now has a résumé and I think he might be eligible for his SAG card.

The movie is due to be released soon. It's called *Think Tank*. If Jerry's scenes don't end up on the cutting-room floor, then I highly recommend this movie. So please go and see it. And if Steven Spielberg is reading this, have your people call Jerry's people (that's me).

The Dinner Party
A Screen Treatment

[Erica Schoenberger and Melissa Webb Wright]

Premise: What social life would be like if people behaved like dogs.

OPENING SCENE:

A living room. Some of the guests have already arrived and are racing around the room, variously hugging, colliding, dancing around each other, patting one another vigorously on the shoulders, and jumping up and down.

Another guest arrives at the door and rings the bell. Everyone runs over to the door, evidently excited beyond belief, and stands or jumps around, jostling one another while staring at the door and yelling, "WHO'S THERE?!?! WHO'S THERE!?!?!"

The guest on the other side of the door yells back, "WHO'S THERE?!?!? WHO'S THERE!?!?"

Somehow, the new arrival enters and the party resumes as before.

THE CAMERA FOLLOWS SEVERAL OF THE GUESTS AROUND, INCLUDING:

A muscular male dressed all in black who carries a Frisbee everywhere, clutched tightly to his chest. If anyone touches the Frisbee, he whirls abruptly around and stalks off, glaring over his shoulder.

Another man, dressed in plaid, rather jolly, who has a drooling problem. Every so often he shakes his head and drool flies onto adjacent guests, who don't even notice.

A depressed-looking woman who spends the entire evening methodically ripping a large, stuffed chair to shreds.

A small group huddled together in a corner. They are all talking loudly and at the same time about completely unrelated subjects.

A huge guy, with jeans jacket and tattoo, who goes up to various people, drapes his arm over their shoulders, and gives them a giant squeeze. Whoever it is immediately hands their hors d'oeuvre to the guy, who eats it.

A very small old lady with frizzy hair who leaps out from behind the furniture at passersby and speaks sharply to them. Even the huge guy is daunted.

The party Lothario who sidles up to anyone, male or female, and tries to smooch, but often misses the other person's face. Nobody seems to mind.

VARIOUS BITS OF ACTION OCCUR:

Someone emerges from the bathroom, and everyone rushes over and crowds in to see what's happened.

A guest, looking out the window, suddenly gets very excited and yells, "A CAT!!! A CAT!!! A CAT!!!" Everyone rushes to the window and joins in, yelling, "A CAT!!! A CAT!!! A CAT!!!"

Two people—one big, one little—grab an appetizer at the same time. They stand stock still, each holding on to it and staring out the corner of their eyes at each other. Suddenly, the big one whirls around and tries to walk off with it. The little person, however, doesn't let go and is flung around in the first one's wake.

In the kitchen, several guests have knocked over the garbage and are going through it.

In the backyard, several people with little spades are digging holes.

A fight breaks out in the living room between two guests, but it's over in three seconds and the opponents hug each other joyfully.

Several guests can be seen hiding bits of food around the living room. They carefully scan for a likely spot, put the food down, then pick it up again and start looking for a better place.

One guest, with his hands full of food, simply holds on to it and snarls at anyone who approaches him. He keeps trying to add more food to his pile, spilling as much as he acquires.

DINNER IS SERVED:

Everyone races over to the table and there's a big to-do while the seating arrangement is worked out.

Then all the guests eat as fast as they possibly can. Every so often, one guest simply grabs something off the plate of the person next to him/her. Sometimes that person grabs it back.

When everyone's finished, they jump up and change places to inspect one another's plates.

After dinner, everyone takes a nap. They are sprawled around the room, some in little groups huddled together, some on their backs on couches with their feet up on the arms and their hands flung over the back, some curled up awkwardly in overstuffed chairs with their chins propped up on the arms. Occasionally, we see limbs twitching and hear little contented noises.

PARTY GAMES:

>Tug of war

>How many tennis balls can you hold?

>A relay race in the backyard where the baton is never passed off. Each member of the team simply grabs hold when his or her turn arrives and everyone runs together.

>Tug of war

>Singing together around the piano, but everyone sings a different song.

>Tag

>Grab the tail of the donkey.

>Musical chairs, where shoving is allowed and you can sit on more than one chair. The big guy in the jeans jacket always wins.

GOOD-BYES:

A real dog party, of course, would never stop. So we have to introduce another group of humans who gradually arrive to pick up the guests. This is no easy task, as the target guest runs off when called. There's a lot of milling around and loud confusion as the caretaker humans go after the guests, sometimes grabbing them by the collar or the arm and hauling them away while the guest looks back at the crowd, waving joyfully.

Outside, on the sidewalk, a passerby is knocked down by a group of departing guests.

Everyone looks very happy, and the good-byes are loud and enthusiastic.

She Who Must Be Obeyed

[Tom Gliatto]

WE KNOW SOMETHING is not right with Her because of Her unenthusiastic inflection on the command "Walkies!" It is the same tone of voice she uses with Charles. She might as well be asking us if we need to be dewormed or deloused. We have often heard Her, in fact, asking Charles the same question. What we mean is that we detect a wariness there, a distraction—an unlikelihood that She will encourage us, as She does when we are all alone, to trail behind Her with the leash in our jaw while She walks before us wearing one of our collars. We believe this is Her form of private amusement. Even so this afternoon we take what pleasure there is to be had running through the tall wild grasses and smelling the odors on the highland breeze. From very far off, we can even pick up the scent of what She has called "paparazzi." They smell like something between a dead crow and raw bacon crammed into a damp woolen sock. It is always somewhat problematic that our legs are so short, and the grasses lash against our snouts, and we inhale the pollen, and we sneeze a good deal. But of course we do not complain, any more than She does. We do not whimper or droop our ears when troubled, although—and again, we find this curious—Charles does. We take from Her our cue and comport ourselves with a—

Hedgehog!
Oh good Christ, a hedgehog!
Where?
There—by that log!
Trap the hedgehog!
Kill the hedgehog!
Yes yes yes yes—!

But this is a meaningless sport, at best, and we leave off the instant She claps her hands and summons us to return to Her side.

We wonder now what act of propitiation will bring her any small ray of sunshine and happiness. We will lick her toes, yes? It is a revolting act: if you ever heard the strange sound of a Corgi gagging, you would know this was the cause. When all is said and done, there is no joy to be had in licking Her toes, but we will do it. It is in our Corgi blood, our very fiber. However, we draw the line when it comes to the feet of Philip. There haven't been such toenails since the time of Merlin.

Back in the castle, things have been no better. We went ahead with the licking of royal toes, calves, inner knee, and so many parts above and beyond that there was concerned talk in the House of Lords, and we have been forced to retreat. We cannot help being somewhat abashed when we hear the phrase "put down," because we are not sure whether it refers to action taken to suppress a common rebellion or something more along the lines of what happened to Anne Boleyn's Collie. She made the mistake of appearing on Anne's behalf before the Star Chamber. Nor did we win ourselves any renewed smiles or nods of the head—no snacks, no treats, no indulgent pats—when in a long afternoon of obsequious fetching we brought Her the newspaper, the Magna Carta, the little metal stick she carries all encrusted with precious metals and silvers, and a small baby. Two feuding mothers of the *EastEnders* variety both claimed it was their child and needed cutting in half. She remains closeted in meetings. She speaks in a very terse voice into the telephone. She talks heatedly with her husband. She shouts to Princess Margaret to stop singing bawdy sea chanteys from the bath.

When it is time for walkies, She leashes us to a great yew tree far from the castle. She steps behind the tree and removes all Her clothes as film star Roger Moore crawls out from beneath a shrub. She knows that we are discreet, because we are Corgis, and She knows that we know that their lovemaking is merely a form of stress-releasing. It is too bad, really, She cannot simply bay at something in the sky.

Another walk, toward sunset, and She seems more dejected than ever. The phrase "walkies horribilis" has occurred to us, and at this point we ourselves have become preoccupied and lag behind Her, lost in thought. We are in fact separated when She crosses a brook, her feet secure and dry in her Wellies, while we are quickly immersed in the current and our own little specialty boots torn from our paws and borne away before us like memories of happy days. We bob and splash until we land on the opposite bank, when—

> *Oh, the hedgehog!*
> *After it, after it!*
> *Kill the—!*
> *Bite its—!*
> *Zwounds!*

And yet we are completely mistaken: this is no hedgehog but a great and royal stag, much as we have seen in paintings in the house, only scaled to our own size—we mean that its grand body sits atop abnormally short legs. It looks like Bambi's father after a terrible accident in a sawmill. In addition it glows with a spectral phosphorescence, and it speaks to us in a voice of limpid grace that is magically comprehensible to us. Under routine circumstances we are sure it would never occur to us that a stag sounds like Laurence Olivier reading the works of the American laureate Maya Angelou: "Oh, Corgies of Windsor," he says, "that this sceptered isle should witness the indignities your Queen hath suffered of late! Her untaintable noblesse has been smeared, as if with cold drippings meant only for the under parlor maids in *Upstairs, Downstairs,* by tragedy and scandal, her dream of being played by Angelina Jolie in a salt-and-pepper wig dash-èd possibly forever! Oh Blair! Oh Diana! Oh black-hearted midnight! Oh—just oh! Do not desert her, brave dogs, nor question whether her actions are dictated by spleen, choler, or melancholy. Offer her nothing but your love and your loyalty. Do not fail your glorious role in history! Did not two Corgis thwart the assassin who lobbed an explosive pineapple at Victoria, swallowing it whole and raining down their puppyish shards on the royal parade? Ah— well, no: those were Pomeranians named Lucy and Drake. But was it not a Corgi, ycleped Dingy, who performed his "business" in the shoes of Wallis Simpson, giving that ignoble whore a strong and aromatic hint of how she should comport herself—viz, out the door of the palace? My time, like your legs and I see mine as well, grows short. Remember me! Farewell!"

With time, Her command of "Walkies!" regains some of its old lilt—it's sort of a quick squeal, as if an inflated bagpipe had been stepped on by Godzilla—and we are rewarded for our steadfast support. We are fed free-range pheasant breast from the Windsor silver, treated to hot-stone massages, and—a dream we would never have admitted indulging in—knighted. Wonderful finally to meet Dame Diana Rigg!

Per Her instructions and design, a beautiful doghouse is built among the topiaries in the west garden. It is made of cedar and cypress and other soft aromatic woods, inlaid with mother-of-pearl and topped by a mad but inspired profusion of Tudor gables and spires. Then She commands, "In, Charles." And in he goes.

Our Twelfth Labor

[Ben Brashares]

 WE HAVE TWO DOGS, Angie and Greeley. Greeley is our good dog and Angie is our bad one. Greeley, though troubled by allergies, nocturnal incontinence, an obliviousness to moving cars, a taste for expensive leather, and a generally weak constitution (which reveals itself monthly in eye-watering vet bills), has always been well-meaning and malleable. Angie has only one problem: she attacks other dogs. But this problem trumps all others because here in Berkeley, California, aggressive dogs are fronts for bad owners, bad people, gang members, or, worse, Republicans. And, sadly, in the world of dogs, Greeley's "good" doesn't cancel out Angie's "bad" to produce a "just fine" dog. Instead, they find the lowest common denominator and morph into what Kate (my fiancée and original owner of Greeley) and I have come to call "Angreeley," a Cerberus-like thing (albeit with two rather than three heads) that wreaks havoc at dog runs.

Indeed, of all Greeley's traits, her worst, by far, is her willingness to do whatever Angie tells her to do. If pressed to fuse our own names (à la Brangelina, Bennifer, Angreeley, etc.) it seems fitting that Kate and I would be "Bate" (as in "bait"). Angreeley uses us to pull in its victims. The attacks happen infrequently enough that Kate and I can be lulled into a hopeful state of dog trust. And that's the real genius of Angreeley. If it happened every time, we'd ban them from dog runs ourselves, take them out separately or whatever, but they know just how often they can do it and remain free and wild.

When it does occur, it goes like this: Unsuspecting dog (always smaller, often arthritic) saunters up for a hello, Kate or I give him a pat, Angie gives Greeley the signal, they touch noses, become "Angreeley," and attack the dog. In response, I summon the strength of Hercules and pull the beast off the poor dog. I chase off Greeley and hold down Angie until her growls fade to soft, demonic gurgles. I apologize to the owner and to the dog, and put Angie on a short leash. This effectively saps the Cerberus of its power. Greeley can frolic and play again, free of her evil burden. Why not just always keep Angie on a leash, you ask? Again, she's a genius. She lulls you with cuteness the way Hannibal Lecter lulled his victims with fine wine and delightful conversation.

After three or four of these incidents (usually over the course of a few days), we are invariably banned, and Kate and I pick up and move Angreeley on to the next dog run. You might say we've developed a "slash and burn" strategy for exercising our dogs. In fact, if you plot our homes over the last two years on a map, you'd find a trail of tears from Brooklyn to Pennsylvania to Connecticut all the way across the country to Berkeley, California. It's not job- or school-related as many tend to think. Sadly, we're just looking for fertile, dog-friendly territory to spoil.

And it's been fine. Until now. The truth is, we've found a dog park we really like. It's big yet mostly contained; has ducks for chasing, ground squirrel holes for digging; it's suitable for jogging; it's on the water with views of the San Francisco skyline and the Golden Gate Bridge; it even has free Mutt Mitt turd bags at stations posted about every hundred yards. We really want it to work out. So we signed up for a private training session for Angie.

We'd been working with Angie for a good twenty minutes when Sharon, our trainer, said she was going into the back office to get Floyd. Judging by how well Angie had responded to Sharon's efforts thus far, Kate and I figured Sharon was going to get help from a more seasoned trainer. She walked back out moments later holding a stick. On the end of the stick, hovering a few inches off the floor, was Floyd, the stuffed bad-dog-baiting Basset Hound. Floyd's job was to coax an attack from the dog in training, and judging by the missing leg, the saliva-matted ear (one), and torn corduroy coat, he'd been working this unfortunate gig for some time.

Angie's hackles shot up when Floyd sauntered over. Sharon told us to notice Angie's body language, her frozen anticipation. She placed a plastic clicker device in my hand and instructed me to "click" when Angie's eyes drifted from the stuffed Basset Hound to me. The click was to be immediately followed by a treat. A click and a treat, easy as that, but the click has to occur at the precise moment Angie looked at me. That was crucial. We needed to reward distraction. Angie's eyes meeting mine meant she was out of fight mode. And that's where I wanted her. But you have to click at the *precise* moment she looks at you, Sharon stressed once again, otherwise the connection between click and moment-of-hackle-free distraction would be lost.

The trick was to wait for that moment. One walk-by after another, Angie leapt at Floyd, snarling and choking at the end of her leash. Each time, Kate's and Sharon's eyes stayed on me, ready to pounce on my late click. During the thirtieth or so walk-by, Angie's eyes finally drifted up to mine. I was paralyzed, out of practice. I heard a click. It was Sharon. Sharon clicked for me. My click wasn't far behind, milliseconds probably, but in dog-time, apparently, that's just too damn long. Kate looked at me as if I'd already failed as a father to our future children.

"Maybe you could click-train Ben to click-train Angie?" Kate said to Sharon. Sharon giggled and I handed the clicker to Kate, muttering something about how it's harder than it looks. She glared back at me in a way that said, *It's always harder than it looks with you.*

Skeptical of my results, I decided to consult the Google Gods. Turns out, clicker training is all the rage. Amid ads for something called Clicker-Expo, one dog-training site offers an article called "Amygdala: the Neurophysiology of Clicker Training." It says that clicks work better than words because words need time to be recognized and interpreted, whereas clicks travel a direct pathway to the brain's bean-sized amygdala, the place where superfast "fight or flight" responses are conducted. Another article boasts about a guinea pig that's been clicker-trained to give high-fives. It says clicker training "helps you engage in more activities with your pet, improve her behavior, clip her nails without a fight, and teach her to come out from behind the fridge, among other results (high-fives)." It goes on to give step-by-step training tips on how to pull this off. When it mentioned rats, I began to wonder how small you could go with this clicker training. Could I clicker-train the mice living in our walls to crap in the trash instead of our silverware drawer? Could I clicker-train the ants to divert their parades away from our kitchen table during meals? Perhaps I've been unknowingly click-training Angie's fleas to perform circus tricks for my entertainment. Come to think of it, maybe Kate *could* click-train me to click-train Angie.

The fact is, it's the first stage of clicker training that Angie and I can't seem to get past. As demonstrated by the session with Floyd, clicker training requires a great amount of patience, not to mention precise timing. For high-fives, I can imagine it's an efficient tool. However, for behavior you *don't* want, it seems fundamentally different, and much harder. For instance, I tried to use the clicker to teach Greeley not to bark at the slightest noise outside our apartment. For each moment she sat on the couch not barking, I clicked the clicker and gave her a treat. She'd lift her head off the pillow for a moment and look at me as if to say, *Huh. Thanks.* A few moments later, another treat. *Me again? That's great. Thank you.* And then back to the snoozing. She seemed to enjoy this training very much, but it didn't help at all with the barking.

And, I had to wonder, what if I misplaced my clicker or took Angie somewhere without it? I can easily imagine going to a friend's house with Angie and her attacking the friend's dog as I frantically search my pockets for a clicker. "Yeah, sorry, I don't have my clicker with me." GrrrrrrrArghghh YELP GrrrrrrrrArrrghgh YELP! Then trying to click my tongue to produce the same sound. When it comes down to it, Kate and I are too lazy, too scatterbrained to stick with clicker training as long as it needs to be stuck with.

But, frankly, we're running out of options. After witnessing Angreeley's bullying, my father said he'd buy us a round of shock collars. My brother suggested we get some muzzles, or perhaps a Hannibal Lecter mask. My mother has, on more than one occasion, offered to put them down herself. According to Greek mythology, Psyche was able to subdue the Cerberus with drugged honeycakes. In Roman mythology, Hercules completed his twelve labors by penetrating Cerberus's well-guarded cave and taming him with brute strength. We don't have the heart, nor the strength, to implement any of these suggestions. And that's where our problem really becomes clear: we're too soft for shock collars, too lazy for clicker training, too weak for blunt force. And the pet store doesn't carry drugged honeycakes.

We're thinking about moving back to New York. It's been more than two years since we burned that bridge. We think there's a good chance they've forgotten about Angreeley. If they haven't, Kate and I are getting married in England, where she's from. We could stay there, see if the cultural differences work in our favor. If that doesn't pan out, we could look into reintroducing them to the wild, finding a congenial wolf pack that'll appreciate their excellent high-fives. More likely, we'll just keep hand-feeding the beast its treats and let it continue its useless job of guarding our cave.

Pyr Pressure

[Franz Lidz]

IF YOU'RE CONTEMPLATING having children, you might consider staying over at my house for a weekend rethink. Car, curfew, and clothes negotiations; the constant keening of self-pitying rock ballads; showers running endlessly with or without people inside. . . . An Australian friend with his own teenagers tells me that if only he had known how much he'd enjoy his dog in his declining years, he "might have given parenthood a swerve." I wouldn't go that far (at least not publicly), but I know what he means. Over the last decade, I've owned six Great Pyrenees. Actually, the Pyrs were not so much owned as adopted into my family: in the morning, we all have breakfast together; at night, they encircle the parental bed. Every adoptee has been a comedian with a wildly different act and sense of humor.

The first two, Cadmus and Europa, came along when I was in the first flush of confident, urban ignorance after my wife, Maggie, and I acquired six wooded acres in rural (or at least rural-ish) Pennsylvania. Like others in similar circumstances of un-preparedness, optimism, and bedazzlement (newlyweds in a home-furnishing outlet, movie stars with their first big paycheck buying a reckless number of vacation homes), we quickly filled up our new barnyard with a Noah's Ark of ill-chosen beasts. The two puppies took their place alongside llamas, miniature goats, chickens, ducks, geese, guinea fowl, turkeys, turtles, cats, and a Vietnamese pot-bellied pig from hell.

If not for their senses of humor, none of my Great Pyrenees would have had any sense whatsoever. These big-hearted dogs of the mountains walk up to and joke around with all kinds of farm animals—even miniature goats—because they are too trusting. Miniature goats, however, tend not to trust Great Pyrenees, and, when approached, try to butt their brains in.

Repeated brain-butting may explain the obtuse Cadmus. Over the years, there has been considerable discussion in my home about whether Cadmus was as dumb as he seemed or dumber. He was a big fellow with a big appetite for food and an even bigger one for attention. The portly clown combined the physical grace of Oliver Hardy and the simpleton destructiveness of Bullwinkle. He was so prodigiously dim that he must have thought his name was "Off the bed!"

Cadmus flunked obedience school. Twice. Then again, he was always more showman than academic. He loved to entertain plumbers and mechanics and babies, especially baby chickens. To the horror of our hens, he would pounce on their chicks and bat them between his paws like badminton birdies. If they stopped chirping, he tried to revive them by slurping their feathers. My oldest daughter, Gogo, used to call the drool-drenched remains Cadmus left in his wake "Chick-sicles."

Among the other loves of this not-quite-Great Pyrenees were seat cushions, oven mitts, barbecue tongs, chaise longues, bags of charcoal, boxes of matches, cartons of cigarettes, and cans of lighter fluid, all of which, at one time or another, he liberated from a neighbor's patio and dragged a quarter of a mile to our barn. There was something faintly comical about the way he piled his booty in a great towering heap, hollowed out a trench in the middle, and fell asleep.

At Thanksgiving, Cadmus was at his most amusing. He would station himself between the stove and the dinner table and bay at whatever holiday fare—stuffing, giblets, Bromo Seltzer—hovered overhead. On his final Thanksgiving, Cadmus howled and slavered as the turkey was handed around the groaning board. After the first pass, Maggie set the bird on a table behind her. When it was time for seconds, she reached back and found only an empty plate. Somebody observed that the baying had stopped; the rest of us searched the house for the obvious suspect. We found Cadmus in the barn, stretched out in mid-heap, a dopey smile pasted on his face and the turkey carcass—picked clean—tucked under his chin. When he died a few months later of bone cancer, I told Maggie, "I never thought I could love anything so stupid."

By comparison, his sister Europa was a veritable Caninestein. Even when she slobbered, she had a certain air about her, a look of exalted weariness one associates with good breeding and scorn for the foibles of the lower orders. Raising her nose haughtily, she'd dodge and dart through underbrush with light-footed elegance. Europa would only lower her snout to search for a scent, and even then she'd maintain a kind of cool dignity: sniff, sniff, sniff, snuffle, snuffle, schnozzle, schnozzle, all nose and no nonsense.

Europa survived on her Chaplinesque wits. Because she weighed only about 80 pounds, she made an easy target for the larger brother who loomed over her, but her quick thinking, agile body, and surprising ingenuity helped her more than hold her own. She'd romp gleefully with Cadmus until she wore him out, then literally run circles around him. As Cadmus panted, Europa would look at him the way a child on a merry-go-round looks at the gaily colored center pole.

Europa was so poised and stately that, on a lark, we once entered her in a town dog show. There—amid a Babel of yips, yaps, and the occasional yowl from barkless Basenjis—a judge evaluated the twenty or so entrants pretty much as if they were guys auditioning for the Chippendales. The judge, whose face could have won Best-in-Show at Westminster, pinched, prodded, and poked. He ran his hand down each dog's back, felt its shoulders, patted its rump trying to tell by feel instead of X-ray just how close its skeletal makeup came to Pyrenees perfection.

The judge clasped Europa's head between his hands and peered into her eyes. With a faint hand signal, he commanded my daughter Daisy to walk Europa, halt, pose. As Daisy matched Europa stride for stride, the judge stepped back and viewed the pooch front, back, and profile, like a fastidious art critic sizing up a newly found masterpiece. Europa reacted as if she were a piece of outsider art. She stopped abruptly in the center of the ring, eyed the judge with regal disdain and, like an ancient sovereign, attended to her bodily functions. As the judge stared in revulsion, I realized Great Pyrenees have their own jokes that do not seem a bit funny to non–Great Pyrenees.

The idea that Great Pyrenees compete at Westminster as "working dogs" strikes me as ridiculous. Cadmus's nephew, the sweet and antic Huck, solved the problem of work: he didn't work. Then again, he was a true aristocrat: work had been bred out of him. His lone aspiration was to be a rug in our bedroom closet, a 150-pound rug.

Huck was the quintessential beta male. Europa was the boss bitch. Though alleged to be a guard dog, the only thing Huck ever guarded was his dog bowl. Then again, Europa could have it whenever she bared her teeth at him. Vacuum cleaners terrified Huck: a burglar wielding a Dust-Buster would have had the run of our house.

Huck was never goofier than when doing impressions of humans. Like Pee-wee Herman, he could pick up and reflect back facial expressions as they flashed across his consciousness: grins, smirks, paroxysmal eye twitchings. Happily, Huck had been neutered, so he was never in danger of getting arrested in the balcony of a porn theater.

He also barked in his sleep. No amount of time in a kennel or lunatic asylum could prepare you for the *warrph* that rumbled forth basso profundo. To silence it, you had to squirt him with a bedside water gun. When my youngest daughter, Daisy, was ten, she invited a girlfriend to the house for a sleepover. In the middle of the night, Huck *warrphed* his way to a drenching. The next morning we learned that Daisy had been shaken awake by her terrified schoolmate. "I think there's a burglar in the house," she told Daisy. "I heard your mom scream, 'Stop or I'm going to shoot you!'"

Alas, Cadmus, Europa, and Huck are all long gone. These days, the Pyr pressure in my home is exerted by Ella and her younger half-brothers, Errol and Tyrone. There's a lot of Keaton in Ella, both Diane and Buster. Diane, in that the steady glitter in her eyes radiates mischief; Buster, because she's acrobatic—her parlor trick is to leap against a sliding glass door and, after stretching her forelegs to the top, slowly, squeakingly descend for maximum annoyance value—and has a serene capacity for absorbing frustration and turning a blind eye to fear and failure. Ella dedicated the first two years of her life to pulling off a single practical joke: grabbing rolls of toilet paper off bathroom dispensers and unraveling them along our property line like crime-scene tape. When she finally got it right, she burped in delight.

Which brings us to Errol and Tyrone, the wet-nosed equivalents of Jack Lemmon and Walter Matthau. A fussy worrywart whose fur coat is as immaculately white as the Cream of Wheat he adores, Errol minces about like a lanky, gonky teenager, on the tips of his toes. A walking mudslide, Tyrone shambles to his own grubby rhythms, trailing a long string of drool that invariably entangles Errol.

As much as Tyrone grates on Errol, and Errol on Tyrone, they need each other; it's the pairing that makes them funny. As with Tom and Jerry, their slapstick is based on a marvelous tension, a mutual incompatibility. Indeed, it seems to conform to what Mark O'Donnell, the noted anima-physicist, has termed the Laws of Cartoon Motion. According to the Second Law, any body in motion will tend to remain in motion until solid matter intervenes suddenly. To demonstrate this principle, Tyrone and Errol require a frolicking squirrel. In hot pursuit, they are so absolute in their momentum that only a tulip poplar will impede their forward motion absolutely. O'Donnell says Sir Isaac Newton called this sudden termination the Stooge's Surcease.

In his book *How to Speak Dog,* Stanley Coren, a psychologist and dog trainer, parses the subtleties of tail-wagging. Coren claims that when a dog holds its tail almost horizontal, pointing away from its body but not stiff, it's saying: "Something interesting may be happening here." That's what Ella does when watching Tyrone and Errol perform one of their anarchic routines. A dog that holds its tail up and slightly curved over the back is saying: "I'm top dog." That's how Europa behaved around Cadmus and Huck until the very end.

James Thurber said death, to dogs, is the "final unavoidable compulsion, the last ineluctable scent on a fearsome trail. They like to face death alone, sharing it with no one." Europa ran off one New Year's Eve, without fanfare or good-bye. Huck left with her, returned without her. We posted signs all over town, everywhere from grocery stores to dry cleaners. We tacked one in the post office next to a wanted poster for Osama bin Laden, who never showed up, either.

I finally found Europa four days later in back of a neighbor's house. She was lying on her side and breathing in weak, raspy gulps. She didn't move until I called her name—a little like the way Argus perked up when Odysseus returned to Ithaca after twenty years.

I drove her to the vet, who hooked her to an IV bag and revived her with steroids, cortisone, Kibbles. Daisy sat in Europa's cage and ministered to her all morning and afternoon.

When we got home, Europa lay down and fell asleep. She heaved terribly. The cancer had spread to her lungs. We gently woke her and got her upright and walked her outside, where she collapsed. She died instantly.

On her final walk, Europa waved her tail in broad sweeps, a tragicomic flourish worthy of the Little Tramp. Coren calls that particular waggle the "closest to the popular conception of happiness."

It might be wishful thinking, but wagging happily is how I like to remember her.

Tool: Retractable Dog Leash $10.95–$39.95

[Jeff Steinbrink]

Flexi-Alternatives:

• Rope
• Chain
• Obedience School

Seems simple enough. You hold on to the business end of the Flexi Classic, clip the other to your dog's collar, and the two of you are good to go, you at your speed, Ajax at his. What puts the flex in the Flexi Classic is its retractable leash, or "lead," a cable that plays out from the handle as Ajax trots away and rewinds (without any help from you) when he comes back. Your walk together becomes a series of partings and remeetings, and if Ajax knows his John Donne he's likely to shoot you a look that says,

> *Thy firmness makes my circle just,*
> *And makes me end where I begun.*

That's the concept, anyway: you at the center of your dog's world, he, your little Magellan, and the Flexi Classic, a spring-loaded reminder of the tie that binds.

In practice, though, this scheme, this very Order of Things, is likely to fall apart. It's clear that the Flexi Classic was designed with the well-behaved dog in mind, the mannerly, picturesque, well-adjusted dog who regards you as he might a god and who trots gladly at your side, drifting briefly away to sport with a butterfly, pee on a hydrant, or scratch where it itches. The Flexi Classic's whipcord winds out easily as he does, winds back noiselessly as he returns, rests as naturally in your grip as a scepter might. You are a champion, my friend.

Maybe all dogs in Germany, where the Flexi Classic is made, are this way: docile, businesslike, orderly. In other parts of the world the Flexi Classic may have a hard time coping with, let's say, less conventional dogs. A lazy dog, for instance, will give the Classic fits. Mine is a lazy dog. As we walk I'll feel his inertia building as he begins ever so gradually taking line with him, from behind. If I slow, so does he. The Flexi Classic is no match for him. He's no more likely to speed up and allow it to reclaim lead than he is to flutter his saddle-bag ears and leave the ground. If I don't resort to yanking and tugging (accomplished by holding down the brake button on the Flexi Classic's handle) I'll soon be at the end of my tether and Ajax will be lying down, his head between his paws.

Or take a belligerent dog, an ornery dog, especially a big ornery dog. The largest Flexi product, the Flexi All Belt 3, claims to restrain dogs who weigh up to 150 pounds. Except for my little brother, I've never had anything to do with an animal of that size, but I have walked my neighbor's 75-pound Collie mix, a sociopath named Mikey. For Mikey the Flexi All Belt 3 is a dream come true, a way to bring down two victims in one fluid motion. He'll begin a walk as innocently as a choirboy, prancing along as if with a clear conscience. But at the sight of a neighborhood cat, rat, ferret, hamster, or guinea pig he'll bolt, every ounce of his 75 pounds developing momentum like a round shot from a chamber. By the time he arrives at the full sixteen-foot limit of the All Belt he will be traveling in excess of 120 mph and approaching his prey with the effective mass of a small planet. Your options are to allow the Flexi to be torn from your hand or to hang on (some models come with a Comfort Soft Grip) and kiss your rotator cuff good-bye.

From the dog's point of view these retractable leashes must reinforce the conviction that their people are fools—lovable fools, but fools. The Flexi line, after all, allows us to be flown like kites. The Mikeys of the world take off running and try to hurl us into space, while the Ajaxes allow us gently to float away as they hold their ground. For the Flexi to function as its (human?) developers intended, it may be necessary to secure a particularly agreeable dog, a cooperative and philosophic dog. A German dog.

Nothing on a Doberman moves in the wind. —Dan Liebert

A Dog for All Seasons

[Patrick F. McManus]

 ONE OF THESE DAYS, they'll probably come out with a mechanical bird dog that locates pheasants with a special scent detector and radar. A small on-dog computer will record and analyze all available information and give the hunter a report: two roosters and five hens in the stubble field—253 feet. A pointer on the dog's back would indicate the exact direction.

There would be luxury models, of course, with built-in stereo and FM sets, a special compartment for lunches, a cooler for beverages. The dog's nose would be a cigarette lighter.

The really high-priced jobs would not only retrieve the bird but pluck it, dress it, wrap it in foil, and quick-freeze it. By the time the bird got back to the hunter it would be neat and trim as a TV dinner.

Since no self-respecting hunter would want to be seen carrying his dog around by a handle, all but the cheapest models would be designed to look like nifty attaché cases. If you passed by some good hunting ground on your way home from work, you could get out and let your attaché case nose around in a thicket or two.

There would be minor inconveniences ("We'll have to go back, Harry. I thought I had my bird dog but it's just a bag of briefs."), but on the whole, the mechanical bird dog would have many advantages over the standard makes most of us have now.

Still, I'm something of a traditionalist, and if the mechanical bird dog were to go on the market tomorrow, I'd probably stick with my old ready-made hound, such as he is. His eyes don't light up much anymore, let alone his tubes, and you can't light a cigarette on the end of his nose. The sounds that come out of him are not stereo (fortunately) and he has never been much on fidelity any way you look at it. But I would keep him nevertheless. There was a time in my youth, however, when I would've swapped my dog for a mechanical job and thrown in my T-shirt decorated with bottle caps to boot.

Take the flaws of character you find in all dogs and most human beings, roll them up in the hide of a sickly warthog, and you would have a reasonable facsimile of my dog Stranger, who was dirty, lazy, bigoted, opinionated, gluttonous, conceited, ill-tempered, and an incorrigible liar.

An old man once summed up Stranger's character succinctly: "He's a prevert!" he said. I didn't know what preverts were but had no doubt Stranger was one of them.

We had called the dog Stranger out of the faint hope he was just passing through. As it turned out, the name was most inappropriate since he stayed on for nearly a score of years, all the while biting the hands that fed him and making snide remarks about my grandmother's cooking. Eventually, the name was shortened to "Strange," which was shorter and much more descriptive.

My mother used to say that Strange was like one of the family. Then my grandmother would bawl her out and say that that was no way to talk about my uncle George. That was one of Mom's favorite jokes and was probably the reason she allowed the dog to stay on the place. At least nobody ever thought of another reason.

I used to beg for a decent dog—a Labrador Retriever, an Irish Setter, or just a regular old mongrel like most of the other guys had—but with no success. We just weren't a two-dog family, and since no one in his right mind would take Strange and Mom wouldn't take advantage of anyone who revealed his low mentality by offering to take Strange, I was stuck with him.

Strange didn't even make good as a criminal. In our part of the country the worst crime a dog can commit is to run deer. As soon as Strange found this out, he rushed out into our clover field and tried to run the deer that grazed there. They would have none of it. They looked at the wildly yapping creature dancing around them and went back to their munching.

Strange had only two chores, but he could never get them straight. He was supposed to attack prowlers, especially those whose character bore the slightest resemblance to his own, and to protect the chickens. He always thought it was the other way around.

Whenever he was caught assaulting a chicken he would come up with some cock-and-bull story about how the chicken had been about to set fire to the house when he, Strange, happened along and prevented arson. "Bad enough we have a dog that attacks chickens, we have to have one that lies about it besides!" Mom would say. (It should be understood that Strange did not actually speak in words, or at least that anyone ever heard, but with his eyes and gestures with feet, tail, and ears.)

As for prowlers, Strange would go out and invite tramps in off the road for a free meal. While the dog was out in the yard apologizing to the tramp for my grandmother's cooking, the womenfolk would peek out through the curtains and try to determine whether the fellow was dangerous. If so, they would wait until he had just about finished his meal and then my sister would bellow, "Do you want the gun, Ma? Do you want the gun?" This usually would bring the tramp to his feet and send him at a fast walk toward the nearest cover, the ditch on the far side of the road. Even had that gun been real, which it wasn't, the tramp would have been in no danger—unless of course he happened to step between Mom and the dog.

As soon as I was old enough to hunt I would borrow a shotgun and sneak out to the woods in search of grouse. I had to sneak, not because Mom disapproved of my hunting, but because Strange would insist upon going along and contributing his advice and services. An army of Cossacks could have bivouacked on our front lawn for the night without his knowing a thing about it, but he could hear the sound of a shotgun shell being dropped into a flannel shirt pocket at a hundred yards.

Just as I would be easing my way out the door, he would come staggering out of the woodshed, his eyes bloodshot and bleary from a night of carousing, and say, "My suggestion is that we try Schultz's woods first and then work our way up Stagg's hill and if we don't get anything there we can stop by the Haversteads' and shoot some of their chickens."

Strange made slightly less noise going through the woods than an armored division through a bamboo jungle. Nevertheless, we usually managed to get a few birds, apparently because they thought that anything that made that much noise couldn't possibly be hunting.

My dog believed in a mixed bag: grouse, ducks, pheasants, rabbits, squirrels, chipmunks, gophers, skunks, and porcupines. If we saw a cow or horse, he would shout, "There's a big one! Shoot! Shoot!"

Fortunately, Strange tired of hunting after about an hour. "Let's eat the lunch now," he would say. If he had been particularly disgusting that day, I would lie and tell him that I had forgotten to bring a lunch, knowing that it was against his principle—he had only one—to ever be caught more than an hour's distance away from a food supply. He would immediately strike off for home with the look of a man who has suddenly been deposited in the middle of the Mojave Desert.

Thus it went through most of the years of my youth, until finally Strange's years totaled what we supposed to be about a dozen. He sensed death approaching—probably the first thing in his life he ever did sense approaching—and one day staggered to a window, looked out and said, "A dog like me should live for a thousand years!" Then he died.

Everyone wept and said he hadn't been such a bad dog after all. Everyone except my grandmother, who simply smiled to herself as she stirred the gravy.

That night at dinner I said, "This sure is lumpy gravy," and "This pie crust sure is tough." It seemed like the least I could do for Strange.

As I say, there was a time when I would have traded a dog like Strange in an instant for a mechanical bird dog. But now? Well, let me think about that for a while.

What is muddier than a muddy Bichon Frise? —Dan Liebert

HOW TO HOUSEBREAK YOUR DOG
BY ERNIE BUSHMILLER

How to Housebreak Your Dog

[Mark Newgarden]

A DOG LIFTS his hind leg and urinates on a man's couch. The annoyed man takes the dog outside, locates a tree and, demonstrating his preference in the matter, leans forward and urinates on the tree. They return home and the enlightened dog immediately follows suit; standing upright like his master, he dutifully leans forward and urinates on the man's couch.

As far as historians have been able to determine, this simple, mildly off-color comic strip first appeared in the 1961 *Dutch Treat Club Yearbook*. A privately printed edition of 750 copies of the yearbook was issued to the attendees of the club's annual dinner in the Sert Room of the Waldorf-Astoria Hotel in New York on May 3, 1961. The Dutch Treat Club, a fraternal luncheon (and cocktail) organization founded in 1905, boasted a prominent membership of creative professionals. The club maintained no home base, operating instead as a floating Tuesday-afternoon gathering at designated Manhattan bistros. The yearbook was launched in 1920 as a souvenir program of the club's bacchanalian annual dinner, which traditionally included a full-fledged theatrical revue, produced by and starring its multi-talented members. The yearbooks continued for decades, and the editions of the 1930s and 1940s boast elaborate production values and arresting graphic design. However sumptuous, those collections found their true niche as showcases for "blue" contributions by the famous illustrators and cartoonists among its ranks, work quite unlike the familiar fare that endeared these pulp entertainers to the general public.

How to Housebreak Your Dog was drawn by Ernie Bushmiller (1905–1982), famed as the creator of the syndicated comic strip *Nancy* and renowned to aficionados as a minimalist who "dumbed down" his gags to their barest essentials, resulting in a strikingly austere visual language. Bushmiller joined the Dutch Treat Club in mid-career, long after the yearbook's heyday. His name first appears in the membership rolls in 1952, and he remained a loyal member until shortly before his death. Despite this longtime affiliation, *How to Housebreak Your Dog* was Bushmiller's sole yearbook effort. Ernie later referred to this strip as "the only dirty thing I ever did."

Although intended as a cheap laugh for his Dutch Treat Club cronies, *How to Housebreak Your Dog* assumed an illustrious afterlife. The irresistible (and uncopyrighted) page was promptly bootlegged, perhaps by a fellow Dutch-Treater gone bad, and was soon launched into the labyrinthine networks through which illicit printed matter of the day was channeled to its eager audience. No other work produced for this obscure social club ever enjoyed such far-flung distinction. Over the past forty-six years, in various modes and media, this mutt has stepped up to the couch again and again. Bushmiller's humble dog-pee joke flows gloriously onward, replicating like mutant bacteria through the dark alleys of our pop culture.

Canine Einstein?

[John Warner]

GREENBROOK, IL—April 5, 1978
See Spot run. See Spot bark. See Spot fetch. See Spot
engage in complex cause-and-effect reasoning previously only observed in humans and other primates?

Yes, yes to *all* of the above, according to researchers at the University of
California Davis Institute for Canine Behavior.

The "Spot" in question is actually a Lab/Shepherd/Setter mix named
Melvin, member of the Warner family—parents Mike and Sue, children
Mike Jr. (12) and John (8)—of Greenbrook, Illinois.

Traditionally, canine intelligence has been measured by a dog's ability
to absorb "conditioning" through the process of repetition. Pavlov's ring-
ing bell at feeding time that induces drool is no different from the basic
"sit" command. The lives of even the most highly trained service animals
are merely a series of discrete actions, each unrelated to the other.

However, Dr. Kathleen Sullivan, head of the research team that recently spent three months conducting observational studies in the Warner
home, says that Melvin is a whole new ballgame. "If we're right, you're
talking to the future Jane Goodall of dogs."

Humble origins

Originally born in an Indiana University fraternity house, Melvin was adopted by the Warners as a puppy from a neighbor as part of a package deal.

"We got half-price tickets to *The Sound of Music* for agreeing to take the dog," says Mrs. Warner.

At first glance Melvin appears to be your average dog: medium-size, predominantly black with brown accents on the muzzle and brow, white chest speckled with black spots from his Setter heritage. He likes to fetch, chase squirrels from the backyard, and sleep, but according to Dr. Sullivan, there's something very different going on behind this pooch's wagging tail.

"Most dogs will break their gaze when looking at a person, recognizing their lower place in the pack order," Dr. Sullivan says. "Melvin will look you right in the eyes, not even blinking, like he's speaking right to your very core."

When asked what Melvin is trying to communicate, Dr. Sullivan says, "'I own you'—that's as close as I can come."

Who's in charge here?

Melvin uses his abilities to hold sway over all the members of the Warner family, but according to Dr. Sullivan, Melvin's favorite target for his "intelligence" is the youngest Warner child, John. "From Melvin's perspective the slower, and—pardon me—dumber target is most inviting. He's zeroed in on the weakest member of the pack."

Like most dogs, Melvin is highly "food motivated," and most of his problem-solving schemes involve separating young Mr. Warner from his lunch or snacks.

One afternoon-long battle over sandwiches illustrates Melvin's ability.

The scenario began with John trying to transport a sandwich from the counter to the kitchen table, and Melvin simply grabbing it from the lowered plate. A second sandwich prepared, John tried carrying the plate extended over his head, seemingly out of the dog's reach. However, before John was able to reach the safety of the table, Melvin delivered a well-timed double-pawed blow to the boy's solar plexus, causing John's arms (and the sandwich) to drop into snatchable range.

In tears, the boy made a third *and* a fourth sandwich, reasoning that he could distract the dog by hurling the extra sandwich into the corner, providing enough time to scurry safely to the table.

Here are Dr. Sullivan's observations: "Where every fiber of this dog's breeding should have been screaming 'retrieve' as that sandwich flew toward the corner, he instead lay down on the kitchen floor and pretended to be asleep. Unbelievable."

Lulled into a false sense of security, John went to pick up the "diversion sandwich" while carrying his own sandwich. The researchers' stop-motion cameras indicate that it took Melvin 1.6 seconds to leap from a prone position and fully ingest both sandwiches.

"Essentially, a three-year-old dog exerts complete control over an eight-year-old child," says Dr. Sullivan. "If the dog doesn't want that child to eat, he doesn't eat. Of course, because Melvin is so intelligent, he seems to recognize that he can't completely crush the boy's spirit or he'll lose the drive to even prepare food. After six or seven sandwiches Melvin usually lets John have one, or at least a handful of bites of one."

Skepticism

However, not all animal behaviorists are impressed with Melvin's feats. "He's a clever dog, no doubt," says Dr. Herman Lodell, dean of Tufts University Center for Canine Research, "but it's entirely possible that we're dealing with a unusually dim kid, as opposed to a unusually bright dog."

When reached by phone, John Warner's third-grade teacher, Barbara Goldsboro, would not comment on his intelligence or school performance other than to cite Mr. Warner's unique ability to simultaneously shove three pencils up his nose.

Michael Warner Sr. is skeptical about the researchers' claims as well. "This is a dog that begs to eat your snotty Kleenex. How smart is that?"

In rebuttal, Dr. Sullivan offers a recounting of what has come to be known as "The Nut-crusted Cheese Ball Incident."

The cheesy part

"This happened at the Warners' holiday party. There were thirty to forty guests at any given time, and always at least two to three people present to prevent Melvin from grabbing a cantaloupe-size ball of cheddar cheese encrusted with walnuts located on a counter-height sideboard. It was delicious, I had some myself.

"Unable to gain free access to the cheese ball, Melvin's first attempted move was to upset the bar cart, which did succeed in toppling the ice bucket, but the diversion wasn't sufficient to give him a clear shot. After that, he went for the nuclear option."

In the words of Michael Warner Jr., "Mel took a big stinky dump."

"He hadn't done that ever," Sue Warner confirmed.

"This was not an accident, not in the slightest," in Dr. Sullivan's opinion.

Only the research-team cameras captured what happened next: as Michael Warner Sr. moved all the guests into the next room, Sue Warner opened the back door to provide ventilation before turning to grab cleaning supplies. That's when Melvin made his move. Gripping the entire cheese ball in his jaws, he bolted for the open door.

"We're confident that he'd consumed forty percent of the ball even before he made it through the door," Dr. Sullivan said.

Dogs rule?

Dr. Lodell of Tufts is once again impressed, but not convinced, and perhaps even a little worried. "If this dog really is capable of this level of reasoning, in a few dozen litters we could be looking at a *Planet of the Apes*–type situation, only with Schnauzers and Dobermans in charge."

"Sounds pretty cute to me," counters Dr. Sullivan.

Although, in reality, as one looks into homes across America where the four-legged creatures spend their days lounging around the house, licking their genitalia and sleeping while the two-legged creatures work long hours to provide food, shelter, and security, one might wonder if we aren't already living on the Planet of the Puppies.

A Pekingese spends half his life trying to keep his tongue in his mouth.
—Dan Liebert

Seven Protective Popeyes

[George Singleton]

 I ALWAYS FELT deep down that my odd assortment of ex-strays all hailed from the Me Generation. Oh, I brought them each into the fold like they were down-on-their-luck drifters, and knew that they didn't carry Will Fetch for Food cardboard signs only because they didn't possess opposable thumbs and Magic Markers. And at first each dog pretty much retained a look in the eyes similar to that of the planet's terrified, hungry, orphan children. They—whether ten or eighty pounds, whether appearing biracial or a mixture of forty breeds—continued the ruse for a week, then felt comfortable enough, evidently, to join the pack under its inherent, ongoing Me First banner.

My dogs' tendencies became apparent this past November when I realized they didn't care whatsoever about my undergoing the pains and side effects of possible *E. coli* infection. There'd been a massive recall of all bagged spinach, and every grocery store in America sent produce managers on an endless beeline between their vegetable stations and the Dumpster out back. The *E. coli* outbreak had killed a few people scattered across the country, and left other healthy-eating individuals somewhere between painful gastrointestinal episodes and outright kidney failure. A panic ensued, of course. Terrorists had struck our food supply! some survivalists declared, as did a few of the more paranoid members of Congress.

Let me say right now that I have never been known as a "healthy eater" in regard to the recommended fifty-six daily portions of fruits and vegetables. That's another story. But for some reason, I couldn't fathom not eating spinach if and when I wanted the stuff. So I got out one of the garden books I rarely open, and learned that, indeed, spinach is a fall crop. So is broccoli. Up until this point, I'd only planted tomatoes (which my dogs took off the vine, thinking that tennis balls ripened), cucumbers (which my dogs picked and carried around like giant green cigars, maybe in hopes of being in the next C. M. Coolidge portrait of dogs playing poker), squash (which my dogs seemed to use as juggling clubs), and so on. They never touched the jalapeños, but then again, I don't have any Chihuahua-mix strays.

I got to work. I bought topsoil. During the last week in September I constructed a raised-bed garden that measured eight feet by twenty-four. Spinach seeds only cost ninety-five cents an ounce, as it turned out, and there were about a million seeds in an ounce. I planted eight rows. Off to the side I planted a dozen broccoli plants, just in case the terrorists struck that lovely plant next. I watered every morning and tried not to pay attention to my dogs sitting in a row behind me, staring. *I hope he's planting something that attracts more moles, voles, and shrews that we can dig up and roll on,* I could almost read on Maggie's and Hershey's faces. Charlie, Marty, and Stella looked as though they wanted Brussels sprouts, of all things, seeing as they would fit their smaller mouths as compared to tomato/tennis balls. Nick and Dooley, kind-of-black-Lab and kind-of-Pointer, respectively, wanted something to attract more slow-moving doves.

I came back inside all smiles each morning from tending the garden. *Tell me I can't eat spinach when I want to eat spinach,* I thought. I took each of my seven dogs aside and said, "You're in charge of making sure no one else digs in the garden. You're in charge of keeping the other dogs from using the new raised bed garden as a gigantic Porta Potti. That would kind of defeat the anti–*E. coli* purpose of this little experiment."

Every one of my dogs nodded. They promised.

––––––––––

In late October, I had to leave for five weeks in order to be some kind of writer-in-residence at an MFA program in Wilmington, North Carolina. Every other writer in the United States must've been busy for a month; perhaps they didn't want to travel around with possible spinach terrorists in their midst, I don't know. I left on October 24. My spinach had come up nicely, in straight rows, maybe an inch high. I thought, *When I come back I'll have to pick the stuff, blanch it, get it into freezer bags quickly.* I had read up on that part of the operation soon after the gardening book, understand.

About ten days into my residency I drove home, feeling guilty for leaving my patient better half, Glenda, with seven dogs to take care of. She couldn't leave her job—oh, I should mention that this Wilmington gig included a house on Wrightsville Beach—and she wasn't exactly ecstatic that I had to work *nonstop* for three hours on Mondays, spend a day reading student work sometime during the week, and use the rest of my time there to make friends with seagulls.

I came in the side door to our house, and the indoor dogs leapt on me as they always did. They didn't make eye contact as usual, though. When I let them outside with me—I wanted to go check on the garden seeing as we'd undergone a dry stretch of weather—they took off immediately for the back corner of the property. They passed Maggie and Hershey along the way, two obviously sated dogs who barely moved from their spots in the sun. I called back to Glenda, "What the hell happened to the spinach?" My dog-members of the Me Generation took up their posts in the garden, growling at one another. *This is my spinach, this is my spinach, this is my spinach* and grazing on it at will. *I will be Popeye, I will be Popeye, I will be Popeye.* They acted the same way they did over a rock, or a dried-up miniature peach that finally fell off one of the trees like a scab, or a scrap of paper that had flown into the yard. I might've cursed loudly. I could hear children being herded in from miles around, could hear drapes and Venetian blinds being closed, could sense the slight populace of Pickens County dialing 911. Marty and Nick got up from their claims first, slowly walked over to the tallest broccoli plant, and lifted their legs. The other five dogs followed.

I took Dooley with me back to Wrightsville Beach. He, too, showed interest in the seagulls. It seemed like he spent a great deal of time looking for vegetation in order to do his business, and the waves coming in only confused him. Other dogs being walked around on leashes didn't fascinate him, and I wondered if he grew homesick for his pack of selfish buddies. Most every dawn, and at midday, and again at night, I walked him out to the beach path, where he sniffed every stalk of sea oats, then pulled me back to the house. He showed no interest in the rawhide chews I bought.

So when my teaching gig finished, I packed up and started the six-hour drive home. Dooley sat in the passenger seat, per usual, staring straight ahead. He didn't bark at cows or horses, and when I stopped at South of the Border on I-95 so that he could check out the giant sculptures of giraffes, gorillas, and rhinos, he looked at me as if to say, *Let's not waste our time; let's get home as soon as possible.*

He whined and wagged his tail when I turned onto Hester Store Road, a mile away. We got out of the Jeep, but he didn't run to the side door where we normally entered. No, he took off—maybe he's part Pointer and part Greyhound—straight for the spinach. He sniffed every remaining leaf in each row, then got down on the ground as close to the spinach as possible, as if waiting for his buddies to come outside so he could tell his stories, so he could listen to them tell their tales of Bluto coming by.

An Open Letter from Miss Ruby to Her Problem Owner

[Miss Ruby]
(who may or may not have used the assistance of one
J. F. Englert and his opposable thumbs)

Dear J. F.:

Recently, I have confirmed that you have been using me as a sort of "muse" for your writing work and that the main character of your new book is a pudgy five-year-old black Lab with a tuft of white hair on his chin and a Felix Unger–like attitude. This makes me feel rather uncomfortable since, despite some differences (gender the most obvious), this fiction hits a little too close to home. Allow me to explain.

As a true Labrador Retriever, I have always been extremely supportive of your struggles with the written word and, for that matter, with whatever you do, especially if it includes food, and generous helpings of it. It would be easy—and disingenuous—to say that I am a genetically programmed pushover and will "love" you no matter what. This is not true. You have, through your words and good behavior, earned my affection and loyalty over the years. For example, you can be counted on to correct anyone who calls me fat by informing them that I am merely well-insulated or better still, a "water dog" and possibly descended from seals. I have done my part by rolling in all available puddles and relishing our infrequent trips to the ocean. You have also consistently delivered my thyroxine pills for my sluggish thyroid (a Lab's Achilles' heel, they say) and have always been sensitive to my need for walks—perhaps this empathy comes from your awful experience when caught with a bladder full of beer in the front row at Carnegie Hall during a performance of Handel's Messiah. *Whatever the cause, I appreciate your sensitivity. Many humans fall short in the walk department.*

In return, I have observed your many eccentricities and conveyed through my muteness and large brown eyes that these things ultimately do not matter and, in fact, somehow make you a better person. We will not speak of your habit of waking in the middle of the night, tripping over my green velvet cushion, scouring the refrigerator for some snack and not giving any thought to whether your dog might also like to partake.

But this "muse" business has really bothered me. I have heard you speak to your friends about how you have "channeled" me, and I cannot help but notice how you strut about our tiny New York apartment of late, unshaven and in boxer shorts, as if you are some sort of animal behaviorist just waiting for Stockholm to call with news of your Nobel Prize.

I would have no problem with any of this if you were right in your assumptions about what goes on inside my brain and heart but, unfortunately, I fear this is not so. Keen observer you might be, but you have missed much about what makes a dog a dog. For example, you spend a great deal of time writing about Number 1's and 2's in your book (I concede your suspicion that I could read was correct, as was your guess about me watching television). But, honestly, Number 1's and Number 2's aren't the stuff of great literature or good manners—it's bathroom humor. I might as well tell you that I did not appreciate you jotting things down in your note pad as I squatted on the pavement or strained on the fringes of the meadow in Central Park. Worse were your knowing comments about my "curious shyness," "melancholy eyes," and "astounding self-consciousness, almost shame" as I assumed these positions to do my "business." I wouldn't think of disturbing you on the "throne" and disrupting your "business." And to suggest that a dog is humiliated or ashamed by doing something so natural as going to the bathroom defies reason. After all, I'm not the one picking up after me, you are.

Your observations of my interactions with other breeds at the dog run are likewise misleading. Dogs are, in fact, very practical creatures. Of course, we like to play and we love being dogs (two points battered to death in your work, I believe), but more than this, we are intent on sharing information with one another. And this involves engaging in strange, ritualistic behavior that might make the uninitiated think that our kind is either obsessive-compulsive or daffy—when, in fact, the behavior is as task-specific as firing off an e-mail or conducting a business meeting. Nowhere in your work do you capture the intricacy and seriousness of dog relations and the amazing speed with which we find out exactly what we need to know and move on to the next dog's hindquarters. You do explore the fact that our sense of smell is 100,000 times greater than man's, and the wondrous world of scents that belong to the canine because of this ability (regrettably, you have not yet taken measures in our own home to add more enticing smells beyond your unwashed socks; may I suggest hanging ham hocks from every doorknob?).

Most of all, though, I dislike the suggestion that behind human and dog relations is opportunism. No doubt when dogs or dog-like creatures first inched up to the primeval campfire of man, a bargain was made that involved the exchange of goods and services. I'm not naive. The junkyard dog still earns his keep, but as for you and me . . . well, this just isn't the case. . . .

Already I feel my calm, even-tempered, and generous Lab spirit get the better of me. I know you were doing the best you could to understand the life of a dog and I forgive you. After all, you're only human.

Faithfully,
Miss Ruby

Pet Quality

[Andi Zeisler]

 I HAVE THE KIND of dog that people—if I may put it delicately—go batshit over. I'm not bragging. I'm just saying, the dude's got charisma. People on the street— people whom I know *only* from the street—have actually screamed his name from thirty paces, and just stood there smiling while we ambled over, me embarrassed, Oscar thrilled at the prospect of strange hands squeezing all over his beefy little body.

When my husband and I want to make Oscar feel bad, we tell him he's "pet quality." That's the phrase the breeder used when explaining why we could have our fat little French Bulldog at a discount. "See his nose?" he asked, pointing at the pink shnozz speckled with black. "It's what they call a dudley, and it'll disqualify him from the breed standard. Unless that nose fills in, he won't be show quality."

As it happens, his nose did fill in, and people at the dog park began asking whether he was a show dog. "He has excellent conformation," observed one gentleman as Oscar chewed maniacally on his Pug's back leg. This is not the kind of stuff I like to talk about at the dog park. I'd much rather hear about how one woman's Pit Bull ate human feces off the street, and top it with the story of how Oscar not only ate human feces off the street, but later regurgitated it on my pants. But dog-show people would much rather talk about stuff like good conformation.

The idea of Oscar as a show dog wasn't particularly appealing. I had no desire to run around a ring in grandma pumps and thick nude hose, and since we'd had Oscar neutered soon after he started humping my husband's head in the mornings, he wouldn't be eligible anyway. But it did occur to me that perhaps I should be thinking about how a dog like this could be making me some money.

I realize that doesn't sound good. I'm not all that mercenary, and I don't believe in exploiting, racing, fighting, or embarrassing one's domestic companions. But the fact was that I was the editor of a struggling nonprofit magazine and my husband was a freelance photographer. We both worked pervertedly long hours for very little money, and watching the hands-down cutest member of our family doing absolutely nothing with his marketable skills was, frankly, a little frustrating. If Oscar was going to spend all day sitting on the couch watching TV and occasionally barking for a treat, why couldn't it be Kelsey Grammer's couch? Why couldn't the treat be dispensed by a nice young production assistant?

The more I thought about it, the more convinced I became that Oscar had a real show-business future. Yes, he had flunked the section of puppy school where the dogs were tested on whether they could walk by a Snausage without stopping to eat it. Yes, he could clear a room with one fart. But he always sat very patiently for my husband's camera, and even let himself be photographed in a fez, an eye patch, and a yarmulke (though not all at once). I didn't want him to be the new Spuds McKenzie or anything, but a dog with his particular good looks could probably move a few units of, say, rug cleaner. Or life insurance. He could even be one of those sitcom dogs who acts as a punch line simply by waddling into the room. I pictured him snuggling into Loni Anderson's ample cleavage, punctuating one of John Lithgow's windy monologues with an exasperated snort, or looking sheepish when a leg of lamb goes missing at Bonnie Hunt and Craig T. Nelson's big dinner party.

I had no idea how much dogs made as sitcom sidekicks, or from commercial residuals, but I figured it was enough to make sure Jeff and I could pay all our bills and maybe take a vacation that didn't involve sleeping in his mom's trailer in Fresno. As for Oscar, I doubted he would find the work too taxing. He lives to meet, sniff, and charm new people, so show business would be heaven to him. Plus, he wouldn't grow up and sue Jeff and me for all his earnings that we'd spent on rent. If we allotted a certain percentage of his monthly take to all-natural dried-liver treats and plush hedgehogs, that would be plenty to keep him happy.

It's not as if I was spending *all* my time thinking about how to make my dog famous. It's more like, after a long day of work, when I was standing on the sidewalk listening to yet another person squeal over him and ask me a familiar series of questions—yes, he's a Frenchie; two years old; from a breeder in the Central Valley; yes, his ears are naturally like that; no, he doesn't have too many health problems, unless you count excessive flatulence—it seemed like only a matter of time before we ran into the person whose questions could actually change our fortunes.

So I wasn't all that surprised the day Jeff came home from the park and announced that he had met a commercial director who had flipped over Oscar and said he would be perfect for a project she was scouting. It was all falling into place: the recognition, the jobs, the extra income from someone who almost wasn't even working. Sure, maybe one of us would have to take a little time off work now and then to escort Oscar to auditions, grooming sessions, and cast parties. Maybe we'd even have to move to L.A. for a while. But it would be worth it.

Or it would have been. "I'm going to call her tomorrow," I said to Jeff. "Can you give me the card?"

But my husband, chronic leaver of jackets, umbrellas, and ephemera, had managed to lose the director's card somewhere in the eight blocks between the park and our apartment. Some fruitless searches through jeans pockets and bags followed, but that was that. My stubby, pet-quality dog had a moment of almost-fame, a nugget of recognition that could have avalanched into a gold mine of glory, fortune, exotic locations, and squeaky toys, and now it was over.

Naturally, I never forgave Jeff. Several months after he lost the director's card, French Bulldogs were storming the media. Here was one selling savings plans for a bank. There was one sheepishly demonstrating the need for room freshener. A particularly ugly—probably show-quality—one showed

up in the new Steve Martin–Queen Latifah comedy. They sold MP3 play-
ers, illustrated computer-graphics capabilities, lounged alongside models in
fashion spreads. And none of them was Oscar.

Oscar likes to watch TV with me, and each time one of these impostors
flickers by, I remind him, "That could have been you, dude. That should
have been you. We should be watching this TV from Topanga Canyon."
He just blinks at me, but Jeff leaves the room every time.

[Editors' Note]

Most dogs are indiscriminately enthusiastic about their meals. We who dish out the food, however, are often more curious. Holding up a spoonful of commercial dog food, we may wonder: What's actually in this stuff and how might it taste? These next two essays, one written in 1989 by Ann Hodgman—before the advent of "gourmandized" dog food—and the other in 2006 by Rebecca Rose Jacobs (with a nod to Hodgman's "analysis"), get to the heart of the matter. Affirming, perhaps, that nothing says lovin' like something from your own oven!

No Wonder They Call Me a Bitch

The intrepid author experiments with dog food,

so you—thank goodness—don't have to.

[Ann Hodgman]

I'VE ALWAYS WONDERED about dog food. Is a Gaines-burger really like a hamburger? Can you fry it? Does dog food "cheese" taste like real cheese? Does Gravy Train actually make gravy in a dog's bowl, or is that brown liquid just dissolved crumbs? And what exactly are by-products?

Having spent the better part of a week eating dog food, I'm sorry to say that I now know the answers to these questions. While my Dachshund, Shortie, watched in agonies of yearning, I gagged my way through can after can of stinky, white-flecked mush and bag after bag of stinky, fat-drenched nuggets. And now I understand exactly why Shortie's breath is so bad.

Of course, Gainesburgers are neither mush nor nuggets. They are, rather, a miracle of beauty and packaging—or at least that's what I thought when I was little. I used to beg my mother to get them for our dogs, but she always said they were too expensive. When I finally bought a box of cheese-flavored Gainesburgers—after twenty years of longing—I felt deli-ciously wicked.

"Dogs love real beef," the back of the box proclaimed proudly. "That's why Gainesburgers is the only beef burger for dogs with real beef and no meat by-products!" The copy was accurate: meat by-products did not ap-pear in the list of ingredients. Poultry by-products did, though—right there next to preserved animal fat.

One Purina spokesman told me that poultry by-products consist of necks, intestines, undeveloped eggs, and other "carcass remnants," but not feathers, heads, or feet. When I told him I'd been eating dog food, he said, "Oh, you're kidding! Oh, *no!*" (I came to share his alarm when, weeks later, a second Purina spokesman said that Gainesburgers do contain poultry heads and feet—but *not* undeveloped eggs.)

Up close, my Gainesburger didn't much resemble chopped beef. Rather, it looked—and felt—like a single long, extruded piece of redness that had been chopped into segments and formed into a patty. You could make one at home if you had a Play-Doh Fun Factory.

I turned on the skillet. While I waited for it to heat up I pulled out a shred of cheese-colored material and palpated it. Again, like Play-Doh, it was quite malleable. I made a little cheese bird out of it; then I counted to three and ate the bird.

There was a horrifying rush of cheddar taste, followed immediately by the dull tang of soybean flour—the main ingredient in Gainesburgers. Next I tried a piece of red extrusion. The main difference between the meat-flavored and cheese-flavored extrusions is one of texture. The "cheese" chews like fresh Play-Doh, whereas the "meat" chews like Play-Doh that's been sitting out on the rug for a couple of hours.

Frying only turned the Gainesburger black. There was no melting, no sizzling, no warm meat smells. A cherished childhood illusion was gone. I flipped the patty into the sink, where it immediately began leaking rivulets of red dye.

As alarming as the Gainesburgers were, their soy meal began to seem like an old friend when the time came to try some *canned* dog foods. I decided to try the Cycle foods first. When I opened them, I thought about how rarely I use can openers these days, and I was suddenly visited by a long-forgotten sensation of can-opener distaste. *This* is the kind of unsavory place can openers spend their time when you're not watching! Every time you open a can of, say, Italian plum tomatoes, you infect them with invisible particles of by-product.

I had been expecting to see the usual homogeneous scrapple inside, but each can of Cycle was packed with smooth, round, oily nuggets. As if someone at Gaines had been tipped off that a human would be tasting the stuff, the four Cycles really were different from one another. Cycle-1, for puppies, is wet and soyish. Cycle-2, for adults, glistens nastily with fat, but it's passably edible—a lot like some canned Swedish meatballs I once got in a care package at college. Cycle-3, the "lite" one, for fatties, had no specific flavor; it just tasted like dog food. But at least it didn't make me fat.

Cycle-4, for senior dogs, had the smallest nuggets. Maybe old dogs can't open their mouths as wide. This kind was far sweeter than the other three Cycles—almost like baked beans. It was also the only one to contain "dried beef digest," a mysterious substance that the Purina spokesman defined as "enzymes" and my dictionary defined as "the products of digestion."

Next on the menu was a can of Kal Kan Pedigree with Chunky Chicken. Chunky *chicken*? There were chunks in the can, certainly—big, purplish-brown chunks. I forked one chunk out (by now I was becoming callous) and found that while it had no discernible chicken flavor, it wasn't bad except for its texture—like meat loaf with ground-up chicken bones.

In the world of canned dog food, a smooth consistency is a sign of low quality—lots of cereal. A lumpy, frightening, bloody, stringy horror is a sign of high quality—lots of meat. Nowhere in the world of wet dog foods was this demonstrated better than in the fanciest I tried—Kal Kan's Pedigree Select Dinners. These came not in a can but in a tiny foil packet with a picture of an imperious Yorkie. When I pulled open the container, juice spurted all over my hand, and the first chunk I speared was trailing a long gray vein. I shrieked and went instead for a plain chunk, which I was able to swallow only after taking a break to read some suddenly fascinating office equipment catalogs. Once again, though, it tasted no more alarming than, say, canned hash.

Still, how pleasant it was to turn to *dry* dog food! Gravy Train was the first I tried, and I'm happy to report that it really does make a "thick, rich, real beef gravy" when you mix it with water. Thick and rich, anyway. Except for a lingering rancid-fat flavor, the gravy wasn't beefy, but since it tasted primarily like tap water, it wasn't nauseating either.

My poor Dachshund just gets plain old Purina Dog Chow, but Purina also makes a dry food called Butcher's Blend that comes in Beef, Bacon & Chicken flavor. Here we see dog food's arcane semiotics at its best: a red triangle with a *T* stamped into it is supposed to suggest beef; a tan curl, chicken; and a brown *S,* a piece of bacon. Only dogs understand these messages. But Butcher's Blend does have an endearing slogan: "Great Meaty Tastes—without bothering the Butcher!" *You know, I wanted to buy some meat, but I just couldn't bring myself to bother the butcher.*

Purina O.N.E. ("Optimum Nutritional Effectiveness") is targeted at people who are unlikely ever to worry about bothering a tradesperson. "We chose chicken as a primary ingredient in Purina O.N.E. for several reasonings [*sic*]," the long, long essay on the back of the bag announces. Chief among these reasonings, I'd guess, is the fact that chicken appeals to people who are—you know—*like* us. Although our dogs do nothing but spend eighteen-hour days alone in the apartment, we still want them to be *premium* dogs. We want them to cut down on red meat, too. We also want dog food that comes in a bag with an attractive design, a subtle typeface, and no kitschy pictures of slobbering Golden Retrievers.

Besides that, we want a list of the nutritional benefits of our dog food—and we get it on O.N.E. One thing I especially like about this list is its constant references to a dog's "hair coat," as in "Beef tallow is good for the dog's skin and hair coat." (On the other hand, beef tallow merely provides palatability, while the dried beef digest in Cycle provides palatability *enhancement.*)

I hate to say it, but O.N.E. was pretty palatable. Maybe that's because it has about 100 percent more fat than, say, Butcher's Blend. Or maybe I'd been duped by the packaging; that's been known to happen before. As with people food, dog snacks taste much better than dog meals. They're better looking too. Take Milk-Bone Flavor Snacks. The loving-hands-at-home prose describing each flavor is colorful; the writers practically choke on their own exuberance. Of bacon they say, "It's so good, your dog will think it's hot off the frying pan." Of liver: "The only taste your dog wants more than liver—is even more liver!" Of poultry: "All those farm fresh flavors deliciously mixed in one biscuit. Your dog will bark with delight!" And of vegetable: "Gardens of taste! Specially blended to give your dog that vegetable flavor he wants—but can rarely get!"

Well, I may be a sucker, but advertising *this* emphatic just doesn't convince me. I lined up all seven flavors of Milk-Bone Flavor Snacks on the floor. Unless my dog's palate is a lot more sensitive than mine—and considering that she steals dirty diapers out of the trash and eats them, I'm loath to think it is—she doesn't detect any more difference in the seven flavors than I did when I tried them.

I much preferred Bonz, the hard-baked, bone-shaped snack stuffed with simulated marrow. I liked the bone part, that is; it tasted almost exactly like the cornmeal it was made of. The mock marrow inside was a bit more problematic: in addition to looking like the sludge that collects in the treads of my running shoes, it was bursting with tiny hairs.

I'm sure you have a few dog-food questions of your own. To save us time, I've answered them in advance.

Are those little cans of Mighty Dog actually branded with the sizzling word *BEEF,* the way they show in the commercials?

You should know by now that that kind of thing never happens.

Does chicken-flavored dog food taste like chicken-flavored cat food?

To my surprise, chicken cat food was actually a little better—more chickeny. It tasted like inferior canned pâté.

Was there any dog food that you just couldn't bring yourself to try?

Alas, it was a can of Mighty Dog called Prime Entree with Bone Marrow. The meat was dark, dark brown, and it was surrounded by gelatin that was almost black. I knew I would die if I tasted it, so I put it outside for the raccoons.

Leave Some for Me, Fido

[Rebecca Rose Jacobs]

 ON THE WAY into my New York office earlier this summer, I stopped at my favorite bakery to pick up an iced coffee. I was feeling hungry after a short run, but didn't fancy tackling one of the store's signature "giant muffins." Fortunately there was a jar of more manageable biscuits next to the till. These were small and plain. Just the thing. "An iced coffee, and one of those," I said.

The muffin man looked over the counter and examined the empty floor by my feet. "You do know those are for dogs?" Humiliated, I left the place with only a drink in hand. What kind of establishment puts dog treats in a glass bowl next to the till?

In New York, many kinds of eateries do just that. As one who finds the sight of dog owners picking excrement off city streets vomit-inducing, I was not pleased to be sharing coffee-shop counter space with the neighborhood dogs.

Eventually I realized I wasn't upset at the thought of the dog biscuits contaminating the human fare. Heck, I'd wanted the dog food for myself. I was jealous—jealous of the dog's healthier options, jealous of the prominent display, jealous generally of all the fuss made about man's best friend. If the doggie tidbits on offer were good enough to eat, I decided to try them out.

I was inspired by a classic essay by an owner who ate her dog's food. Ann Hodgman's "No Wonder They Call Me a Bitch," written for *Spy* magazine in 1989, is now a favorite text in writing classes. In it, Hodgman tries the food she's feeding her dog, from Milk-Bone Flavor Snacks to Kal Kan Pedigree chunky chicken. It offers a harrowing description of eating a can of meat containing a "long gray vein."

I started my adventure in the safety of a specialty dog food shop where the employees claimed to try all the food themselves. Indeed, their Fido Eats oatmeal cranberry dog biscuits contained nothing more unsavory than organic white flour, organic oatmeal, organic cornmeal, and cranberry juice (for fighting urinary tract infections, as the sleek, minimalist packaging explains). I popped one in my mouth, then another. They didn't taste bad, although they also didn't taste very strongly of cranberry. They were a little hard, I suppose, and, at about the size of a 5p coin, difficult to dip into my coffee. This is good for dogs, since hard food is what cleans their teeth.

The only really distasteful aspect of the Fido Eats treats was the price: $18.99 for what couldn't have been more than five ounces of food.

Izzy Yum Yums' Sushi Snacks for Dogs, at $19 for two rolls and eight pieces of sashimi, contain rice, seaweed, chicken broth, and, weirdly, Parmesan cheese and ham flavoring. It was also the one item I tried that I really couldn't bite into for fear of cracking my teeth. The bits of uncooked rice I managed to gnaw off didn't taste like fish, and a small mound of "wasabi," which I could do little more than lick, seemed to be mostly sugar.

Sugar is the one thing most treats avoid, perhaps because dogs can develop adult-onset diabetes from eating too much of it, according to Pratikshya Patil, a vet at the New York Veterinary Hospital.

So the Kung Fu Fido Fortune Cookies for Dogs (at $10) are infused with chicken livers, not sugar—not that I could have detected the difference. The cookies resemble those served at any Chinese restaurant. The only telling difference is the fortunes: "Someday you will find yourself barking up the right tree," for example, or "Confucius say, dog who pee on electric fence get real zinger."

After a morning of eating organic oatmeal-cranberry dog crackers, followed by dog fortune cookies and a fairly tasty, if hard, carob-and-peanut coated homemade dog biscuit, I felt glum. I had crossed a line drawn far back in evolutionary time, and while I was still hungry, human food now also felt diminished, like mere calories dressed up as dinner.

Still, as demoralizing as my initial encounters had been, they did not approach the repulsive experiments Hodgman conducted. Maybe it is simply that all food—dog and human—marches ever upward, becoming more sophisticated, clean, and refined with each decade. After all, the 1960s recipe book *Saucepans and the Single Girl,* recently rereleased for the nostalgic and post-modernist among us, contains recipes for Humbleburger Soup and Sardines and Cream Cheese. I'm no gourmet, but I'd sooner serve my dinner guests dog food crackers than steaming bowls of burger soup. Mind you, in ten years, some other single gal living in a studio apartment in Brooklyn may choke at the thought of serving prosciutto-wrapped figs at a cocktail party.

A conscientious pet owner recommended that for high-end wet food, I try Wellness brand, which according to its Web site makes dog food with ingredients "fit for human consumption," if not officially "human grade." Peeling back the top of the can of Lamb & Sweet Potato Formula, I was met with a slightly shimmery surface of light brown meat, ground so finely it might have been mistaken for grains of overcooked barley.

It tasted like lamb at first bite, with an emphasis on "like" lamb, as distinct from "as if it were" lamb. Indeed, its main ingredients were: lamb, lamb broth, and lamb liver pulsated into a smooth, soft consistency and mixed with grains and root vegetables. Its aftertaste, however, was 100 percent whitefish. In fact, that wall of whitefish, in combination with the gelatinous, push-back consistency of the stuff, made me realize why I didn't find Wellness all that bad: I'd been conditioned by a lifelong fondness for gefilte fish.

Merrick brand's Campfire Trout Feast was a different story. The label suggests you crack open this can of wet food while "on the banks of the Rio Grande River next to a campfire with your beloved dog . . . under the stars, the two of you feast on freshwater trout and all the fixin's." Those fixin's include trout, salmon broth, fresh Yukon gold potatoes, fresh carrots,

fresh courgettes, and olive oil. Not bad, I thought. I had almost been persuaded to buy a can of the Napa Valley Picnic as well.

The trout feast was spookily odorless and looked like old chocolate
gone white. It slid from the can only after some prising, and then in a massive chunk. It's amazing that something completely lacking in flavor can
nevertheless produce a gagging effect. I spat out my first bite. On my second try, I detected what for a second I thought might be a hint of trout
spread, but then identified as the pure taste of preservatives. The nothing
taste flooded back and I gagged again.

I learned my lesson, and decided to dress up the next selection: Stella &
Chewy's freeze-dried chicken steaks, which the proprietors at my favorite
West Village pet store, Canine Styles, assured me were very popular with
their customers. The "steaks," at $16.99 for nine pieces, contained U.S.
Department of Agriculture–inspected free-range chicken, which buoyed
me. However, that free-range product includes bone, which sank me once
again. Cartilage aside, the ingredient list seemed perfectly acceptable, with
sweet potatoes, alfalfa, blueberries, and ginger.

The steaks crumbled into sawdust when sliced. After putting on a pot
of water to boil for pasta, I sautéed some garlic and tomatoes and added a
cutting-board's worth of chicken-steak. What I learned was that if a cruel
restaurateur ever tries to serve you pasta with dog food, even high-end dog
food, you'll detect the trick by the overpowering, unmistakable smell of
low-grade meat. The price of that lesson was biting into what may have
looked like browned sausage, but tasted like gristle, tendons and, yes,
ground-up bones.

During my first visit to Canine Styles, I was invited to a dog ice cream
social. I had assumed dogs were lactose intolerant, maybe because it seems
half the population of New York is, but it turns out they can eat ice cream
(sugarless) with abandon. On learning this, I first felt a creeping annoyance
that canines had managed to horn in on yet another of our food groups.
Then I remembered the times when Meggie, our family dog, felt sick, and
how comforted she was by the healing diet we would give her of cooked
rice mixed with yogurt. For the first time, I began to understand what these
owners must be thinking as they buy their pets outrageously expensive

snacks and put them on raw-food diets: human food for dogs isn't always an attempt to erase lines between species; sometimes it's just because we care about the critters.

At the ice cream social itself, my sympathy for the animals increased. The ice cream was great—a homemade blend of yogurt, honey, and peanut butter (the humans got ice cream sandwiches, full of preservatives, I'm sure)—and the social scene was friendly and open. No one seemed to mind that I didn't have a dog. But as I spooned up my ice cream happily, I looked around and noticed the dogs licking away desperately as their containers slid around on the sidewalk. Opposable thumbs are a privilege, I thought— there but for the grace of Dog go I.

I stopped eating dog food on the day I ate a dog biscuit simply because I was hungry. I was at work, with a snack machine in the office and a mélange of human options outside, but I had at my desk one of the garlic- and-chicken bones from that original muffin shop. I took one bite—hard but subtly flavorful. Better than the hardtack the pilgrims ate on the *Mayflower.* I took another—it hit the spot. But by the time I had finished the bone, hiding it from my coworkers, I knew I had to stop. After all, defe- cating on the street was only a few logical steps away.

Our dogs not only give us joy and laughter, they also enrich our lives with their constancy and immediacy. For the endpiece of this collection, we have chosen a work with a slightly different twist— Meghan Daum's contemplative essay on her experiences as one of today's "dog people." It is a fitting bridge to the heart of Howl's *raison d'être.*

Dog Is My Co-Dependent

[Meghan Daum]

HOW DOES ONE own a dog without becoming a dog person? The answer, I suspect, depends upon whether or not you have a dog and the degree to which you're inclined to buy in to the idea that pet ownership, like child rearing, isn't what it used to be. Of course, most things aren't what they used to be, but when it comes to the relationship between helpless creatures and responsible adults, many of us aren't in Kansas anymore. In my case, I mean this literally. When I got my dog, a Collie/St. Bernard mix named Rex, I lived on a farm in the central plains. He slept in the barn, flanked by a horse on one side and a pig on the other. On frigid mornings I'd come in with his food and often find him curled up with the cat. He was just eight weeks old when I got him, a squiggly fluff ball of black and brown fur, and he knew nothing of the inside world for several months. I remember the winter day when I first brought him indoors. Negotiating the strange new surface of the polished floors, he actually slipped and fell down several times as though he were on another planet. I remember the combination of alarm and delight he seemed to take at spotting his image in a full-length mirror on a closet door. He lurched back, startled, then looked behind the door in search of the strange dog lurking there. He soon grew restless so I led him back outside and watched as he trotted back to his familiar environs, a ten-acre pasture where he convened with horses and pheasants with such obvious pleasure that even my fear that he'd be hit by a passing truck was not enough to make me do anything but let him run free.

Now, seven years on, I live with Rex in Los Angeles. His world is a 900-square-foot house and a small fenced yard he can access through a dog door. He has a microchip implant in case he gets lost, an assortment of stuffed toys so he won't get bored, and eats prescription low-calorie dog food because he's gotten fat. Every day, I put on his leash and take him to a wilderness area where he can run free for 45 minutes and socialize with other dogs who have microchips and follow prescription diets. Whereas I used to give him baths in the river, he now goes to a groomer who hoses him off in a giant sink and then sets a fan by a cage to dry him. Whereas he used to spend his nights in a nest of hay, lulled to sleep by the secret world of the barn, he now sleeps with me in my bed, sometimes with his head on the pillow next to me.

I am not so far gone that I don't recognize that Rex's life, albeit safer than his life on the farm and better than the lives of the vast majority of animals in the world, took a turn for the worse when he stopped being a dog and became a pet. At the same time, I would be a liar if I didn't admit that having a pet brings a level of happiness to my life that I wasn't able to experience by merely having a dog. Having an animal, like having a child, is the kind of pursuit to which you can ascribe the world "selfless" only up to a point. There are the obvious hassles—feeding and sheltering and the handling of excrement—but once you put aside the logistics you are looking at a relationship that is almost entirely wrapped up in the need for unconditional love. When I lived on the farm (and I lived there with a man who'd no sooner let a dog in the house than invite a mountain goat over for drinks), the love I felt for Rex was intense, unqualified, and respectful. Here in Los Angeles, where it's not unheard of to take your dog to dinner parties, that love is intense, unqualified, and more akin to the kind of affection traditionally reserved for romantic partners. Since leaving the barn, Rex's responsibilities have increased dramatically. No longer simply my dog, he is my friend, my confidant, and my greatest solace. Though he no longer has to keep himself warm at night, he's been charged with the far weightier task of keeping me warm.

Rex is not the only dog in the neighborhood carrying this kind of burden. When we go walking in the park—and our proximity to these 600 acres of trails is the primary reason I depleted my savings to buy a house here—we encounter many others like us. The dogs are overwhelmingly mixed breeds who, unlike Rex, have been rescued off the streets or from shelters. The owners are overwhelmingly female and overwhelmingly single. Like me, they have purchased homes in this neighborhood not only for the disheveled charms of the overgrown vegetation and absurdly steep and narrow streets but because this is an indisputably "dog friendly" place. Flyers advertising dog walkers, pet sitters, subsidized spaying and neutering, and lost and found animals are perpetually pinned to telephone poles. An organized alliance of concerned pet owners (though they prefer the term "human guardian") maintains a lively online message board, gathers food and bedding donations for local shelters, and runs a "pet photos with Santa" booth every year at the neighborhood holiday crafts fair.

I call this group the Dog Squad. I suppose I'm one of them, though the extent to which I want to be swings on a sort of pendulum between my visceral love for animals and the remaining vestiges of my ability to be rational about the way the world works. It bears mentioning that in addition to being mostly female and mostly single, the members of the Dog Squad are overwhelmingly Caucasian and middle to upper-middle class. That is to say we've bought or rented homes in this neighborhood mostly in the last decade, which is roughly how long it's been since the neighborhood began to shake off its reputation for having some of the worst gang violence in the city. We are the ones paying upwards of $500,000 for small bungalows because we know more of us are coming and despite the shifts in the market, the values are only going up. We are the ones with the hybrid cars and the Democratic-candidate signs in our yards, the ones on whom no one will ever file a noise complaint, the ones who place a simple wreath on the door at Christmastime rather than an entire team of high-wattage reindeer. We are the ones who don't care how crappy the public schools are because we either don't have school-age kids or, if we do, make a second career out of finding private or magnet schools that offer German classes and diving teams.

This is a fairly standard portrait of gentrification, of course. You'll find it from Brooklyn, New York, to Oakland, California, and minus a few regional specifics, it all looks pretty much the same. This neighborhood, for its part, has always straddled the line between the bohemian mythology of its radical leftist roots and the majority rule of the Spanish-speaking immigrant population that has dominated it since the 1960s. On balance, tensions around here don't run as high as you'd think. The white people, even the recent gentrifiers (among whose ranks I have no choice but to count myself) define themselves in distinct opposition to the kinds of white people who live in L.A.'s pricier areas. Our combination of earnestness (we have a pottery studio and a weekly antiwar rally) and tough, urban pioneer posturing (we have green-haired hipsters smoking outside the coffee shop) gives us a liberal, egalitarian sheen you tend not to see in quieter, more manicured communities.

But my status as both a white person and a dog owner (I'll continue to say "owner," if only to convince myself I haven't joined the cult entirely) has made me complicit in a pernicious kind of bigotry. More than once I have found myself entangled in a "rescue operation" involving a dog whose guardians have been deemed unsuitable by the Dog Squad. Depending on which Squad member you ask, "unsuitability" can run the gamut from having a debris-strewn yard to not registering adequate concern when the dog is found to be wandering the neighborhood. Depending on how politically correct that Squad member is, the underpinnings of these issues will either be chalked up to vague assertions like "people are so irresponsible" or the thornier—and more honest—recognition that what we're dealing with has less to do with animals than with a treacherous gulf between two cultures. Though most Squadders won't say it out loud, the majority of the pet owners who are deemed unfit are economically disadvantaged, Latino immigrants from countries where dogs run loose as a matter of course. Though most Squadders would no sooner trade their Priuses for Hummers than admit to racism, there is little denying that their work load (or do I mean "our" work load?) would be significantly lighter if not for the fact that even though we live in the United States, a good portion of our neighbors are still playing by the rules of Central America. This begs the question of whether, when we rescue a dog, we're really saving an animal or merely attempting to save our culture while disregarding someone else's.

My best guess is that it's a little of both. It would be entirely wrong to suggest that all or even half of the Latinos in this neighborhood are letting their dogs roam the streets. In fact, most are as responsible and loving (if not as self-congratulatory about it) as the Dog Squadders themselves. And to their credit, the Squadders go to great lengths to solve these problems without running roughshod over the humans who have ostensibly caused them. They will offer to walk neighbors' dogs themselves, procure vouchers for free spaying and neutering, and assist in finding good homes for pets whose owners need to surrender them. They maintain relations with the Department of Animal Control, work with the dogs of homeless people, and build fences and dog runs for neighbors who can't afford them. But I cannot ignore the fact that every time I've joined forces with the Dog Squad to help an animal in need, I've found myself feeling less like a Good Samaritan than a crazy white lady who needs to get a life. I've provided foster care for dogs who needed homes, taken my neighbors' dog to the vet for neutering, and jumped out of my car more times than I can count to scoop a wayward dog away from oncoming traffic. But when I look out my window, past the fence that confines my dog and into the valley of quiet streets below my house, I can't help but see a free-running dog as a thing of fragile beauty. And every time I've assisted in the "re-homing" of one of these animals to a place that will offer a fence and stuffed toys and, I hope, a little love to go along with the amenities, I wonder if I'm doing the right thing. I wonder if I'm making life better for this dog or simply preserving the value of my real estate.

To be honest about the conditions of any dog's life requires being honest about the conditions of our own dogs' lives. And as most urban dog owners know, this sort of assessment is little more than a series of small lies we tell ourselves so that we may continue to function as human beings in the modern world. I can tell myself that Rex's quality of life is somewhere in the 90th percentile—he's developed a taste for sushi, he accompanies me to the Redwoods, he is the recipient of no end of tummy scratching and gooey declarations of love—but the truth is that any measure of his happiness can only be calibrated in relation to my own. I can tell myself that our happiness is symbiotic, that I take pleasure from his apparent pleasure so it all works out in the end, but that would be an insult to his truest essence, which is not that of a love object or even a pet but, simply, a dog.

How does one love a dog and respect him at the same time? The answer, I suspect, is that we cannot. As humans, we are genetically programmed to give love in a singularly human way. We can, of course, choose to extend that love to animals, but to presume that that affection translates into anything resembling the way *we* experience love is to cross the line between keeping our pets safe from harm and keeping our hearts safe from loneliness. There is a reason I fell (and continue to fall) so easily in step with the blurred logic of the Dog Squadders: Like me, they are women who live alone, who've made their own way in the world, and who, by choice or circumstance, have channeled their inherent nurturing instincts not toward children or even men, but toward dogs. As it has with me, the hard work of this kind of independence has made them blind to the privilege that bequeathed it.

There is no doubt in my mind that dogs should not be allowed to run loose in city streets. But I say that knowing that my own dog's life changed for the worse the minute I brought him inside the farmhouse on that chilly afternoon seven years ago. Though it would be more than a year before I'd leave the farm, I knew then that his days as a free-range dog were numbered. I knew I'd eventually do not what was best for him but what was best for me and that all the bed-sharing and doggie playdates and expensive groomers in the world would never give him half as good a life as he'd had when, like the dogs I now see fit to "rescue," he lived in perpetual danger of getting run over on the road. I knew then, as I know now, that when he looked in the mirror on that first day indoors he was seeing not himself or even another dog, but the reflection of insatiable human need. We call that love, but there is no love that doesn't come at the cost of some degree of freedom. To love our dogs is to hope they love us back enough that it was worth their sacrifice.

Permissions Acknowledgments

GRATEFUL ACKNOWLEDGMENT is made to the following for permission to reprint previously published material.

DAVE BARRY: "A Gentleman's Ideal Companion," originally published in the *Miami Herald* (December 19, 2004) as "Man's Best Friend Is Always Ready," copyright © 2004 by Dave Barry. Reprinted with permission of the author.

JON BOWEN: "Two Pooch or Not to Pooch?" originally published in the *Washington Post* (July 17, 1998), copyright © 1998 by Jon Bowen. Reprinted with permission of the author.

SCOTT BRADFIELD: "Doggy Love," copyright © 2003 by Spilogale, Inc., originally published in *The Magazine of Fantasy & Science Fiction* (August 2003) and also included in *Hot Animal Love* by Scott Bradfield (Carroll & Graf, 2005). Reprinted with permission of the author.

BONNIE JO CAMPBELL: "What My Dog Has Eaten Lately," originally published in *The Bark* (Summer 2002), copyright © 2002 by Bonnie Jo Campbell. Reprinted with permission of International Creative Management, Inc.

MARGARET CHO: "Dog Whores," originally published on Margaret Cho.com/blog (November 10, 2005), copyright © 2005 by Margaret Cho. Reprinted with permission of the author.

Copyright Acknowledgments

"Can We Interest You in a Piece of Cheese?" copyright © 2007 by Alison Pace; "One-on-One with Triumph the Insult Comic Dog" copyright © 2007 by Catie Lazarus; "Excerpts from Great Books in the Canine Canon" copyright © 2007 by Francis Heaney; "One Step Out of the Dog House" copyright © 2007 by Frank Gannon; "Seven Days of Finny" copyright © 2007 by Ann Brashares; "Newman" copyright © 2007 by Thomas Cooney; "Let the Heeling Begin" copyright © 2007 by Bill Scheft; "She Who Must Be Obeyed" copyright © 2007 by Tom Gliatto; "Our Twelfth Labor" copyright © 2007 by Ben Brashares; "Pyr Pressure" copyright © 2007 by Franz Lidz; "How to Housebreak Your Dog" copyright © 2007 by Mark Newgarden; "Canine Einstein?" copyright © 2007 by John Warner; "Seven Protective Popeyes" copyright © 2007 by George Singleton; "An Open Letter from Miss Ruby to Her Problem Owner" copyright © 2007 by J. F. Englert; "Pet Quality" copyright © 2007 by Andi Zeisler; "Dog Is My Co-Dependent" copyright © 2007 by Meghan Daum; "Brevities" copyright © 2007 by Dan Liebert.

ILLUSTRATIONS

All illustrations included herein are protected by copyright and may not be reproduced without written permission of the copyright holder.

Brian Biggs: 131, 247
Bill Charmatz: 12, 38, 63, 107, 110
Greg Clarke: 5, 18, 23, 303
Jacob Collins: 223
Randy Glass: 207
Donna Grethen: 253
Eric Hanson: 1, 155, 188
Jason Jägel: 57, 61
Einat Peled: 24, 36, 39, 96, 126, 169, 202, 211, 225, 258, 280
Thorina Rose: 219
Graham Roumieu: 140, 165, 185–187, 240, 244
Ward Schumaker: v, 9, 13, 19, 52, 64, 68, 81, 87, 100, 102, 105, 133, 141, 156, 160, 173, 182, 194, 230, 233, 269, 275, 287
Christian Slade: 249
Mark Ulriksen: Title page
Michael S. Wertz: 77, 199, 213, 267

Acknowledgments

OUR GRATITUDE GOES to Michael Rosen, Susan Tasaki, and Ben Brashares for their invaluable editorial assistance. A special thanks to Lee Harrington and Christopher Schelling for their timely introductions. Our appreciation to Annik La Farge and Allison McCabe, our editors past and present; and to Lisa Bankoff of ICM for shepherding this project. A word of thanks to the contributors, representatives, and assistants who graciously and unselfishly made this book possible, and funny. Most of all, a pat and a treat to all the dogs who inspire us—Nellie, Lenny, Callie, and others too numerous to mention.

Kudos to the many individuals and groups who have created and maintain dog parks across the country—havens for dogs and their people, a place where play, good humor, and laughter thrive on a daily basis.

Plus a grateful appreciation to Patrick McDonnell—creator of Mutts and friend to all animals.

Check thebark.com and *The Bark* magazine for more *Howl* exclusives! Photos of your smiling dogs can be sent to smiling@thebark.com.

About the Contributors

BONNIE THOMAS ABBOTT is an Ohio-licensed humor essayist whose first novel, *Radical Prunings: Officious Advice from the Contessa of Compost,* was published by Emmis Books. She shares a home with Gracie, a part-Dalmatian, part–Courtney Love mix.

HENRY ALFORD has contributed to the *New York Times* and *Vanity Fair* for over a decade, and to *The New Yorker* since 1998. He is the author of a humor collection, *Municipal Bondage,* and of an account of his misadventures as a struggling actor, *Big Kiss,* which won a Thurber Prize.

PHIL AUSTIN is best known for his many years of work as a writer/performer with the Firesign Theatre, America's favorite surreal comedy group, wherein he portrays Nick Danger, Third Eye, among many others. His "Blog of the Unknown" contains much of his writing.

MUTTS *Patrick McDonnell*

DAVE BARRY is a humor columnist whose work has appeared in more than five hundred newspapers in the United States and abroad. He is the author of thirty books, including his latest, *The Shepherd, the Angel, and Walter the Christmas Miracle Dog,* although virtually none of them include any useful information. He received a Pulitzer Prize for commentary in 1988. Many people are still trying to figure out how this happened.

Artist GARY BASEMAN has been named one of the "100 Most Creative People in Entertainment" by *Entertainment Weekly,* and *Dumb Luck,* a book showcasing his work, was recently published by Chronicle Books. garybaseman.com

ROY BLOUNT JR. is a columnist, sportswriter, editor, screenwriter, and the author of nineteen books, including *I Am Puppy, Hear Me Yap: The Ages of Dog;* a biography of Robert E. Lee; a memoir, *Be Sweet;* and *Feet on the Street: Rambles Around New Orleans.* His work has appeared in 166 periodicals, including *The New Yorker, Gourmet, Playboy,* and *Vanity Fair.* He is a regular panelist for NPR's *Wait Wait . . . Don't Tell Me.*

JON BOWEN lives with his wife, children, and two dogs in Charlottesville, Virginia. His writing has appeared in the *Washington Post,* Salon.com, *Runner's World,* and other publications. His dogs continue to be a rich source of inspiration, frustration, amusement, and companionship.

SCOTT BRADFIELD is the author of *Good Girl Wants It Bad, The History of Luminous Motion, Animal Planet, What's Wrong with America,* and *Hot Animal Love: Tales of Modern Romance.* Born in the San Francisco Bay Area, he now lives, writes, and teaches in London.

ANN BRASHARES is the author of *The Sisterhood of the Traveling Pants* novels and *The Last Summer (of You and Me).* JACOB COLLINS is a painter and the founder of The Water Street Atelier and The Grand Central Academy of Art. Together they live in New York City with their three children and their large and beloved black Labrador, Finny.

BEN BRASHARES, who recently completed his MFA in creative writing, lives in Berkeley, California, with his girlfriend, son, and two dogs. His work has appeared in *Rolling Stone, GQ, Men's Journal,* and *Maxim.*

BONNIE JO CAMPBELL is the author of the novel *O Road,* and the story collection *Women and Other Animals.* She lives outside Kalamazoo, Michigan, where she trains her donkeys and tries to convince her dogs that if they don't want to be chased, they should stay out of the pasture.

MARGARET CHO is a comedian and writer. Her successful 1999 off-Broadway show, *I'm the One That I Want,* was made into a film and was the basis for her bestselling book of the same name; her second book, *I Have Chosen to Stay and Fight,* was published in 2005. She is the recipient of the First Amendment Award from the ACLU of Southern California, and has also been honored by the National Organization for Women, the Gay and Lesbian Alliance Against Defamation, the National Gay and Lesbian Task Force, and the Asian American Legal Defense and Education Fund. She maintains an award-winning blog at MargaretCho.com.

NEVA CHONIN is Critic at Large for the *San Francisco Chronicle.* Her journalistic duties include a weekly column, "Live!Rude!Girl!," in which she ruminates on cheese, Harry Potter, epistemology, and French Bulldogs. The four are not connected. Dogless but still hopeful, she shares her studio apartment with a mouse named Mouse.

NANCY COHEN has written for numerous television shows, including *The King of Queens; Sabrina, the Teenage Witch;* and *Blind Date,* where she met her husband while writing thought-bubbles. She is currently developing her own series, *Baggage,* for Channel 4 in the UK.

SUSAN CONANT is the author of one Cat Lover's Mystery and seventeen Dog Lover's Mysteries, and a six-time winner of the Dog Writers' Association of America's Maxwell Award. She lives in Newton, Massachusetts, with her husband, two cats, and Alaskan Malamute, Django.

THOMAS COONEY is a writer and a bargain hunter, and has had a past (albeit brief) career of being mistaken for a Bollywood film idol. MFA Program Coordinator at Saint Mary's College of California, he shares his couch with his Oakland Terrier, Newman.

CATHY CRIMMINS is the award-winning author of twenty-two books, including *Where Is the Mango Princess?* and *How the Homosexuals Saved Civilization.* Her work has appeared in the *Village Voice, Redbook, Working Mother, Parent's Digest, Hysteria, Funny Times, Glamour,* and other publications. She lives in Hollywood, California, where her dog Silver is trying to break into the movies.

ALICE ELLIOTT DARK is the author of two short-story collections, *Naked to the Waist* and *In the Gloaming,* and a novel, *Think of England.* Her work has appeared in *The New Yorker, Harper's, Doubletake, Book Magazine, Five Points, Redbook,* and *Best American Short Stories of the Century.* She frequently writes essays for the *New York Times* and various anthologies. The dogs on her bed at the moment are a Miniature Dachshund and a Schipperke.

MEGHAN DAUM is a columnist at the *Los Angeles Times* and the author of the novel *The Quality of Life Report* and the essay collection *My Misspent Youth.* Her work has appeared in *The New Yorker, Harper's, Vogue, Elle,* and the *New York Times Book Review,* among other publications.

GREGORY EDMONT is an author and screenwriter. His first book, *Spotted in France,* chronicles his extraordinary journey across France by motor scooter with his Dalmatian, JP, and is being adapted as a film. Their adventures continue in his new book, *Château Stray*. He and his adopted son split their time between New York, California, and the south of France, with JP and his own liver-spotted son, Sketch.

J. F. ENGLERT is the author of *A Dog About Town* and *The Collar*. He is a graduate of the Columbia School of Journalism, attended Fordham University School of Law, and has written for the *New York Times*, among other publications.

AL FRANKEN, who hosted the *Al Franken Show*, flagship program of Air America Radio, is an Emmy Award–winning television writer and producer; *New York Times* bestselling author; Grammy-winning comedian; and, most recently, candidate for U.S. senator from the state of Minnesota. Franken was part of the original writing staff that created the groundbreaking late night show *Saturday Night Live*. His books include *Lies and the Lying Liars Who Tell Them: A Fair and Balanced Look at the Right*, *Rush Limbaugh Is a Big Fat Idiot and Other Observations*, and *The Truth (with Jokes)*.

BRIAN FRAZER is the author of *Hyper-chondriac: One Man's Quest to Hurry Up and Calm Down*. His work has appeared in *Esquire*, *Vanity Fair*, *Premiere*, *ESPN*, and *Los Angeles*.

KINKY FRIEDMAN is a singer, songwriter, novelist, humorist, and politician (most recently, he ran as an Independent in the 2006 Texas gubernatorial race). Originally a country-and-western singer, he went on to write a

succession of crime-thriller detective novels featuring himself as the hero. A former columnist for *Texas Monthly,* he also supports animal rescue work through donation of his share of the proceeds from the sale of his "private stock" salsa.

FRANK GANNON has written four books and is a frequent contributor to *The New Yorker, Harper's,* and *Soldier of Fortune* magazines (just kidding on the last one). He was not allowed to have a dog when he was a kid, so he has neurotically overcompensated by having many, many dogs as an adult. He lives with his mixed-breed Terrier, Otto, and his wife, Paulette, in the mountains of north Georgia. To Otto, he is "The Great One Who Takes Me on Walks."

GEORGIA GETZ is an acclaimed essayist, novelist, screenwriter, and director. No, wait!—that's Nora Ephron. But Georgia did *dream* of one day becoming these things and more—just as soon as she finished college at the age of thirty-five. In the meantime, she wrote several unacclaimed essays, TV pilots, and screenplays, and raised two children and one humor blog: iambossy.com. You'll find Getz's name featured on the cover of the finest magazines—right on the subscription tag.

JON GLASER is a writer and actor. Several of his stories have appeared in the *New York Times Magazine.* His television writing credits include *Late Night with Conan O'Brien, Saturday Night Live,* and *The Dana Carvey Show.*

TOM GLIATTO is a television critic for *People.* He is also a contributor to McSweeney's humor Web site.

MARGA GOMEZ tours nationally as the writer/performer of seven solo plays and as one of the first openly gay comedians in America. Her television appearances include HBO, Showtime, and Comedy Central. Ms. Gomez has been nominated for New York's Drama Desk Award and is the recipient of several performance honors, including Theatre LA's Ovation Award and the GLAAD Award. Her dog Tabasco took second place for "Best Butt" in a Brooklyn dog parade.

LEE HARRINGTON'S award-winning series "Rex and the City" has been appearing in *The Bark* since 2000. Her bestselling memoir, *Rex and the City: A Woman, a Man, and a Dysfunctional Dog,* based on this series, was published in 2006, and her first novel, *Nothing Keeps a Frenchman from His Lunch,* is forthcoming from Villard in 2008. She is at work on the second volume of *Rex and the City.*

ANTHONY HEAD lives in Austin and is editor in chief of *Directions: The Magazine of the Texas Hill Country* (hillcountrydirections.com). He is *not* Anthony Head the distinguished English actor. This means that, despite having lived in Hollywood for fifteen years, this Anthony Head has less silver-screen time than his dog, Jerry.

FRANCIS HEANEY is the author of *Holy Tango of Literature* and several puzzle books. He is a former editor-at-large for *Games* magazine; the composer and co-lyricist of the off-off-Broadway musical *We're All Dead;* and the author of the highly irregularly scheduled webcomic *Six Things.*

ANN HODGMAN is the author of several humor books, a number of cookbooks, and more than fifty books for children, most recently, *The House of a Million Pets.* She and her family live in Connecticut.

PAM HOUSTON is the author of the novel *Sighthound;* two collections of short stories, *Cowboys Are My Weakness* and *Waltzing the Cat;* and a collection of essays, *A Little More About Me.* She has received a Western States Book Award and her stories have been selected for the Best American

Short Stories, the O. Henry Awards, the Pushcart Prize, and the Best American Short Stories of the Century. She is the director of creative writing at UC Davis and has been the grateful recipient of the love and wisdom of (so far) five Irish Wolfhounds.

REBECCA ROSE JACOBS is a journalist who writes for the London *Financial Times.*

HAVEN KIMMEL is the author of the novels *The Used World, Something Rising (Light and Swift),* and *The Solace of Leaving Early;* the memoirs *A Girl Named Zippy* and *She Got Up Off the Couch;* and the children's book *Orville: A Dog Story.* She studied English and creative writing at Ball State University and North Carolina State University and attended seminary at Earlham School of Religion. She lives in Durham, North Carolina.

KATHE KOJA writes adult and young-adult fiction. She is the author of *Straydog,* which was honored by the ASPCA and the Humane Society. Her novels include *The Blue Mirror, Talk, Going Under, Kissing the Bee,* and *Buddha Boy.*

JEAN-PIERRE LACRAMPE lives in San Francisco and is currently earning his MFA in creative writing at Saint Mary's College of California, where he is the fiction editor of *Mary* magazine. His work has appeared on McSweeney's Web site.

CATIE LAZARUS, a comedian and writer, has appeared on *The Daily Show with Jon Stewart,* Fox News, and the CBS Evening News, and has been heard on NPR. Awarded "Best Comedy Writer" by Emerging Comics of New York, Lazarus has contributed to the *New York Post, Forward, Time Out New York, The Jerusalem Report,* and the books *Nobody Reins, Insomnia,* and *The Complete Idiot's Guide to Jokes.* Currently, she is writing for the show *Dr. Lazarus,* as well as working on her first novel, *Me Inc.* lazarusrising.com.

FRANZ LIDZ is a *Sports Illustrated* writer, a *New York Times* film essayist, and the author of *Unstrung Heroes: My Improbable Life with Four Impossible Uncles* and *Ghosty Men: The Strange but True Story of the Collyer Brothers.* He lives on a six-acre farm in Pennsylvania's Brandywine Valley with two llamas (Ogar and Edgar), three Great Pyrenees (Ella, Errol, and Tyrone), two cats (Yojimbo and Sanjuro), three dozen chickens and guinea fowl (don't ask), two daughters (Gogo and Daisy), and one wife (Maggie).

DAN LIEBERT, author of *discontinuous soup*, is known as the Verbal Cartoonist. He is one of the few modern aphorists included in the forthcoming Bloomsbury USA book *An Encyclopedia of Aphorisms*, and his work has appeared in anthologies. He lives in Lawrence, Kansas, surrounded by dog memories.

DAVID MALLEY has worked in various editorial capacities for the Discovery Channel, *Rolling Stone*, and most recently *Maxim*. He currently lives in Berlin, Germany, where he is writing, performing with Belgian theater director Michael Laub's Remote Control Productions, and trying, with great pains, to learn the German language.

MERRILL MARKOE, as the multiple Emmy Award–winning head writer for *Late Night with David Letterman*, created "Stupid Pet Tricks." In addition to a wide variety of television and print, she has penned eight books, including *What the Dogs Have Taught Me* and *Walking in Circles Before Lying Down*. For more, including dog videos, try MerrillMarkoe.com.

ROBERT MASELLO is a journalist, television writer, and bestselling author based in Santa Monica, California. His most recent book is a supernatural thriller entitled *Bestiary* (Berkley Books). He has written for several popular television series, including *Early Edition* and *Charmed*, and also serves as the visiting lecturer in literature at Claremont McKenna College.

PATRICK MCDONNELL, children's book author and creator of *Mutts,* lives in New Jersey with his wife, Karen, their dog, Earl, and their cat, MeeMow. Patrick's cartoons, as well as his efforts on behalf of humane and shelter groups, have received awards from the National Cartoonists' Society, HSUS, and PETA.

ROB MCKENZIE wrote a funny article about his dog that nobody wanted. Then one day he saw a *Bark* bumper sticker. He sent the article to *The Bark* and voilà, a meeting of minds. Rob lives in Ontario, Canada, with his wife, Pam, daughter McKenzie, and dog Kiki J. His day job is TV critic for the *National Post* newspaper.

PATRICK F. MCMANUS's columns for *Outdoor Life* and other magazines have been collected in several books, including *The Bear in the Attic, Never Cry "Arp!," How I Got This Way, The Good Samaritan Strikes Again, Real Ponies Don't Go Oink!, The Grasshopper Trap, Never Sniff a Gift Fish, They Shoot Canoes, Don't They?,* and *A Fine and Pleasant Misery.*

SUSAN MILLER is a playwright best known for her critically acclaimed one-woman show *My Left Breast.* Winner of two OBIE awards and a Guggenheim Fellowship, Miller has had plays produced at The Public Theater, Second Stage, Mark Taper Forum, and Naked Angels. Her articles appear in *O, The Oprah Magazine* and *American Theatre.* Miller was a consulting producer on the hit Showtime series *The L Word.*

MARK NEWGARDEN is a cartoonist whose work has appeared in alternative weekly newspapers and publications ranging from *Raw* to the *New York Times* op-ed page. His work has also graced the walls (and screens) of the Smithsonian Institution, the Cooper-Hewitt, the Brooklyn Museum, the Museum of Television and Radio, and the ICA in London. Mark has also worked as a novelty creator and has conceived, scripted, and designed programming for Nickelodeon and the Cartoon Network. He is the author of *Cheap Laffs, We All Die Alone,* and, with Megan Montague Cash, has recently created a number of "Bow-Wow books" starring a dog that looks suspiciously like their little Terrier. laffpix.com

LAURIE NOTARO is the author of six books, keeps a jar of dog cookies on her desk, and is an idiot who regrettably taught her dog Maeby to nudge her when in need of something. Like dog cookies from the jar on her desk. She lives in Eugene, Oregon, and spends a great deal of her day dressing Maeby in raincoats and washing Oregon mud off her paws.

ALISON PACE is the author of the novels *If Andy Warhol Had a Girlfriend, Pug Hill,* and *Through Thick and Thin.* She lives in New York City with her extremely cool dog, Carlie.

ALYSIA GRAY PAINTER's work appeared in *Dog Is My Co-Pilot;* the humor compilations *May Contain Nuts* and *More Mirth of a Nation;* and Mc-Sweeney's anthologies, *Created in Darkness by Troubled Americans* and *Mountain Man Dance Moves.* She lives in Los Angeles with her husband and two Pugs who are skilled at turning any new lap they encounter into their very own chaise longue in under twenty seconds flat.

MELISSA HOLBROOK PIERSON is the author of three books, one of which, *Dark Horses and Black Beauties,* is about our equine companions. Her next will be about shifting styles in dog training, as well as about the dogs with whom she has been honored to live and learn.

NEAL POLLACK is the author of the bestselling memoir *Alternadad,* hailed as "the most offbeat parenting memoir ever written." In addition to his four-year-old son, he's also dad to Hercules and Shaq, two gassy Boston Terriers. Because of the dogs, he's having a hard time persuading the boy

that incessant humping and licking aren't acceptable human behaviors. They all live in Los Angeles.

MO ROCCA, author of *All the Presidents' Pets,* appears regularly on CBS's *Sunday with Charles Osgood* and NBC's *Tonight Show.* He can be heard on NPR's *Wait Wait . . . Don't Tell Me.* He began his career in television as a writer for the Peabody Award–winning PBS children's series *Wishbone,* about a heroic Jack Russell Terrier who in his dream life becomes the heroes of classic novels. (And you find that strange?) A native of Washington, D.C., he lives in New York City.

MICHAEL J. ROSEN, a writer and editor of humor (he created the biennial series *Mirth of a Nation*), has also created a shelf of books about dogs as a children's book author, poet, kid-trainer, illustrator (*Kids' Best Dog Book*), and editor (*Dog People, The Company of Dogs,* and *21st Century Dog: A Visionary Compendium*).

GRAHAM ROUMIEU'S signature art has appeared in advertising, magazines, newspapers, and books, including *Some Really Super Poems About Squirrels, In Me Own Words: The Autobiography of Bigfoot,* and *101 Ways to Kill Your Boss.* His work has been honored by *American Illustration, Applied Arts* Magazine, and the National Magazine Awards. He lives in Toronto.

BILL SCHEFT is the author of two novels (*The Ringer, Time Won't Let Me*) and a collection of humor columns (*The Best of the Show*). He has been a writer for David Letterman since 1991, which means he responds to the command "Stay!"

ERICA SCHOENBERGER is a professor of geography at Johns Hopkins University. Her Australian Shepherd, Sasha, teaches there as well.

GEORGE SINGLETON has published four story collections and one novel. One collection is *Why Dogs Chase Cars,* and he continues to ponder his hypotheses as his rescued ex-strays (eleven of them at one point) sit close at his side. His fiction has appeared in *The Atlantic Monthly, Harper's, Playboy, Zoetrope, The Georgia Review, Shenandoah,* and elsewhere, and has been anthologized in *New Stories from the South* eight times. His new novel is *Work Shirts for Madmen*. He lives in Dacusville, South Carolina.

ROBERT SMIGEL is *Saturday Night Live*'s longest-running writer, having been there for more than twenty years. A multiple Emmy Award–winner, Smigel has also written for *Late Night with Conan O'Brien,* where he is best known for Triumph the Insult Comic Dog, whose first CD earned Smigel a Grammy. In addition to writing for *SNL, Conan,* and *The Colbert Report* and collaborating with Adam Sandler on a number of films, he has advocated for and raised money on behalf of autism awareness, including producing Comedy Central's *Night of Too Many Stars* to support autism education.

DAVID SMILOW is an actor and writer who now lives in New York's Hudson Valley, where he participates in a readers' theater company called—appropriately enough—Actors & Writers. He has won an Emmy and two Writers Guild awards for his television work. As an actor, he has portrayed (in addition to the dog in *Part Pooch*) *another* dog, a deer, a monkey, a snake, a crocodile, a house, a Samsonite hard body suitcase, and the occasional biped.

MARC SPITZ is the author of two novels, *How Soon Is Never* and *Too Much, Too Late,* and two adult nonfiction books, *We Got the Neutron Bomb* (with Brendan Mullen) and *Nobody Likes You: Inside the Turbulent Life, Times and Music of Green Day.* He is currently working on a biography of David Bowie. He is a former senior writer at *Spin* magazine, and his work has appeared in *Uncut, Maxim, Nylon,* the *Washington Post, Vanity Fair,* and the *New York Post.* Seven of his plays have been produced in theaters of varying size and cleanliness levels.

JEFF STEINBRINK's commentaries have aired on NPR's *Marketplace, Marketplace Morning Report, Maine Things Considered,* and *Morning Edition.* Print pieces of his have appeared in *The Believer, McSweeney's,* and the new online magazine *Lost.* He teaches American literature and creative writing at Franklin & Marshall College.

Proof that you *can* teach an old dog new tricks, MARK ALLEN SVEDE occasionally stops writing about Eastern European art long enough to write something a bit funnier. (And proof that you can teach young pups all sorts of things, he has taught various film and art history courses at Ohio State University and other pedigreed institutions.)

ABIGAIL THOMAS is the author of five books for adults, including *A Three Dog Life* and *Safekeeping,* and two books for children, *Lily* and *Pearl Paints.* She lives in Woodstock, New York, and teaches fiction writing in the graduate program at The New School.

MARK ULRIKSEN lives in San Francisco, painting pictures for *The New Yorker,* the San Francisco Jazz Festival, and a growing roster of clients who commission him for dog portraits. His days center around deadlines, children's homework assignments, and finding the tennis balls Henry, his Labrador, always manages to lose.

JEFF WARD has written comedy for *Saturday Night Live, All Things Considered,* and BBC Radio 4. His comic essays have appeared in *Modern Humorist, The Big Jewel, Lowbrow Reader, Jest,* and the humor anthology *May Contain Nuts.* He lives in New York City with Mrs. Ethel Cohen and Chester, two Welsh Terriers.

MICHAEL WARD is a product of suburban Boston. His attempts at humor writing have appeared in *The New Book of Lists, Created in Darkness by Troubled Americans,* and *Mountain Man Dance Moves,* as well as on the Web sites mcsweeneys.net and yankeepotroast.org. His dog Jasper looks suspiciously like a common house cat.

JOHN WARNER is the editor of McSweeney's Internet Tendency and the author most recently of *Fondling Your Muse: Infallible Advice from a Published Author to the Writerly Aspirant.* He teaches at Clemson University and lives in Greenville, South Carolina, with his wife, Kathy, and their dogs, Scully and Oscar.

Though WILLIAM WEGMAN is popularly known for photographic collaborations with his Weimaraners—Man Ray, Fay Ray, and assorted

puppies—he is also an accomplished painter and videographer. His photo
graphs, videos, paintings, and drawings have been exhibited in museums and
galleries internationally. Wegman lives in New York and Maine. wegman
world.com

MELISSA WEBB WRIGHT is associate professor of geography and
women's studies at Pennsylvania State University. Surprisingly, she does not
at present live with a dog, but has two cats, one partner, and an enchanting
daughter.

ANDI ZEISLER is a writer, illustrator, and the cofounder and editorial/
creative director of *Bitch: Feminist Response to Pop Culture.* She got over an
early childhood fear of dogs and now embraces, often literally, all dogs. A
New Yorker by birth and temperament, she lives in Portland, Oregon, with
her human and canine companions.

DAN ZEVIN, who teaches journalism at NYU, is the author of three
books—*The Day I Turned Uncool* (currently in development as a feature
film), *The Nearly-Wed Handbook,* and *Entry-Level Life*—and numerous
magazine pieces. He and his wife live in Brooklyn, New York, with Chloe
(their first-born, who happens to be a dog) and their two recently arrived
human babies.

IN 2005, when the Gulf Coast was ravaged by Hurricane Katrina
and the floods that followed, media coverage of this natural disaster revealed the importance of the bond between humans and
their companion animals. To honor this bond and assist with the
ongoing rebuilding effort, all royalties earned by *Howl* will be
donated to animal shelters and other humane organizations in
the Gulf Coast region.

About the Editors

CLAUDIA KAWCZYNSKA AND CAMERON WOO founded *The Bark,* the world's premier dog magazine, in 1997 in Berkeley, California. Created initially to rally support for a local off-leash area, *The Bark* quickly grew from a modest newsletter into a glossy, award-winning magazine lauded for its intelligence, wit, and design. Hailed as "*The New Yorker* of dog magazines," *The Bark* aspires to live its motto—Dog Is My Co-Pilot—by being the source for impassioned, thoughtful dog lovers. The editors' first anthology, *Dog Is My Co-Pilot: Great Writers on the World's Oldest Friendship,* was a *New York Times* bestseller. The editors live and work in Berkeley with their dogs and cats. To learn more about *The Bark,* see thebark.com.

[Also from the editors of *The Bark*]

For people who love great writing and, yes, great dogs, a book to be both shared and treasured.

DOG IS MY CO-PILOT
Great Writers on the World's Oldest Friendship
978-1-4000-5053-6
$14.00 paper (Canada: $21.00)

Dog Is My Co-Pilot is an anthology of essays, short stories, and expert commentaries that explores every aspect of our life with dogs. Included are pieces by Lynda Barry, Rick Bass, Maeve Brennan, Margaret Cho, Carolyn Chute, Alice Elliott Dark, Lama Surya Das, Pam Houston, Erica Jong, Tom Junod, Caroline Knapp, Donald McCaig, Nasdijj, Ann Patchett, Michael Paterniti, Charles Siebert, Alexandra Styron, Elizabeth Marshall Thomas, and Alice Walker.